BL 51.E29

# KING OF THE CASTLE

Choice and Responsibility
in the Modern World

# KING OF
# THE CASTLE

Choice and Responsibility
in the Modern World

## Gai Eaton

PUBLISHED IN ASSOCIATION WITH
THE IMPERIAL IRANIAN ACADEMY
OF PHILOSOPHY

THE BODLEY HEAD
LONDON  SYDNEY
TORONTO

© Gai Eaton 1977
ISBN 0 370 30062 9
Printed and bound in Great Britain for
The Bodley Head Ltd
9 Bow Street, London WC2E 7AL
by W & J Mackay Limited, Chatham
Set in Monotype Imprint
*First published 1977*

# CONTENTS

'Now,' said she, 'I know the cause,
or the chief cause, of your sickness.
You have forgotten
what you are.'
BOETHIUS

# INTRODUCTION

If, by some strange device, a man of our century could step backwards in time and mix with the people of a distant age he would have good cause to doubt either their sanity or his own. Mountains, forests and the blue sky would look familiar enough, but they would not be seen by the people around him in the way he saw them. Their physical features might be the same, but their meaning would be different.

He would know what common sense is and what constitutes human normality. So would the people amongst whom he found himself, but their common sense would differ from his and their normality might seem to him abnormal. Questioning everything they took for granted and amazed that they should be so unquestioning in their assumptions, he would find that all he took for granted was brought into question. His 'Why?' would be met with their 'Why?', and he would not know the answer.

From our present position we can see how limited were the beliefs and ideas of earlier times and other cultures, how many avenues were left unexplored and how many opportunities missed. It is easy to suppose that, in changing our perspective, we have escaped from the limitations inherent in human thinking and human vision. Yet our faculties and our senses are the same. We are not a new species, and to compare our own world view with any other is merely to compare different kinds of limitation, as though a man tunnelling his way out of prison were to emerge within the perimeter, exchanging one cell for another.

So it must always be unless the prisoner learns that freedom lies in quite another direction, never through the tunnel of time.

Like those who came before us we have chosen—or had chosen on our behalf—certain particular objectives out of the multitude of possibilities open to man and, like them, we ignore everything that seems irrelevant to our purpose. This purpose is determined by the assumptions we take for granted, the axioms which seem to

7

us to demand no proof, the moral imperatives which appear self-evident and therefore unarguable. We are rational creatures, certainly, but reason does not operate in a vacuum or spin the premises of argument out of its own substance. It must start from somewhere. Certain propositions must be accepted as self-evident before our minds will function, and one can reason as well on the basis of a false proposition as upon that of a true one.

A man in a dark place mistakes a coil of rope for a snake. From then on his logic may be impeccable, his behaviour entirely reasonable ; but he is still wrong. It is the basic assumptions which determine all the rest.

My intention in this book is to take a long, hard look at some of the basic assumptions of our age, to question the unquestionable and to cast doubt upon propositions which appear self-evident. This cannot be done without, at the same time, suggesting the outlines of quite a different perspective.

No one can extricate himself completely from the conditioning of his own period and environment. Consciously or unconsciously, we are all of us to some extent held captive by the clinging vines of our particular jungle and at home in these bonds. They are, indeed, like extensions of our selves and correspond to deeply rooted habits of thought and of feeling. It is not easy to break free, but, precisely because we are human, it is not impossible. Between earth and sky, among all living creatures and all the earth's ornaments, man alone is capable of some degree of detachment from his temporal matrix.

But to break free is not to float away into the void. No one could live and think in a moral and intellectual no-man's-land. To be able to look critically and objectively at the ground upon which the people of our time have taken their stand, one must have firm ground beneath one's own feet. To diagnose the ills of the time one must possess standards of health.

The point of view from which this book is written is, in the first place, Islamic. This does not mean that Muslims in general would necessarily endorse the views expressed or that I propose to put forward a specifically Islamic critique of Western, post-Christian civilisation. What it does mean is that this view is rooted in the Muslim faith and in a soil quite different to that which supports either the modernistic Christian or the modern atheist.

Secondly, this perspective is founded upon a belief in the essential unity of the great religions as deriving from a single source of Revelation, and in a perennial wisdom expressed not only through the religions but also in the myths and symbols of ancient peoples (and of what are commonly called 'primitive' human groups up to the present day), a wisdom which may be said to inhere in the deepest level of our being so that we need only to be reminded of it in order to rediscover the truth within ourselves. This belief is in fact an extension of the Islamic perspective, for Islam is by definition the final Revelation in this human cycle and the final crystallisation of that wisdom.

Lastly and, one might say, as a logical consequence, my concern is with human 'normality' as it has been understood through the ages and in a vast diversity of cultures : the nature and the status of man as man, the two-legged creature standing upright in his blue and green world, face-to-face with his God. Only in terms of an immutable norm can one even begin to consider what choice men have in their lives and what responsibility is theirs.

Whether we praise or condemn contemporary civilisation, none can deny that it is—in terms of what men had been and thought and done until quite recently—different, peculiar, abnormal. There are those who think that this abnormality represents our long-delayed emergence from darkness into the light of reason ; for others it represents the terminal stage of a mortal sickness. But none dispute that we are different and unrecognisable, like creatures from outer space who have descended upon the earth's carapace and taken it over. Whether we see this strange new figure of a man as godling or monster, there has been nothing quite like him before or elsewhere. If we were to substitute for 'abnormality' the word 'deformity' we might see more clearly what is at issue, for to be deformed in this sense 'is to be infinitely odious in His eyes, Whose love of Beauty is the hatred of deformity'.*

And yet this misshapen creature is convinced that he is what man was always meant to be—warts and all—and he defines human nature in terms of his own nature, his own weaknesses and his own vices. He may be aware that there is a great deal wrong in the human situation, but he defines this in terms of current progressive ideals. To suggest to him that it is precisely these ideals which are mistaken and that our troubles are due, not to the obstacles in the way of reaching our goal, but to the initial choice of goal is to

* *Centuries of Meditation:* Thomas Traherne, II:4.

propose the unthinkable. A superstitious faith in progress endures even when the dogma of progress has been exposed as an illusion.

So deeply rooted is this superstition that one hardly dare tell people that anything is wrong. Their reaction, comparable to an involuntary muscular spasm, is to spring into ill-considered and often destructive action. Problems, they believe, exist only to be dealt with at once, usually by wielding the surgeon's knife on the body politic, and they cannot admit that such solutions—revolution, reform, new legislation, further technological development and more extensive exploitation of the earth's resources—only too often breed a new generation of even more intractable evils. Such an admission might compel them to keep still for a while, to look and to listen, and perhaps even to learn to live with the shadows which are inseparable from the light of day.

In any case, obsessive concern with the future of the human race is a uniquely modern phenomenon. We can live—and live well—without optimism and, for that matter, without the pessimism of so-called 'doomsters' who are, for the most part, only disappointed optimists. These are sentimentalities we can ill afford under present conditions and, particularly from the Islamic point of view, they have no real meaning. The Muslim does not easily forget that, as men and women, we are all 'doomed' since we must surely die, and that societies, civilisations and worlds are equally mortal: 'Everything that is upon the earth passes away, and there remains only the Face of thy Lord, infinite in Glory and infinite in Bounty.'* Eternity is One; and One alone is eternal.

This, in a sense, is all we need to know, and indeed the sensible man, though he may pretend a fashionable concern for the human future, behaves much like an actor who cares little how long the theatre in which he is playing will stand, after the play is done. Moreover, for the Muslim as for the Christian of earlier times, this earth and all its people are in the hands of God, whose will is unchangeable; and it scarcely matters whether he means us to continue for a thousand years or for a hundred—or to enjoy our final dawn tomorrow—since all things must take their course and all is ultimately well disposed. Our business is to fulfil, here and now, the function we were born to fulfil.

This book is concerned, above all, with what it means to be a man in terms of the traditional view of human nature. There

* Qurān, 55:27.

exists no common ground between this view and the image which the man of our time sees in his mirror ; the image of a clever animal born to exploit the earth's wealth, whether for his own enjoyment or in the service of his society, until his little light is extinguished and darkness takes him. In the traditional view, the fulfilment of the human function is to live as a 'symbol' rather than as a transient individuality—one of numberless motes of dust caught briefly in a shaft of sunlight—and to live in this way is, in a certain sense, to represent man as such. The height of this function reaches the heavens, and its breadth encompasses the furthest horizon.

But since man as we know him is a fragmentary being, it is wholeness that he seeks in order to become what in truth he is. In the Christian context this wholeness is to be achieved through the imitation of Christ. Equivalents exist in every religion, and in each case the fragmentary being left to his own devices and without a model—the masterless man—is seen as a stray dog foraging on the outskirts of the human village. The role we are offered in the mirrors we hold up to ourselves—novels, plays and films—is, precisely, a stray dog's role and it is played out in a remote and sunless wasteland ; for our present locality is so far distant from the world inhabited by the men of earlier times that we have no yardstick by which to measure it. We can only attempt to describe such remoteness in images that may seem fanciful.

Let us imagine a summer landscape, bounded only by our limited vision but in truth unbounded ; a landscape of hills and valleys, forests and rivers, but containing also every feature that an inventive mind might bring to thought. Let us suppose that somewhere in this measureless extension a child has been blowing bubbles for the sheer joy of seeing them carried on the breeze, catching the sunlight, drifting between earth and sky. And then let us compare all that we know of our world, the earth and what it contains, the sun, the moon and the stars, to one such bubble, a single one. It is there in our imagined landscape. It exists. But it is a very small thing, and in a few moments it is gone.

This, at least, is one way of indicating the traditional or— taking the word in its widest sense—the religious view of our world and of how it is related to all that lies beyond it. Perhaps the image may be pursued a step further. The bubble's skin reflects what lies outside and is, at the same time, transparent. Those who live within may be aware of the landscape in quite different ways. Those whose sight is weak or untrained may still surmise its existence and, believing what they are told by others who see more clearly, have faith in it. Secondly, there are some who will perceive within the bubble itself reflections of what lies outside and begin to realise that everything within is neither more nor less than a reflection and has no existence in its own right. Thirdly, as by a miracle of sight, there will be a few for whom transparency is real and actual. Their vision pierces the thin membrane which to others seems opaque and, beyond faith, they see what is to be seen.

These three kinds of people differ greatly, but this difference is as nothing compared with the gulf which separates them from those who take the bubble for all-in-all and deny that anything real lies outside this tiny sphere. What is truth for the men of faith and the men of vision is, for those others, illusion. No common language exists, and the very names given to the objects of experience mean different things. The physically blind still believe in a world described to them by the sighted even though they may not be able to imagine it, but these blind hearts deny sight.

For Islam this distinction between 'believer' and 'unbeliever' is the most fundamental distinction that it is possible to make between human beings, and beside it differences of temperament or character, let alone of race or class, fade into insignificance. The 'unbelievers' are not simply people who do not share a particular belief; they are the *kafirūn*, the people who are 'covered over', muffled—as it were—in tissues of illusion from the impact of reality, shrouded from the light 'as if', says the Qurān, 'their faces had been cloaked with darkness.'

No less a gulf divides those who 'know' from the 'ignorant' in the context of Hinduism; and Christians, before the modern age undermined their faith, thought it legitimate to put unbelievers and heretics to death rather than allow the contagion of their blindness to spread. However shocking such severity may seem to the people of our time, for whom everything outside the bubble is either fiction or, at best, a pious hope, we would be wrong to imagine that the Christians of earlier times were therefore lacking in charity. They would have seen little virtue in sparing those who, they believed, were poisoning the wells of charity itself and gravely endangering the souls of their fellow men, their neighbours and their kindred. In this century in which such vast numbers of people have been slaughtered in the name of mere political opinions, secular ideologies, it would be absurd for any of us to feel self-righteous or to speak condescendingly of 'fanaticism' in relation to the wars of religion or the suppression of heresy and infidelity.

There is a saying of the Prophet Muhammad which again underlines the difference of proportion between the world as we know it and all that lies outside. 'I swear by God', he said, 'that this world in comparison with the world to come is as though one of you put his finger into the sea ... Let him consider what he brings out on it!' Between droplet and ocean there can be no common measure.

No one, of course, would suggest that every believer of earlier times, Muslim, Christian or Hindu, was aware of the disproportion between the world of his day-to-day experience and the surrounding ocean of reality or even that piety necessarily requires such awareness. But the bedrock truth of a religious doctrine is not established by holding an opinion poll among its adherents. The moment the idea of a revealed religion presents itself, the moment we speak of God or of the supernatural (properly understood), this disproportion is implied, and it colours all that is said or thought. Take it away, and you remove the fulcrum upon which the whole structure revolves. You are left with a religion that is little more than sentimental idealism, idle day-dreaming or wishful thinking; worldly religion, on the same level as the secular ideologies.

In a period of history which readily makes an idol of 'knowledge' and in which people treat with derision the 'ignorance' of past ages, there is an astonishing ignorance of what—only a few generations ago—was regarded as the most important of all subjects and is still so regarded among at least half the world's population. The extent and depth of this ignorance, not only of religion in general and its metaphysical bases, but even of quite elementary aspects of their own religion—if they claim to have one—among 'educated' people might be compared to the ignorance of nuclear physics one would expect to find among the pygmies of Zaire; and yet they have no hesitation in expressing firm and even dogmatic opinions on the subject.

In Britain the educational system provides classes in what is humorously described as 'Religious Knowledge', although no doctrine is taught and the distinction between religious and secular thought is never touched upon. A culture which shows such casual indifference to the subject which has dominated human lives and human minds throughout history, at least until very recently and in a particular locality, is indeed abnormal, to say the least, and, in view of its attitude towards the beliefs which have determined and validated—or invalidated—all other forms of knowledge, can hardly expect to be taken seriously when it makes portentous pronouncements upon politics or morality or upon the human situation as such.

If in the course of this book I appear to dismiss a great deal of 'modern thought' with something less than the respect and attention it is assumed to merit, this is not least because these 'thinkers' have seen fit to dismiss equally casually all that had been considered until quite recently, by the wisest and noblest men whose records are known to us, to give weight and validity to human thinking. Those who refuse to listen should not expect to be heard.

I do not mean to suggest that theoretic knowledge is a prerequisite of faith or that a man cannot love God unless he is a philosopher. Far from it. But the simple believer of earlier times who knew very little yet possessed great faith could scarcely survive in the modern world, bombarded ceaselessly with the arguments of unbelief. Doctrinal knowledge has become almost essential for those who would hold fast to their religion against the tide. A hundred years ago a man could be a good Christian and remain so without ever having heard of St Augustine or Aquinas; ignorant faith was protected, and therefore sufficed. Today a Christian who does not have some knowledge of the doctrines upon which his faith is founded stands in mortal peril, unless protected by an impregnable simplicity.

But it is not simply arguments that threaten him and must be answered. It is something more overwhelming and yet less easily definable: a climate of opinion, even an unspoken 'consensus'. As Frithjof Schuon says: 'When people want to be rid of Heaven it is logical to start by creating an atmosphere in which spiritual things appear out of place; in order to be able to declare successfully that God is unreal they have to construct around man a false reality, a reality that is inevitably inhuman because only the inhuman can exclude God. What is involved is a falsification of the imagination and so its destruction.'*

* *Understanding Islam:* Frithjof Schuon, p. 37.

Just as each age has its pattern of assumptions which are taken for granted, so, in every age, there are certain ideas which appear by their very nature improbable. No process of reasoning is required to establish this improbability; and because the products of the period—its art and architecture, the human environment, the things men do and the things they make—both reflect and reinforce current assumptions, the improbable soon becomes quite unimaginable.

Everything in the environment except virgin nature and certain relics of the past then confirms these assumptions, and an effort of will is required to think about them critically, let alone sceptically. It is as though a process of osmosis took place between human beings and their immediate surroundings; the outward reflects the inward and is shaped by it, while the inward is moulded by the outward. The religious point of view, with all that it implies in the way of a sense of the sacred and awe in the face of that which transcends us, comes naturally to the average man only if he lives in an environment which reflects the light of heaven, however inadequately, and which feeds some glimmer of this light to his senses. In a completely opaque environment the landscape outside our bubble becomes unimaginable and God himself is the Great Improbability.

The particular difficulty pious Muslims untouched by modernism have always had in understanding the unbeliever or recognising him as a man of the same nature as themselves derives from the fact that, for such true believers, the truth of their religion —the divine Unity and all that it implies—is so overwhelmingly self-evident that to deny it is like denying the desert sun when one stands in its full glare. The notion that the unbeliever's views are in some way to be respected would strike them as both foolish and wicked.

On the other hand, the difficulty most people in the modern world experience in trying to understand 'this terrifying faith' (as a French Islamicist has described it) derives from the fact that the overwhelming and, above all, exclusive reality of the everyday world seems to them equally self-evident and equally unquestionable. In either case it is almost impossible to doubt what seems so obvious. Such is the power that a climate of opinion and the environment it forges have over us.

It might be objected that Western Europe and the United States are still 'Christian' in a rather general sense. Whether people who lived at any time in the first fifteen centuries of the Christian era would have recognised them as such is another matter. For those earlier Christians, as for traditionally minded Muslims, Hindus or Buddhists today, there are certain things which take priority in human living, and there is one priority which dwarfs all others. There is the Absolute and there is the relative, and no common measure exists by which we might compare the importance of the one with that of the other. No such sense of priorities directs the humanistic morality of our time nor, for that matter, does it impinge upon those of our contemporaries who have some vague belief in a cosy afterlife available to anyone who behaves decently and 'does his best'.

Today the dividing line between mutually irreconcilable views— between belief and unbelief—has become blurred and neither faith nor infidelity are followed through to their logical conclusions. There is a kind of twilight region inhabited by the many who are neither believers nor unbelievers, but are carried along by the tide of these times while daylight lasts. There must, they think, be 'something' beyond all this, but they doubt whether anybody really knows what this 'something' might be and seem quite unaware of great voices, still audible, telling them precisely what it is and summoning them to attend as a man attends when he stands in mortal peril. Living in a culture which has become in its very nature the *kafir's* cloak of darkness, nothing that lies outside their little pool of light seems quite real, and, if they think of divine reality at all, they think of it as something ghostly, abstract, attenuated—the desert sun no longer scorches or dazzles.

It is hardly surprising therefore that religion, if it survives at all in such a hostile environment, has been cut off from what might be called its vertical dimension and has been engulfed in worldliness; not worldliness as we have become accustomed to hearing the word used—wine, women and song (or their equivalents) have never had much power against religious conviction—but in the sense of an exclusive concern with the things of this world, a concern which has proved all the more seductive because it has been made to seem so worthy. It is true that the virtue of charity flows from the love of God, but this does not mean that a 'social conscience' is an adequate substitute for that love.

The new religious morality which gives priority to social and economic considerations stands condemned in the light of all that was believed by men of faith until quite recently; condemned for the good reason that it has adopted the unbeliever's scale of priorities and surrendered itself to the process of change, abandoning the immutable principles of which religious institutions are the custodians. This however is a situation which suits the irreligious very well; they might be disturbed by a real priest, like grubs under a stone when their covering is lifted by some mighty hand, but they can fraternise happily with a social worker in clerical garb. The people, on the other hand, the real people who ask almost shamefacedly for faith, hope and *caritas*, true love, get little comfort from men as uncertain and insecure as themselves. All they are offered is a bland religion which has fitted itself only too well into the framework of contemporary civilisation, a civilisation which derives its basic assumptions, its values and its logic, from profane sources; from the humanism and rationalism of the French 'Enlightenment', from the Titanic self-assertion of the Renaissance and, more remotely, from the worst features of two ancient cultures, those of Greece and of Rome, which were already decadent in terms of the human norm when they bequeathed to us our classical heritage and over which Christianity triumphed all too briefly.

So many ruins bear witness to good intentions which went astray, good intentions unenlightened by any glimmer of wisdom. To bring religion to the people is a fine and necessary undertaking, but this is not a situation in which the proposed end can be said to justify the means. The further people have drifted from the truth, the greater is the temptation to water down the truth, glossing over its less palatable aspects and, in short, allowing a policy of compromise to become one of adulteration. In this way it is hoped that the common man—if he can be found—will be encouraged to find a small corner in his busy life for religion without having to change his ways or to grapple with disturbing thoughts. It is a forlorn hope. Standing, as it were, at the pavement's edge with his tray of goods, the priest reduces the price until he is offering his wares for nothing: divine Judgment is a myth, hell a wicked superstition, prayer less important than decent behaviour, and God himself dispensable in the last resort; and still the passers-by go their way, sorry over having to ignore such a nice man but with more important matters demanding their attention. And yet these matters with which they are most urgently concerned are, for so many of them, quicksands in which they feel themselves trapped. Had they been offered a real alternative, a rock firm-planted from the beginning of time, they might have been prepared to pay a high price.

It is even possible, had the priest turned his back upon them, attending only to the divine sun which seizes and holds his gaze, they might have come up quietly behind him, knelt down—looking where he looks—and forgotten all their care and all their troubles. It might be said that the basic command of religion is not 'Do this !' or 'Do not do that !', but simply 'Look !' The rest follows.

Since unbelief lies at the root of almost all that is said or thought or done in our time, it follows that the believer's critique of the modern world cannot be less than radical. One does not try to prettify a leper or to treat his 'lion face' with cosmetics. But radical criticism must have an end in view, and since the world's course will not be reversed by any action we can take nor the ages of faith return before the end of time—as we understand time— it might reasonably be asked what point there is in playing Canute and trying to defy the tide. Great men and wise men in the past have readily turned their backs on a heedless world or a hell-bent society, setting an example to those few who were prepared to come their way, but never supposing that the mass of people could be persuaded to walk a different road. Were it possible for those who reject the whole structure of opinion and ideology upon which contemporary societies are based to go their way in peace, one might say—and even fifty years ago one could have said—that this would be the better course.

The justification for adopting a different policy today and for raising the dust of polemical argument lies in the uniqueness of our present situation, the uniqueness of the attempt secular societies are now making to absorb into their process the whole man, body and soul. There is going to be no more 'opting out'. Cornered, one has no alternative but to turn and fight ; and those of us who do not accept the assumptions of this age, its priorities and its moral imperatives, are indeed driven into a corner. In judging our world—and it is not for nothing that men have been given some power of discrimination—we are compelled to weigh one society against another no longer in terms of relative excellence (though some, obviously, are greatly superior to others) but chiefly in terms of how far they have gone in seizing and possessing their citizens.

Just as growing populations in Africa and elsewhere encroach more and more upon the open spaces in which the wild beasts roam, and a time may be foreseen when no space remains and such beasts as survive are confined to game reserves (like the 'savages' of Aldous Huxley's *Brave New World*), so the men of independent mind who cannot take this bubble-world for all-in-all will soon have nowhere to go and no possibility of escape from the demands of society or from the conditioning which it imposes upon all its citizens from an early age. That conditioning or, to use a current phrase, that 'brainwashing' process will undo their truth if it can, and will in any case prevent coming generations even from surmising that such a truth exists or that men have any other function but to be socially and economically useful.

Since there are no longer any sacred societies—except perhaps in a few distant and isolated corners of the globe—the question which must be asked is not whether a particular social system is benevolent, efficient, well-ordered, but whether it still leaves breathing-space for the sacred and still tolerates outsiders and eccentrics who resist incorporation. What is at stake is of such magnitude that those who still have sight of another shore, if only in imagination, and of a beauty beside which all earthly colours are reduced to monochrome cannot be other than 'extremists' in this context; no middle way remains open and we are compelled by the circumstances of our time to make a choice, having the doubtful privilege of living, here and now, in a decisive moment.

The earlier part of this book is concerned less with the role of religion in the world today than with the nature of modern secular societies as seen from the point of view of religion and with their clear, often explicit, tendency to close all the exits, level all the heights and confine the human being, made in the divine image and fit for greatness, within his purely terrestial modalities, his economic function and his role as a social animal. This tendency cannot be resisted on its own level, for on that level such trends have a power—almost an inevitability—such as we associate with the forces of nature. The religious standpoint alone provides solid ground for resistance, but here it must be emphasised that the reference is to an implacable religion rooted in the transcendent, not to sentimental religiosity and pious platitudes.

Only on this basis is it possible to help those who, though they may submit to the pressures put upon them to conform to the collectivist morality of the age, do so in doubt and uncertainty. Only from this standpoint is it possible to assure them that their doubts spring from a sound and healthy instinct and are supported by the whole weight of human tradition. It is with the nature of this tradition that the second part of the book is concerned.

But how is it possible to speak of 'religion' in this context, when there are many religions and they appear to differ on so many points? This is not the place to enter into complex arguments in proof of the essential unity of the religions, but something must be said about the doctrine of 'perspectives' which provides a key to the understanding of this unity.

Truth is one, but it is also infinite and therefore beyond form (since, in the nature of things, one form excludes others: an object cannot be at the same time both square and round). On the human level however truth necessarily conforms itself to the contours of the human mind, but for which it would be totally inconceivable, and it is shaped by the environment in which it finds expression, as it is also by the character of the people among whom it assumes a body of images, concepts and moral prescriptions much as light is fragmented into visible colours by the medium through which it passes. The display of diversity is, in a certain sense, the *raison d'être* of existence, and it would be astonishing if the religions through which men have apprehended reality did not partake most richly of that diversity. This may perhaps be illustrated in terms of an imagery different to that of the 'bubble' and its boundless landscape, but complementary to it.

Let us now imagine another landscape, surrounded this time by a desert which has no discernible end, but in itself fertile and inhabited by many nations, many tribes, set as it were in a circle around a great mountain which stands alone, filling the view. This mountain, in its overwhelming grandeur, may be known in a variety of ways by those who live within sight of it as, being human, do all the nations and all the tribes.

There will be some few who know it as a whole, either because they have climbed it or because their sight has been inspired and has miraculously embraced its many aspects in a single identity.

There will be others who see it from a particular and necessarily limited point of view, discerning certain features very clearly and therefore, so far as their perspective permits, seeing truly. Thirdly there are many whose eyesight is faulty or who are handicapped by distance so that mist intervenes, distorting vision, and among these there is bitter disagreement and much uncertainty. Finally there are those whose faculties may be sound enough but who stand with their backs to the mountain, describing quite accurately what they see on the drab plain before them; but what they see is of little consequence, and so long as they stay in this posture they can make no useful comment on the mountain or any of its aspects, disqualified as they are from taking part in the controversies of those who looked in the right direction. For their part however they are convinced that no one sees anything more than is visible to them. There is nothing there, no power and no glory; nothing.

The mountain, of course, is an image of the truth. The mountain is what *is*. The mountain is Reality, beside which nothing else is entirely real. The mountain is at the centre of the circle; and all ways, if they do not lead to it, lead into the desert where men die of thirst, plagued by chimera.

Among those who have seen it as a whole or, at the very least, surmise its wholeness there is no cause for controversy, unless over semantics, but among the others a conflict between rival perspectives is almost inevitable. In this context—and only in this context—both sides in a war may be right (and rightly claim that God is with them), for both have truth, albeit a partial truth, on their side; and it is in the nature of things that truth, fragmented, should be a source of conflict. So great is their power and their radiance, when such splinters of truth are embedded in the hearts and minds of combative men, that life seems of little account and death a bagatelle.

We are told by those who have received the gift of clarity that the truth is of a dazzling simplicity; but the variety of ways in which it may be perceived, understood and expressed is of vast complexity. This fact need not be in any way daunting, since it corresponds to the variety and complexity of the human minds to which truth is directed; but there can be little excuse for those who, while they reject simple and unquestioning faith as too naive for their taste, ask questions but will not wait for the answers. Among such as these are many who will devote a lifetime of effort and study to some trivial subject of entirely transient interest, but who regard the acquisition of the supreme knowledge—once thought to be the greatest treasure which this world secretes among its gold and jewels—as a matter scarcely worth their trouble unless it is easily accessible. So it is that they by-pass their human heritage and fritter away their powers.

This age in which we live stands condemned in terms of human normality precisely because it encourages men to dream their lives away in forgetfulness of their heritage and of those few things which they really need to know. Here lies the root of its sickness and there, in that heritage, is the rock to which those who refuse to slide away in the current must for ever hold fast.

# I

## UNREAL CITIES

With every choice we make some detail is added to the picture which, when it is completed, will show what we are uniquely and unrepeatably, and the effects of this choice will spread out, as rings spread from the stone tossed into a pool. The people around us will undergo some change, however small, but, far beyond this neighbourhood, the effects reach out to shores of which we scarcely dream. The choice we make is ours and no one else's; ours too are its numberless repercussions. We are responsible and answerable, here or elsewhere, now or later, for all that bears our stamp.

For this to be understood in an immediate, practical sense, men must have a certain freedom of movement and the space in which to deploy their possibilities. Choice is not enough. There must be the opportunity to exercise it, for good or ill; and without this opportunity the very idea of personal responsibility is drained of meaning. There are limitations inherent in human choice, which reflect the limitations of the human state as such when it is considered, so to speak, from above and in terms of an absolute Will of which our powers are only a fragmentary image. But this is another matter, and in what follows we are concerned with the human level, the human experience. At this level and in terms of this experience, men are creatures made for choosing and are, as such, responsible beings, accountable for what is done in their little world, but with a responsibility which extends far beyond its limits since we are not, by nature, entirely confined in our mortal shells. So long as true common sense is not overlaid by the complex falsities and sophistries of an unwise age, we know this well enough.

Children show, by the questions they ask when they first discover the use of words, their need to make sense of the world. Faced with the broken vase, spilt milk or eyeless doll they ask:

23

Who did it? Older, with the gift of simplicity behind us, we still want to ask the same question, though far less certain that it can be answered. The need to attribute acts and events to the person responsible for them is a universal human need.

Of all the changes that have taken place in the human condition over the past hundred years none is more significant than the increasing difficulty we now have in tracing acts to their owners. In earlier times and in more simple societies each act was branded with its owner's name. In the complex societies of today it might take the combined efforts of a detective and a moral philosopher to trace any given act to any one person. The State, the society or the organisation acts. 'They' act. But 'they' cannot be loved or blamed or touched. The need to attribute acts to men or women like ourselves finds no satisfaction.

It has become essential to redefine the idea of human responsibility in relation to a society of jobholders and civil servants, a world in which the majority of men are absorbed into vast collectivities and appear to have as little personal stake in their own actions as the slaves or bondmen of other times. This has become all the more necessary because, so far as it is possible to make any predictions about the future, there are good reasons for believing that our world is moving towards ever more complex degrees of organisation and that the man who is neither a jobholder nor, directly or indirectly, a servant of the State will soon be regarded as a complete eccentric if not as an outcast. For socialist societies this is the acknowledged aim. Under capitalism it is the unintended but nonetheless unavoidable outcome, witness the fact that in that home of 'free enterprise', the United States, ninety per cent of the employed now work in organisations of one kind or another, whereas at the beginning of this century ninety percent were self-employed.

The survival of the kind of world we have made for ourselves —in the context of advancing technology and of the growth of populations—depends upon a high degree of organisation and increasing collectivism, whatever the ideological flag under which it may sail. This world will try to survive for as long as it can, whatever the cost that has to be paid in loss of freedom and destruction of values.

To those who believe men to be more adaptable than in fact they are, it seems strange that an age in which so much responsibility is lifted from individual shoulders and transferred to the impersonal machinery of the State should yet be an age of acute anxiety and insecurity. But most men need some weight well adjusted to their strength if they are to walk well and confidently. Without this weight their feet no longer cleave to the ground and, though still incapable of flight, they lose the power to walk. Here, then, is a further basic need. We must not only know to whom acts belong, if the world is to make sense; we must also understand the nature of our own responsibility and have some notion of the obligations natural to us. Otherwise we swing in uneasy alternation between, on the one hand, an irresponsibility that is seldom free from the sense of guilt and, on the other, an exaggerated notion of our duties and obligations. Both scamp and busybody are products of a land without boundary marks.

If the thought of boundary marks and guidelines brings with it a flavour of constraint this is because we think of them as artificially imposed, disfiguring the landscape in which we live—a line of slick white posts marching up the hillside—whereas the only truly effective fences are either inherent in the landscape itself or else so timeworn and familiar as to be virtually invisible. Men need a framework but they should not know—or at least should not be constantly reminded—that they are living within the limitations of a framework. Few people are troubled by the limitations which their bodies impose upon them—the need for sleep, the unremitting demands of hunger and thirst—but if our bodies changed in form and in capability from week to week our existence would be a nightmare.

That it should be necessary to think about frameworks and to talk as though they could be devised and constructed according to convenience is itself a sign of the revolution that has taken place in the conditions of human living. Although it has its roots in changes initiated some hundreds of years ago, the effects of this revolution have only now encompassed the mass of mankind, and even in the Western world it is only in the past century that the majority of men and women have felt its full impact. Gustave Thibon, the French Catholic writer, wrote eloquently some years ago of that 'millennial equilibrium' which, by the very fact of its endurance, had every chance of being in conformity with the needs of human nature; an equilibrium only quite recently shattered. Powerfully aided by modern technology, our contemporary 'myths'—evolutionary, egalitarian, materialistic—have, as he said, torn the individual away from the great cosmic and social continuities, the earth, the craft, the family, which had been the normal setting of human lives.

The framework has never before been transformed in such radical fashion. Changes in the conditions of living had always, until now, taken place within a pattern that seemed unchanging to the men within its bounds, however it might appear to the bird's-eye-view of the historian. A dozen generations would hardly provide time enough to assimilate what has happened since the turn of the century and to assess it. We do not have the time. We come to terms, as any creature concerned with survival would do, but the greater part of what is happening escapes our full attention.

Everything becomes a blur when you travel beyond a certain speed. Distant objects may still be clear in outline, but the blurred foreground makes it impossible to attend to them. This landscape is unreal and the passengers in the express train turn to their books, their thoughts or their private fantasies.

The subjectivism of our age has a good deal to do with this imprisonment in a speeding vehicle, and the fact that we made this vehicle ourselves, with all the tireless care that children give to a contrivance of wood and wire, does not save us from the sense of being trapped without hope of escape.

A further effect of such vertiginous speed is a kind of anaesthesia, entirely natural when the operation of the senses by which we normally make contact with our environment is suspended. With no opportunity to assimilate what is going on, our powers of assimilation are inevitably weakened and a certain numbness sets in ; nothing is fully savoured and nothing is properly understood. Even fear (which exists to forewarn us of danger) is suspended. This would be so even if speed of change were the only factor involved, but the kind of environment in which a large part of humanity lives today—the environment created by technology at the service of immediate, short-term needs—does much to intensify this effect. Outside of works of art which embody something beyond our physical needs, our own constructions bore us. Those who, when they have built something and admired the finished product for a decent moment, are ready to pull it down and start on something new have good sense on their side. To live in an entirely man-made environment, in the midst of a clutter of our own products, is to be isolated in a narrow world which gives no play to the capacity we have for reaching out to what lies beyond the human realm as such.

In its ugliness and also in its remoteness from the natural world, this environment is a kind of projection of the unbeliever's psyche, as it is of his philosophy. It does not set out to provide spiritual nourishment—why should it, since the intention is only to satisfy certain 'practical' exigencies?—and, though it may excite them, it does not appease the senses. It offers only a setting in which cease-less and, for the most part, aimless activity can take place.

There is nothing in common between, on the one hand, the stupor produced by an environment which offers no nourishment and, on the other, that 'sleep of the senses' induced by a beauty which melts the barriers between one world and another—or by such concentration of attention upon what lies beyond the im-mediate grasp of the senses that perceived reality becomes, not blurred, but transparent. For beauty to penetrate or for concentra-tion to become stabilised, time and stillness are necessary. The speed with which events follow one upon another in the modern context, the speed with which the very framework in which these events occur changes shape, must banish both from our lives; and, in a landscape of blurred outlines, the exercise of responsible choice between sharply perceived alternatives—which also re-quires time and stillness—becomes doubly difficult.

An environment that never stays still can only breed men whose capacity for choosing is maimed and shaken. How can one choose between the waves of the sea? And man himself, neither physically rooted nor spiritually nourished, is far from being a fixed point in this shifting scene. His changing environment compels him to adjust to unstable currents and veering winds, conditioning him in terms of an instability which undermines all capacity for judg-ment. Indeed, if the world his kind have made is to maintain its momentum, he must adapt and keep pace or fall—so he is led to believe—into some no-man's-land of unreality: for this, he is told, is the real world; there is nowhere else to go, so make the best of it.

He, the ordinary man, the member of the multitude, has been ripped out of the environment of solid, tangible things which—in terms of human generations—stay put, and has been made into something functional and interchangeable.

The peasant farmer who mistreats the soil or neglects his crops is very soon made to know the error of his ways, and the fact that one kind of reality presses so hard upon him and refuses to be ignored or falsified teaches him to discriminate in other fields between the real and the fantastic, the necessary and the super-fluous. Whereas the official or the jobholder, a unit in a vast organisation, may survive a lifetime of gross errors and mistaken notions before reality catches up with him. Thibon, who was himself of peasant origin, wrote: 'If peasants have as many faults (as other men), they have less perversions. Rather than their virtue, it is their health that I praise'. He did not mean by 'perversion' quite what moralists would understand by this term. Perversion is essentially an act of turning away from reality at any level, from the earth at our feet or from the sky above us, a retreat from the light into private darkness.

To our sophisticated palates the peasant is not altogether an attractive figure, but he represents—take him or leave him—a way of life that shows up, by force of contrast, the fragility and rootlessness of the new ways which have taken its place. The Communists, those high professionals in the craft of manipulating and exploiting human material, have often found him a prickly mouthful to swallow.

The small businessman or trader is also brought constantly face to face with the consequences of his own actions in a way that the member of a big organisation is not. The latter depends, for his success or failure, upon the uncertain and often unrealistic judgment of his fellow men (already the decisive factor in his personal and social life) rather than upon the firm pressure of natural forces which would fling back at him the results of his acts with an infallible precision such as his fellow men can never achieve. For the jobholder, the consequences of action return to him filtered through human media, so that he can always attribute them to the good will or malice of his superiors rather than to his own actions. What was once a simple and direct connection be-tween naked act and equally naked effect has become immensely complex and open to a variety of interpretations. Subjectivism intervenes at every level and it is hard for any man to learn what truth means and how it differs from falsehood and fabrication.

The effects of an unstable and, at the same time, artificial environment are plain enough, as are those of work in which consequences cannot be directly related to their causes; but there is a further element in modern societies which does at least as much to undermine the free exercise of choice and responsibility. This is the protection which society is now expected to give its citizens: protection not only against ill fortune and disaster, but also against all the ills they might bring upon themselves. And here we enter a region of moral ambiguity. It is natural to shelter from a storm and equally natural to share this shelter with our neighbours. Only a fool exposes himself willingly to injury and only a rogue ignores his neighbour's danger. But there is a limit to the obligation we have—or even to the right we have—to protect others against the results of their own follies or vices. Just as pain is necessary to warn us of the body's malfunction, so there are misfortunes which fulfil a necessary function and but for which human beings would never achieve maturity or learn the nature of their world.

To assume that people will behave like irresponsible children if given the chance and, on these grounds, to deny them the chance leads to a suffocating paternalism which ends by destroying what it most cherishes; and to insist upon protecting us against every possibility of injury from other men involves binding them securely, and binding us too, since we are the 'other' in relation to them. There is a morality which insists that men's arms must be bound to their sides because some might want to use their fists and insists that their ankles be tethered because some might want to walk into trouble. There is only one logical conclusion to such overwhelming concern for our wellbeing: we must all be locked up where we can do no harm either to ourselves or to others.

There will be more to be said at a later stage regarding the curtailment of liberty in the supposed public interest, but it is worth noting here a phrase which recurs again and again in the press, on television and in conversation: this is to the effect that when human lives are weighed against 'a small loss of personal freedom' one should not hesitate to make the necessary sacrifice. This phrase may one day be carved over the grave of our liberties, for those who use it seem quite unaware that a number of 'small losses' soon add up to one great loss. There have indeed been thousands, if not tens of thousands of such losses in recent years. They have been readily accepted because the majority of people think they know the limits beyond which they themselves would refuse to tolerate further deprivations of personal freedom.

It is assumed that there is some kind of natural, regulative mechanism which can be guaranteed to stop the process of confinement and enslavement before it reaches a point either absurd or intolerable. The fact is that conditions of life which would have seemed both absurd and intolerable to an earlier generation are accepted without protest by a later one which has started out, so to speak, from a point lower on the scale. There is, strictly speaking, no limit set to the accumulation of small losses. What we have always to bear in mind is not the significance of one new law or regulation—possibly trivial in itself—but the direction in which it points, the tendency it betrays and the place it occupies in the context of similar laws and regulations preceding it or likely to follow it. With this in mind, we may begin to see a great number of the measures imposed upon us for our own protection as points in the plotting of a graph which is both sinister and menacing in its implications.

Meanwhile, in our relatively comfortable straight-jacket and filled with a sense of virtue (are we not the first people who have ever truly *cared* for our fellows?), we become increasingly dependent upon the paternal—or perhaps one should say, maternal—society and accept its benefits without really considering the price that must be paid; for one effect of such protected environments is that they destroy the normal human awareness that everything in this world has its price tag. Another effect is that the sense of personal responsibility atrophies like an unused muscle; what need is there for us to do anything for this child or that old person when everything can be safely left in other hands? When we meet with injury and injustice we call upon 'them' to do something about it and, if we take action at all, it is to demand new laws, new regulations to deal with the situation. Unfortunately such legislation is comparable to generalised radiation treatment, which kills the healthy cells with the malignant ones.

Those who meet the consequences of their actions day in and day out do not need to have the idea of responsibility—the idea that each act has an owner to whom its effects return—explained to them : its physical demonstration is imprinted on their flesh. Others—the jobholder, the functionary, the children of the paternalistic State—are provided with no such object lessons and they lose, in consequence, their sense of reality. This loss of the sense of living in a world which rings true when struck is accompanied by a weakening of man's idea of himself as a being capable of acting upon an environment which includes not only the middle world in which his daily life is passed, but also the dimensions of heaven and hell. Perhaps the very idea of responsibility, as applied to the image of man presented by contemporary beliefs, is ridiculous : this mannikin is too small and too impotent to be the creator and owner of acts which reverberate throughout the worlds.

Whether or not man in the abstract, the alleged conqueror of nature (able for the first time to inflict enduring wounds upon the very earth he treads) seems to us a powerful figure, the ordinary individual in our time feels very little sense of power. He does not control the campaign of 'conquest', but is subordinated to it so that it may at times seem like a grotesque accident in which he happens to have become involved. Few, if any, believe that the process of scientific and technological 'advance' could be halted by an act of will on their part, even though many are aware that it contains the seeds of its own reversal or destruction. If we are merely spectators of a process that advances—whether to glory or to death—regardless of our intentions or desires, while demanding from us all that we have to give of mind and heart and sinew, then we have little enough upon which to pride ourselves.

People of other times have been blamed and even despised for the 'fatalism' with which they accepted the conditions of human life, facing their losses or sufferings as though these things were unalterably decreed ; and yet it is as fatalists that most people in our time accept the process in which they are caught up. 'Progress', it seems, is inevitable, as are its painful side-effects. If it becomes necessary to use the full resources of nuclear and biological warfare now available—and our age does not willingly leave its resources unused—this fatalism will suggest the condition of beasts driven to the slaughterhouse and perhaps recall to memory those trudging crowds who went so quietly to death in the gas chambers of Auschwitz and Treblinka.

When things go wrong or, to be more honest, when things get worse instead of better it is readily assumed that this is a temporary aberration and will soon be put right because there is a natural law which guarantees progress. Now natural processes carry with them a strong sense of fatality and inevitability ; the sun has been rising and setting with predictable regularity for a very long time; and although there is strong criticism of certain particular aspects of our present situation and it is often said that man's 'moral evolution' has failed to keep pace with his 'mastery' of the physical world, the majority of people accept without question that the direction in which we are travelling is the direction dictated by laws as inevitable as those which govern falling bodies (but in this case they imagine the body to be a rising one). It is astonishing, however, that those who have so little regard for natural laws in general, believing that they can be manipulated at will, should accept this particular one so meekly; unless, of course, it turns out to be a law that they, not nature, invented. Men who scorn the idea of submission to the divine Will and are outraged by the notion of a God who requires submission are among the first to demand total submission to the process in which we are involved and seem to attach a kind of moral imperative to willing participation in it. Any other attitude, so they say, is reactionary or escapist or anti-social. Perhaps, after all, they have found a divinity to worship; and, if they have, the only charitable comment must be: God help them!

Escaping, as we have done, from the so-called tyranny of absolute principles derived from religious doctrine which, because they are not altogether of this world, possess a certain elasticity as to their practical application and leave room for a variety of interpretations in terms of the practical life, we have fallen under the very real tyranny of majority opinion as to what is right and what is wrong.

The old morality was stable and lasting, yet it left space for manoeuvre; the new one is rigid and unintelligent but, as though to compensate for this rigidity, it changes from year to year in terms of fashions in popular opinion and under the influence of propaganda. Each new doctrine of 'right' and 'wrong' kicks aside the previous one and struts its little time upon the stage as an absolute monarch. The man who is filled today with self-righteousness because he acts in accordance with crowd opinion here and now would have been considered a sinner yesterday and may be thought a villain tomorrow. It is instructive, in this context, to study the political speeches of leaders in the West or in the Eastern Bloc if one wishes to understand the techniques of moral blackmail. Their appeal is always to right-thinking people, decent people, who only want to act for the best. It is by this technique that men are gulled, if not into supporting rampant evil, at least into unwillingness to oppose it.

We do not have the right to despise our fellow men as men. We do not know their innermost 'secret'. But we have every right to turn away in contempt from the Great Beast—the term which Simone Weil, surely among the most compassionate of women, applied to society—and to treat with contempt the opinions which, in its impersonal stupidity, it strives to thrust upon us.

It is strange that in a supposedly cynical age the exponents of the current morality which, at this particular moment in time, has to do with 'social justice' and 'equality', should be as self-righteous as any seventeenth-century puritan or nineteenth-century missionary. One might have expected them to be more self-critical. And the new Puritanism readily adopts the jargon of the old one; differences in wealth are 'obscene', the notion that some people might be better than others is 'indecent' and so on. No Calvinistic deity speaks here, but only an historical trend which seeks to express itself through a multiplicity of masks, seldom showing its raw face. Those who serve it do not know it; and their innocence serves its purpose very well. A rogue who consciously deceives the people and deliberately leads them up the wrong road cannot go far in politics. A man must believe in himself if he is to be believed, and he must be convinced if he is to convince. Above all he must be at one with the obscure yet powerful currents of opinion which sway men's minds and hearts when they have lost faith in an absolute and changeless Principle from which, in the ages of faith, all opinions flowed.

The beliefs which now hold sway could have little appeal were it not for an emptiness that demands to be filled and an ignorance which cries out to be assuaged by certainties, however absurd. Men need to *know*. If true knowledge is denied them, they will seize upon error and make it their knowledge; but this can only happen to those who, being unacquainted with truth at the mundane level of wind and weather, have little hope of acquaintance with truth at any more exalted level. The veils which hide from them the normal realities of human living hide much else besides, for such veils not only protect but also exclude: they enclose us within a dream world in which folly may be wisdom and falsehood may be truth, and no one can tell the difference—for the bright light by which he might discern it is shut out. What will such vulnerable creatures do when they are cast out into the open like pet animals left to fend for themselves? They are not equipped to face reality in any shape or form. And yet the structure which for the moment protects them against the forces of nature as it does against the results of their own folly or improvidence is very frail and may already be threatened with destruction. Its existence is a by-product of a period of unprecedented wealth and prosperity in the so-called 'developed' countries. We must wait to see how the compassionate society behaves when it is no longer the fat society.

Sadly but, perhaps, not altogether unexpectedly this society has had very limited success in achieving what is supposed to be the justification for its existence—the greatest amount of happiness for the greatest possible number of people. In so far as its citizens are saved from the major anxieties and responsibilities which normally surround the business of being a man, they transfer what appears to be an unvarying human capacity for worry to the most trivial things, making mountains out of molehills on a vast scale; and they have 'nervous breakdowns' over problems which men and women living under sterner conditions would hardly find time to notice.

It is revealing that so many people in Britain and the U.S. who are old enough to have been involved in the Second World War look back upon that time of trial and danger as the 'happiest time of their lives'. But happiness is an elusive quality, not easily imposed through legislation, and human beings have a way of behaving like a contrary child who squats in the midst of a pile of Christmas presents wailing that the one thing he really wanted is missing. This is profoundly discouraging for those whose only desire is to please, yet they are not easily put down. In imperial times the Anglo-Saxons made by far the most determined and uncompromising missionaries, and the missionary spirit endures (particularly in left-wing circles) but is now turned inwards upon our own societies. The new morality or the new 'normality' is imposed in the same earnest and self-righteous spirit which animated those intrepid exponents of the less orthodox sub-cults of Christianity when they confronted the naked heathen and told him what was good for him. Only the tropical topee has been discarded.

The man who, in spite of these pressures, has difficulty in

accepting what his mentors regard as self-evident and fails to conform to the 'normality' in fashion at this particular moment, is clearly a case for treatment. When we criticise the Soviet authorities for confining their dissidents in mental hospitals we tend to forget that, for them, anyone who does not conform to 'socialist morality' is indeed less than sane. Simone Weil's 'Great Beast' has become a god denied only by madmen, and to be 'anti-social' is to be out of touch with reality. In the West 'gradualism' takes the place of revolution and the issues are therefore less clear-cut; but we are travelling in the same direction and psychiatry already plays its part in encouraging conformity.

In theory the psychiatrist conceives his job as one of helping people to live as happily as may be possible in the world in which they find themselves, without making moral judgments any more than the motor mechanic concerns himself with the direction in which a car will be driven after he has made it roadworthy. Unfortunately the human situation does not permit us to take up positions of neutrality. Psychiatrists are men, with an ineradicable tendency to see human actions in a moral context, and their clients also are men, not motor cars. The difference cannot be ignored, for cars do not choose their direction whereas men—at least in a partial and limited sense—do.

The question which the psychiatrist tries at all costs to avoid answering is whether men should be persuaded to adjust to a bad society or to a society on the way to self-destruction. To answer it would be to make value-judgments which most psychiatrists are determined to exclude from their work, although the very notion that this can be done betrays a singular ignorance of human nature.

Which, in fact, do we admire: the slave who adjusts to his position and is happy in slavery, or the slave who escapes and becomes a free man? Most people would favour the escaper, but the psychiatrist is dedicated to combating tendencies to 'escapism', whatever form they may take, and to counsel adjustment to the circumstances of our time simply because these circumstances exist, rather as though a man in the path of an avalanche were advised to adjust to his situation—which certainly exists—and allow himself to be engulfed, since to get out of the way would be an act of 'escapism'. To those who have no belief in principles situated outside the realm of ceaseless change, reality appears to be neither more nor less than what happens to exist at a given moment and what exists at this moment is all that there *is*. The notion that there may be degrees of reality is quite alien to this mentality, although the fact that waking life is more real than dreaming or that hallucinations differ from the clear vision of objects is not denied.

People easily mistake for courage and realism attitudes which are, in truth, their opposites and, because a calamity cannot be prevented, call it a benefit and make a virtue of their inability to escape from it. Realism would require quite a different approach, for it implies discrimination and valuation. At the simplest level we know well enough the difference between what is pleasant and what is painful, and the fact that we may have to endure the latter does not prevent us from recognising it for what it is. To refuse to recognise those features of the modern world which are clearly evil, ugly and destructive of the qualities which constitute the nobility of the human state, simply because they exist and we do not know what to do about them, is to compound the injuries we suffer by allowing our innate capacity for judgment to be falsified.

The major problem, however, which faces those who would like to ensure that their fabricated system is proof against all incursions of reality concerns emotional distress. In the first place, swift change is extremely uncomfortable and unsettling : required to readjust every few years to major changes in their environment, many people become depressed and forget to smile. Secondly, we are all of us exposed to grief: the people we love die, as we shall ourselves in due course ; expectations are disappointed and ambitions are thwarted by circumstance. Finally, there are some who insist upon feeling guilty over the ill they have done or simply on account of the ugliness which they perceive in their own souls. A solution of a kind has been found to this problem in the form of sedatives and anti-depressant drugs, so that many human experiences which used to be accepted as an integral part of human life are now defined and dealt with as medical problems. The widow who grieves for a beloved husband becomes a 'case', as does the man saddened by the recollection of the napalm or high explosives he has dropped on civilian populations. One had thought that guilt was a way, however indirect, in which we might perceive the nature of reality and the laws which govern our human experience ; but it is now an illness that can be cured.

Death, however, remains incurable. Though we might be embarrassed by Victorian death-bed scenes or the practices of mourning among people less sophisticated than ourselves, the fact of death tells us so much about the realities of our condition that to ignore it or try to forget it is to be unaware of the most important thing we need to know about our situation as living creatures. Equally, to witness and participate in the dying of our fellow men and women is to learn what we are and, if we have any wisdom at all, to draw conclusions which must in their way affect our every thought and our every act. It was with good reason that Walid I, one of the Umayyad Caliphs, wore always on his finger a ring inscribed 'Walid, thou must die'.

We cannot begin to consider what we are or what we should do until we know in heart and mind and body that we are mortal and that death walks with us from the moment we are born. It is not only in Islam that the wise man lies down each night knowing that he may not awaken and greets each new day in the knowledge that he may not see its ending. But those who live in this awareness find in their days a savour that is missed by all who hide themselves away from it. They know, as these others do not, what it is to be a man.

We are witnessing now an attempt to eliminate the darker, more painful aspects of human living, no longer by rising above them (and thereby gaining in stature), but either by abolishing them— which is impossible since they lie in the nature of things—or by pretending they do not exist. It was possible for the men of other times to accept these conditions because life as such was situated in an infinitely wider context. They knew that however deeply involved they might be in the scenario of suffering and loss, they were not by nature totally submerged in it. Experience taught them to look elsewhere for peace and for perfection, and faith assured them that there are indeed other dimensions than those which seem to hem us in. Today most people are confined in a place that knows no 'elsewhere', trapped with wild beasts that tear their flesh and from which they cannot escape. It is hardly surprising that they need to be drugged to be able to exist in such a situation.

This has inevitably drawn us into a vicious circle. The more we try to insulate ourselves, however temporarily, against the harsh realities of the human condition, the more unreal our world becomes and the further it is removed from all contact with Truth. The awareness of other dimensions—an awareness through which we might achieve freedom—becomes inaccessible; there is no place for God in an artificial world since it is realities that point towards him and remind us of him, not fictions; and the idea that anything good—any joy or reconciliation—or any light is to be found outside the bubble in which we live is inconceivable. We can imagine only darkness and a fearful emptiness, black as interstellar space: we hide our faces from it and wait to die.

When a man is mad we say that he has 'lost contact with reality', which is a fair enough definition though it leaves room for considerable differences of opinion as to what we mean by 'reality'. Not every psychiatrist, however, defines sanity in terms of adjustment to a given, uncritically accepted situation. In his study of human behaviour in the Nazi concentration camps,* Bruno Bettelheim (himself a survivor of the camps) writes of the common tendency to deny that any basic problem exists in connection with the increasing mechanisation of the human condition. 'Like the person suffering from addiction', he says, 'our society seems to be rushing ahead unthinking into an ever greater mechanisation of life, expecting more extensive technology to solve the problems it creates. Here we operate like the alcoholic who tries to escape from his hangover by going on a new binge.'

'Modern man', he adds, 'suffers from his inability to make a choice, as he sees it, between renouncing freedom and individualism, or giving up the material comforts of technology . . . This, as I see it, is the true conflict of our times.'

This, of course, assumes an awareness of the possibility of choosing. The speed with which we are being carried onwards in our express train, the blurring of outlines in our changing environment and the fatalism with which people are encouraged to accept these conditions makes it difficult to see that a choice exists or has ever existed. There is, in any case, a common human tendency, more pronounced in our time than ever before, to believe that one can 'have one's cake and eat it'. This belief is encouraged by evolutionary theory and by the bastard notion it has begotten on wishful thinking: the concept of progress. It is

* *The Informed Heart:* Bruno Bettelheim.

readily assumed that the benefits of the modern world—comforts, material prosperity, protection from many natural disasters, 'richness' of human experience and so on—accrue to us in the way that certain advantages accrue to a man or woman when they reach adult status.

Among the worst of the many misleading lessons drummed into our children at school, where the hypotheses of contemporary science are presented as though they were unquestionable facts, is the flattering fiction that our age represents the 'grown up' condition of mankind. Picture books show our hairy ancestors discovering fire, our childlike but promising predecessors inventing primitive machines and ourselves, both wise and clever, travelling at breathtaking speed and reaching out towards a heaven on earth. Implied (but not illustrated, for this would be tactless) is an image of Western man bearing gifts of knowledge and civilisation to those less fortunate than himself.

Inventiveness has become the touchstone both of intelligence and of excellence, and qualities peculiar to one particular human group at a particular moment in history are seen as the qualities proper to man in his 'evolved' form. The fact that such one-sidedness is developed only at immense cost and through the sacrifice of many of the qualities which were once thought to mark the real distinction between men and beasts is ignored. And yet the human situation does not really change. Man is still man, compelled to choose between this good thing and that one, never allowed to enjoy both together. To possess one he must, in the long run, sacrifice another; and, for that matter, to possess some worthless trifle he may be called upon to give up such valuables as he has inherited, buying fantasies at the cost of reality and paying in sound coinage for trash. What the world can offer us is limited by its very nature, and we must decide what we want to have from it. There is nothing to suggest that men have succeeded, in this age, in escaping from these laws of compensation.

We need, then, to be shrewd and canny merchants, choosing with care what we buy and sell, constantly on guard against those who offer us something for nothing, and parting with our goods only when we see the colour of the purchaser's money. To a man such as Bettelheim after his prison experience, the true nature of liberty must have been transparently clear; such men will not give up the smallest particle of their liberty unless the value of what they are offered in return has been certified beyond all possible doubt, nor will they readily sacrifice their freedom of choice even in the smallest matters.

The theory upon which contemporary societies operate is that we must have complete freedom to make the right choice. We are to be prevented, so far as may be possible, from making the wrong one, not only because this would be bad for us but because it would very probably injure other people as well. Unfortunately many of us do insist upon choosing wrongly all too often, and our benefactors feel obliged, in the public interest, to narrow the field of choice and restrict our opportunities for making mistakes. In this fashion the trap closes, not with a sudden snap which might provoke a violent struggle to escape, but inch-by-inch year-by-year.

It would be foolish to suggest that the alternatives to letting the trap close upon us are pleasant or palatable. Our situation invites us to make a choice of evils, not a choice between black and white. The beliefs which must be questioned in any radical criticism of the modern age are beliefs which have led, among other things, to advances in medical practice, the elimination of hardship in many areas of human activity and a quantitatively richer life than was ever before possible. The fact that this century has also provided examples of cruelty and mass slaughter on an unprecedented scale is generally considered irrelevant, for these things are regarded as accidents which, with a reasonable amount of luck, we shall avoid in future. The critic is therefore open to attack on the grounds that he would like to see half the babies born dying in infancy and the majority of those who survive being denied most of the joys of life.

The question of what we would or would not like has very little to do with the issue. We would always like to enjoy the best of all possible worlds, or to be more honest, the best of all impossible worlds; but we are bound to the wheel of fact, of what exists and of what is practicable. Those who reach out avidly to grasp the impossible find that they have lost what little they had that was good and solid. At the end of the day they hold only fantasies in their hands; fantasies which, like parasites, destroy their host.

It is also quite common to ask the critic if he wants to see 'the clock put back', as though the process of time could be reversed or an old man become young again. We must learn from the past but we cannot return to it, and patterns of living or social systems which have had their day are done with and cannot be brought back; but they may still provide a touchstone, and without such touchstones, such indications of the human path, we are no more than children lost in the wilds. The putting-the-clock-back argument is, in any case, a prime example of the modern tendency to dismiss as pointless any criticism which is not accompanied by an instant remedy. Yet a building with unsound foundations will fall, regardless of whether the builders are ready to put up another in its place, and in their personal lives people are still allowed to recognise that a wrong decision was made and to regret the fact, even when the decision cannot be reversed.

For countless generations in that past from which, if we were less arrogant, we could learn so much that we need to know before it is too late, men lived and died with a picture of themselves and of their world which seemed as real and as immutable as the physical environment itself. The picture varied in detail from place to place, just as human languages and styles vary from one people to another, but in its basic substance it was a single, universal image and the variations fade into insignificance when comparison is made with our contemporary view of things. To most people in the West today and to an increasing number in every part of the world, this image appears to be false since it seems to have no foundation in physical observation and experiment.

We should consider what is implied in the assumption that we are right and everyone else was wrong. If the vast majority of human beings of every race, from the beginning of time until yesterday or the day before, were mistaken in their most fundamental beliefs and lived out their lives in error and illusion, then it is utterly unreasonable to suppose that human beings could now or ever be right. The notion that, after such ages of ignorance and superstition, this silly creature has suddenly become wise is too improbable to be entertained; 'for a being absurd by nature', as Frithjof Schuon has said, 'does not contain the possibility of ceasing to be absurd'. With every word that casts derision upon the traditional beliefs of mankind we dig away the ground from under our own feet and disqualify ourselves from making true judgments in any field. We are the same men they were, with no sixth sense or special power of intelligence over and above what they possessed.

There are indeed some who, taking this point, maintain either that there is no truth to be known or else that such truth as there may be is for ever beyond man's reach: he must therefore be content with the one thing he knows for certain—the fact of his own subjective experience. There can be no more total abdication of human intelligence. These philosophers have found a subterranean place where no thunder can shake them, no lightning dazzle them, and it is sometimes suggested that God himself will respect their dreadful privacy and leave them for ever alone. And yet we possess, as human beings, an inborn conviction that we are capable of true knowledge and that the possibility of being objectively right exists. We have, in fact, a sense of the Absolute. The denial of this capacity shakes and uproots us; it threatens to isolate us in an absurd realm of weightless fantasies with which we cannot hope to grapple—for they are not really there at all.

In this way, as also by the environment we have built around ourselves and by the work we do, we are unmanned and made ready for enslavement. For every prey there is a predator, and ours may be closer than we know.

# 2

## THE COST OF WEALTH

According to a Muslim story Jesus, son of Mary, came once upon an old man who lived on a mountain in the open air, without any shelter from heat or cold. Jesus asked him why he had not built himself a house. 'Oh Spirit of God,' said the old man, 'Prophets before thee predicted that I would live for only seven hundred years. It is not worth my trouble to settle down.'

Those who expect to live an even shorter span may well hesitate to set up house here; and we are assured in the wise doctrines handed down to us that the world is to be treated as a bridge, not as a stopping place. 'I am like a rider who shelters under a tree, then goes on his way,' said the Prophet Muhammad. But to be, in this sense, a traveller or one who lives unconfined is not at all the same thing as being a rootless vagabond. Those who are not firmly established in heaven must at least have their feet firmly planted on earth; for we are, through our earthly nature, embedded in its matrix, dust of its dust. Its minerals run in our veins and its natural forces play within us as they do in the world beyond the skin's thin membrane.

A man stands firm if his roots are well sunk in one place (whether we understand this literally or in a deeper sense), his own particular location, his property, his home. These things are like extensions of his own body; stripped of them he is a tortoise without its shell—a flayed, pulpy creature, and a ready prey for the predators. To suppose otherwise is to be deceived by the false idealism which preaches that men can be freed through violent revolution and liberated from their embeddedness by a simple uprooting, rather than through a transfiguration which encompasses both man and matrix. When, allegedly in the interests of a wider and richer life for all, we deprive men of the private and limited field within which they can effectively exercise their powers of choice and understand their responsibilities, we produce, not a

43

liberated being, but a naked creature. There are reformers who, like wise doctors, labour to keep us in health; but there exists also a malignant passion for change which readily sacrifices the real goods we possess to ideals which are both unrealisable on the level of human living and unrelated to the actual needs of real men and women.

From the time of the French Encyclopaedists onwards our daily life has been increasingly at the mercy of theorists who, in their quiet studies or in university libraries, have let their thoughts and their fantasies run free, intoxicated often enough by a passion for abstract good and abstract right, convinced that the distant world of people and of things can be transformed into something closer to their dreams. Behind the dry exterior and behind the equation which seems to offer a solution to complex human problems is a flood of strangely rarefied emotion which requires no human contact for its satisfaction. Such men often go unrecognised in their lifetimes, but the moment comes when a spark from their secret passion lights on tinder. Young minds take fire, lost men find a direction and the masses begin to stir. Once we have lost contact with the true source of answers which appease the questioning mind, a theory which appears to provide answers and a basis for action is like a draught of cool water in the desert, and there remain no touchstones in terms of which it might be assessed objectively.

Put into practice, these passionate theories come up against the obtuseness of human material: dreams of universal justice are obstructed by flesh and blood, and 'people' (an easily manageable abstraction in the mind of the theorist) block the way of progress; soon there are real bodies in the street and real blood stains the pavements.

But change need not always be so abrupt. There are more subtle ways of removing obstructions and gentler techniques of man-management. Why destroy a man if, with patience, he can be persuaded to destroy himself? And when this patient persuasion appeals to a moral sense that is all at sea, having been cut adrift from the very notion of an immutable Good which is never bent to human convenience, its effectiveness is not in doubt.

In the long run all private goods present themselves as obstacles in the way of change and in the way of the forces which, though they operate in the shadows, direct the course of change; but without some corner of his environment, however small, that belongs to him a man is as easily tipped over as a ninepin. Belongings take up space and restrict mobility, like hillocks dotting the flat surface of a map upon which we could otherwise draw straight lines or like little houses which prevent a 'developer' from realising his grand design for a site on which all else has been demolished. The pride of industrialism in its early stages was the railway, ideally a straight line ruled across the map, but at that time technical problems made it impossible completely to ignore the natural features of the landscape, while social conditions forced the planners to take into consideration private interests—the great estates owned by men so well entrenched that they could insist upon a diversion around their property. The contemporary world however insists upon straight lines, whether on the social, economic or political level. Technology enables us to iron out the natural obstacles, and ideology justifies the elimination of man-made obstructions.

The railways were the precursors of what was to come. Modern techniques of government, like the industrial techniques which increasingly determine them, go straight to the point. Required to twist and turn around islands of individual idiosyncrasy or to respect vested interests and entrenched positions, they could not function at all. But to deprive men of their idiosyncratic individualism, of their vested interests, however small, and of their entrenchment in a given milieu is to uproot them. Only then can they be marshalled into files, and only so can their general interest and their general usefulness be reckoned statistically.

In the economic realm, which is in itself a kind of abstraction of man's earthliness, uprooting takes the form of the substitution of public wealth for private property. These are of entirely different natures, as Hannah Arendt has pointed out in her remarkable study of the subject.* 'The present emergence everywhere of actually or potentially very wealthy societies which at the same time are essentially propertyless, because the wealth of any single individual consists of his share in the annual income of society as a whole, clearly shows how little these two are connected. Prior to the modern age, which began with the expropriation of the poor and then proceeded to emancipate the new propertyless classes, all

* *The Human Condition:* Hannah Arendt (University of Chicago Press), p. 61.

civilisations have rested upon the sacredness of private property. Wealth, on the contrary, whether privately owned or publicly distributed, had never been sacred before. Originally property meant no more or less than to have one's location in a particular part of the world . . .'

Property, as Miss Arendt understands it, is not simply a particular form of acquired wealth but a protective and familiar shell, so assimilated to its owner that it can scarcely be thought of as disposable. To sell it would be comparable to selling oneself, to have it seized in payment of taxation would be comparable to mutilation (hence, no doubt, the age-old loathing for tax-gatherers). A house, a plot of land or durable goods which can be handed down from generation to generation are qualitatively different from a car or a television set which soon become obsolete.

It is this durability in the personal environment that enables men to see their own short and changeful lives against a background of relative permanence and, in doing so, to achieve a stability which may be the foundation of greater and more transcendent achievements. The man who is born and dies in the same bed has lived in a context in which he could sink roots and from which he could draw nourishment. He moved, perhaps he travelled far, but his environment could be relied upon to stay still; and movement should be a quality of men, not of environments.

Understood in this sense, property is something handed on from generation to generation. The modern mind, conditioned as it is to the devouring needs of a fast-changing world and reflecting these needs even in its moral judgments, is disturbed by the very idea of inheritance. It is not only socialists who believe that everyone should start out stripped of inherited advantages and make his way, win his wealth (in capitalist terms) or his position (in the socialist context) by his own efforts. This might be splendid if life in the human community were no more than a glorified School Sports Day, but our race is run through a forest in which wild beasts abound—and even more dangerous creatures. If all cannot take part armed, then at least let some carry weapons of defence. It is even possible that those who are armed may offer some protection to those who are not. If ten men face a host of enemies and only one has a gun, who would ask him to throw it away in the interests of fairness and equality? Those who are fortunate enough to live under a benevolent government and see no danger in placing themselves trustingly in its hands can know little of the world and still less of history if they imagine that this happy state of affairs is in some way guaranteed to endure indefinitely.

Miss Arendt points out that the modern age began with the expropriation of the small man or, in other words, with the creation of a proletariat fitted to the requirements of a machine civilisation. It was with good reason that Marx told the workers they had nothing to lose but their chains. It would be wrong however to suppose that such a dispossessed class has always existed, in Europe or elsewhere; the only historical parallel is probably with chattel slavery. The dispossessed must always represent an element of grave danger for any society, precisely because they have nothing to lose. Take from a man the little he has that is truly his own, his 'locality', and make a slave of him as men were enslaved by developing industrialism; then take note of his condition, raise him up and give him a fair share of the wealth created by his labour : he is now 'better off', he may well be happier but he no longer knows what it means to possess property and he is so effectively integrated into the social machine that he will never obstruct its course, no matter which way that course may lead.

The process of expropriation however may very well start at the other end of the social scale. Attack the big man first—small men, having their normal quota of envy, will be delighted to see him put down. Once the big man has been incapacitated, the small ones can be mopped up easily enough. In the matter of property (and of inheritance) we are sure to hang separately if we do not hang together; and in troubled times the small man's cottage is indefensible once the big man's castle has fallen. The castle, after all, was not merely the local magnate's home ; it was also the refuge, in changing and turbulent times, for all the neighbourhood.

The distinction between the dispossessed and those who are free of possessions—opposites which may superficially resemble each other—must again be stressed to avoid any possible misunderstanding. The saint is essentially a man stripped and naked in this world, but he is one who no longer needs to draw strength and sustenance from earthly roots; he is supplied with these in quite another way and from quite another source. The ordinary man's potential for sanctity is too deeply buried to be wrenched to the surface by the brutal technique of cutting off his earthly attachments. He needs his private plot and, however paradoxical this may seem, is unlikely to rise above it if he is deprived prematurely of this support; a caterpillar will not become a butterfly if it is denied its chrysalis stage.

This is something completely ignored by the cruel and unrealistic 'idealism' of our theorists. There is no limit to the risks they are prepared to take with human souls, and in this age of psychology and 'psychologising' one finds a quite astonishing ignorance of human nature and human needs. If men as they really are do not fit the categories of post-Christian morality, then they must adapt themselves or perish. On the same principle one might fling a group of children who have never learned to swim into deep water. Some, no doubt, will swim; the rest will drown.

The propertyless state is for saints or brigands, homelessness for the wandering friar or the tramp. The majority of people need to find some repose in the things around them if they are to avoid a kind of inward dissolution in the time-stream; and we need this more urgently today than at any time in the past because we live in a machine civilisation, and machines, in the regularity of their movement, have something of the character of clocks which impose the laws of mechanical time upon the human mind as well as the human body.

But we also need to find more than repose and stability in our environment if we are to be nourished by it—nourished, that is, as whole men and not simply as bodies in motion. We need to discover meaning in it, a meaning not easily exhausted and into which shafts can be sunk. This is lacking in fabricated environments, unless the fabrications in question are works of inspired beauty upon which love and wisdom as well as skill and sweat have been lavished. It is profoundly unhealthy for men to live always among the products of their own minds and their own labour, for this is in essence a second-hand environment and is not sufficiently worthy of their attention to prevent them from withdrawing into private or, for that matter, collective fantasy; their contact with reality is attenuated, and without this contact no creature can survive—or deserves to survive—either physically or spiritually.

Such environments have been compared to stage sets, and upon them the most improbable and irrelevant dramas may be acted out. A time comes when error alone seems plausible and truth would be as out of place as a live animal in a gathering of teddy bears. Our cities are just such stage sets, engineered rather than built and, in spite of their appearance of massive solidity (or, from another point of view, because of it), constantly changing in the process of demolition and reconstruction. They offer only geometrical patterns to the eye and, since nothing in visible nature, except the crystal, is perfectly symmetrical, these patterns intensify the sense of artificiality. The laws of geometry stand opposed to the laws governing living organisms and provide, when rigidly applied to the human environment, a Procrustean bed which can provide no rest or refreshment. Moreover the geometrical environment, by its nature, lays claim to a kind of perfection—a quantitative perfection (every angle, every measurement being mathematically exact)—that is at odds with our earthly context in which nothing is final, finished or perfected; but it accords only too well with the false perfectionism which is so readily applied to the organisation of human societies and with an idealism which insists upon fitting humankind into symmetrical patterns.

These cities are fitting barracks for workers whose metabolism, mental as well as physical, must be adjusted to the requirements of the machine. The man who lives in a natural environment has a fair chance of reaching out to something beyond nature; but he who lives in an artificial one has done well if he succeeds simply in remaining human. To do so the worker at a conveyor belt in a vast modern factory needs to possess the kind of strength and heroism which, in another place, might have carried him to sanctity.

A mechanised world, says Frithjof Schuon, is particularly impermeable to spiritual realities: 'It requires machinery and therefore metal, din, hidden and treacherous forces, a nightmare environment, incomprehensible comings and goings—in a word, an insect-like existence carried on in the midst of ugliness and triviality ... When the industrial worker says he has no time to pray he is not far wrong, for in this way he is merely expressing what is inhuman or, one might say, subhuman in his condition.'* Meanwhile, if some spark of the desire to understand survives in the midst of this din he is offered, not such truths as might satisfy the whole man, but empty abstractions and the unbeliever's thin gruel.

* *Language of the Self:* Frithjof Schuon, pp. 153-4.

An environment of abstractions and 'incomprehensible comings and goings' offers nothing to satisfy man's need to find meaning in his daily life. To starve this need was one of the most effective techniques of demoralisation employed in the Nazi camps. Senseless tasks, a hideous environment, cruelties that seemed unrelated to the known laws of causality—these were the means employed to construct a world not only of pain and humiliation but also of non-sense. Torture and punishment no longer bore any logical relation to the persons upon whom they were inflicted. If a work gang showed signs of rebellion, the most docile member of the gang was as likely to be shot as any other. If a flogging had been ordered, it did not matter who was flogged; all were interchangeable units and the very term 'punishment' became meaningless, unless one wishes to think in terms of a faceless mankind punishing itself.

In keeping the camp records it was found simpler to correct errors on human beings than in the books.* If the number of men, women and children in a new intake failed to tally with the figure shown in the records, then some were killed or more were arrested according to whether the figure was too low or too high. Nothing personal was involved. The organisational machine functioned in accordance with the law of simplicity which governs such operations. And yet the motives behind all this might be traced to certain personal roots, for those who contrived the system had fallen from the human level into the lower reaches of natural process, where the light of sense no longer penetrates. Our age is painfully aware of the 'blind' side of nature : jungle proliferation, the riverbed solid with catfish waiting for the sewage that will give them the strength to wait for more sewage, the busy ants and all the business of 'eating and being eaten'. Since man as microcosm contains within himself all that is or can be, the dark shadow of natural process must sometimes fall across our hearts and our minds. There is, in consequence, a kind of satisfaction for certain despairing souls in bringing others to a like state and in reducing proud men to their own level. Already in hell, abandoned—so it seems to them—by the light they have themselves abandoned, they still seek confirmation that there is nowhere else to be.

Those who undertake to destroy, if they can, the imprint of God, there where it seems to offer itself most vulnerably to their

* Bettelheim, op. cit. p. 245.

hands and their instruments, that is to say in the human form,
find their task made easier if their victim is already dispossessed,
a unit in the multitude, an 'ordinary' man.

Within the earthly framework men have sought to assuage the
sense of their own mortality and to build fixed islands in the
stream of natural process by producing objects more enduring
than themselves; but, since this is not mere beavers' labour, the
aim has generally been to create objects which reflect at least some
glint of an eternal light and so recall, however crudely, an unchanging order in the midst of ceaseless change. This is why the possessions of 'primitive' peoples almost invariably have a sacred character, their very construction being accompanied by rituals which
relate them to their heavenly archetypes. Men's labour and their
rest then take place, not in the context of natural process, but in
the midst of fragments fallen, as it were, from heaven; and these
fragments—tattered as they may be—are handed down from father
to son, preserving continuity and reminding those who handle
them that men are not entirely submerged in time and not wholly
subject to its destructive course. Seeing this made plain in their
outwardness, in the furniture of their brief lives, they may the
more readily perceive elements in themselves which are set above
the flood and which indicate the mark of eternity implanted in
their hearts, that Kingdom of Heaven which, Christ said, is
'within you'. Such men are not easily moved by the fickle currents
of theory and fashion.

The products of industrial civilisation are more ephemeral
than ourselves. We outlive our products. The furniture of our
homes will be out of fashion in a decade or less if it does not come
to pieces even sooner, and the time is approaching when our
houses themselves will be less enduring than we are. These things
no longer provide an anchor; on the contrary, they carry us along
with them in the rushing stream. And the ephemeral character of
all our works is underlined by the fact that we cannot visualise the
shape of the world in which our children—let alone our grand-
children—will live. Troubled by the possibility of nuclear destruction and dizzied by the pace of technological change, many would
hardly dare to visualise it, but we cannot doubt that it will bear
little resemblance to the context that is now our home; and because men's characters and outlook are so closely linked to their
environment, we are cut off even from the bond of kinship with

those who will come after us. We can be sure only that they will be different and we would not know what to say to them.

It is forgotten however that swift change is a characteristic of decay, not of growth, and that the body which took some eighteen years to come to maturity dissolves into its constituent chemicals in a far shorter time.

Now, when we tend to think of ourselves as in some measure emancipated from nature and shielded from it by the man-made structures of civilisation, men are absorbed as never before into patterns reminiscent of natural process rather than of human living, occupied almost exclusively with the quantitative and the repetitious. In a certain sense one might claim that the Australian aboriginal, trekking from one water-hole to the next, is more independent of natural process and more distinctively a man than the modern factory worker, for he is on a purposeful journey. There are no such journeys for the factory worker, whose labour is no more than the constant repetition of essentially meaningless actions and who moves to and fro between his living quarters and his place of work like a shuttle on a loom.

In a world of intensive production and equally intensive consumption we have begun to imitate the wastefulness of what are usually called the 'lower forms of nature', that is to say those aspects of nature which are most impenetrable to intelligence. While men were still parsimonious they stood out in sharp relief from this process and what they drew out of the river of change for their own use crystallised around them into a condition of relative durability. Now things pour from the machines much as tropical vegetation proliferates and, as soon as they emerge, they are used up and returned into the cyclic process. In man's biological functions there is just such a pattern of regularity and repetition; but, as man, it is his nature to go his unique way, striding over the wave-pattern of biological life towards a goal which infinitely transcends this pattern. To condemn him to the repetitious production of objects which have no intrinsic value, ministering not to real needs but to an insatiable greed for consumer goods, is to condemn him to futility.

'We must consume, devour as it were, our houses and furniture and cars as though they were the "good things" of nature, which spoil uselessly if they are not drawn into the never-ending cycle of man's metabolism with nature. It is as though we had forced open the distinguishing boundaries which protect the world, the human artifice, from nature—the biological process which goes on in its very midst as well as the natural cyclical processes which surround it—delivering and abandoning to them the always threatened stability of a human world.'*

It is important in this context to understand that 'nature' is the mother of ambiguity: on the one hand, it reflects a light which far transcends it and is shaped into signs and symbols which indicate the realities inherent in that light; on the other, in so far as it is unreflective, it may be compared to a swirling darkness which dissolves both men and things into dust.

The 'artifice' of which Miss Arendt speaks is therefore nature ennobled by form and by the operations of intelligence, contrasted with the destructive and senseless aspect of natural process. There is an obvious significance in the fact that social wealth, unlike private property, thrives upon destruction. Two great world wars which wiped from the face of Europe so much that was 'obsolescent' and gave a new impetus to technology led within a few years to vast increases of public wealth. Stability, on the other hand, and the conservation of property slow the machine down.

If momentum is to be maintained—and we may already have reached a point at which the whole structure will collapse if it is not maintained—everything must be grist to the mill. 'Both the concentration camps and the death camps—and what happened in them—were an application beyond reason of the concept of labour as a commodity,' says Bettelheim; 'In the camps, not only human labour but the total person became commodity.'† But such concepts are bound, sooner or later, to be 'applied beyond reason' in the kind of world we now inhabit; and once the human person becomes 'commodity', responsibility—if it can still be said to exist—adheres only to impersonal forces, to the great wind which sweeps the earth, flattening everything in its path into uniformity, reducing it to dust. Though the wind is not to blame.

Meanwhile, men hug small things to themselves protectively —protecting the thing, but also protecting themselves. There is a special pathos in the image of the old peasant who keeps his life's savings under his mattress. He distrusts the banks, for he senses

* Hannah Arendt, op. cit. p. 126.
† Bettelheim, op. cit. p. 243.

behind them the marauding forces which would snatch his fragments of stability from him. He refuses to cast back into the flux—
in this case, his country's economy—the little he has won from it.
He is an enemy of society, for he does not understand that what he
earned was not really meant to be 'his'; it was only loaned to him
as 'purchasing power'. Above all he was led to believe that the
printed notes or metal coins which came his way represented
*value*. Being human and therefore the heir to a certain knowledge,
a certain sense of order which cannot be totally eradicated, he
associated the concept of value with something stable, something
to which one might hold fast in shifting sands; he imagined that
the value of his currency would endure. No one had explained to
him that it was nothing more than a ticket with which to purchase
consumer goods and that if he tried to hold onto it he would find,
not gold, but worthless paper in his grasp; for the process of
inflation is a most effective means of dissolving all fixed islands in
the stream and destroying all local privileges.

There are no watertight compartments in the human realm,
and devaluation on one level provokes a corresponding devaluation
on others. Men unify by instinct, however theory may divide. If
the money which would have purchased some degree of security
yesterday is worthless today, then it is all too easy to assume that
everything of value is equally at the mercy of senseless change and
that today's good may be tomorrow's evil. No doubt it is for this
reason that coinage possessed a sacred character in earlier times
and that gold, with its rich symbolic significance, was until quite
recently the linchpin of major currencies. Remove from any
object its sacred or symbolic aspects, tossing it into the flux of
purely quantitative phenomena, and value dissolves like flesh
from bones in a vat of acid.

Not only does the depreciation of currency undermine faith in
enduring principles of any kind but, once the process accelerates
beyond a certain point, it ensures that no one can attempt to stand
on his own feet or to establish his own base of security; all must
turn to the State for protection. It is no wonder that those who
harbour a deep loathing for human independence in any form,
driven as they are by a thirst for the amorphous, welcome the
inflationary process which breaks down crystallised forms and
engorges all solid, stable things. Their thirst for the amorphous
is closely akin to the need to abolish meaning which played its part

in motivating the worst excesses of the Nazis. Both relate in their turn to the deep-rooted desire—more common than is often realised—to slough off the burden of one's humanity, with all that it implies in the way of choice and responsibility, and lose oneself in anonymity and indistinction.

Like many great evils this is the dark side of a great virtue: the bitter longing to lose oneself in the subterranean shadows and be rid of the tyrant 'me' once and for all reflects, in monstrous parody, the holy longing to be perfected and extinguished in the supernal light. Those who are content with their own littleness will never understand either the saint or—taking the term in its most profound sense—the sinner; but the fact remains that the latter means to destroy us and is not easily stopped.

To those whose whole thinking process is separative by nature the practice of relating phenomena which belong to very different levels of experience must always appear strange and savours of confusion: to speak in almost the same breath of monetary inflation and of the magnetism of the infernal regions may seem to them to negate the distinctions inherent in logic; and yet, since all things are connected and all derive ultimately from one source, discursive thought cannot ignore the web of inter-connection. Touch but a single string of a single instrument, and others beyond number vibrate in regions beyond our ken.

Fragmentation, however, is the order of the day, and it extends from the operations of the intellect to the realm of physical labour, as though it were the nature of the disintegrative process to break all things into small, easily digestible pieces. Coomaraswamy, in this context, speaks of an industrial order in which 'none takes all knowledge for his province, and the workman is specifically conformed to the making of small parts of things and can make nothing whole.' 'This excessive division of labour,' he adds, 'can result only in the production of goods that are useful, not of those that are beautiful; for integration, co-ordination and lucidity are essential to beauty, and with these the labourer has nothing to do; he who makes only parts of things cannot be an artist, but only a coolie.'*

The labour of the artist and the craftsman has indeed its special dignity, but the claptrap that is often talked about the 'dignity of

* *The Rg Veda as Land-Nama-Bok:* Ananda Coomaraswamy (Luzac & Co.).

labour' in the industrial context is misleading, since it misses the point. In the traditional view, labour which is not, at least in some measure, a ritual operation (therefore 'imitating' the action of the 'gods') and of which the products are without beauty or significance is unfit for free men. Value is reflected in wholes, not in fragments or fragmentary operations, and men's innate repugnance to futility is aroused by involvement in valueless activities. Our lives are too short for us to spend them in such a way as this; and if we deprive men of the things that are whole and, in some measure, enduring and deny them the opportunity to make such things, we must expect in the long run to produce sick men, rootless men, flotsam in the stream of time.

The corroding sense of futility arises also wherever people are denied the opportunity to act responsibly; the opportunity to do good and, thereby, to straighten what is crooked in themselves, or to do ill and suffer for it; in short, to save their souls or to damn them. In essence, freedom is not so much a matter of being loosed from certain bonds, except in so far as these bonds inhibit action, but rather the opportunity to do something and, in doing it, to show what we are. Since the late eighteenth century there has been an obsessive concern with the idea of freedom from things, rather than freedom to do things. Although these two aspects are often inter-dependent, they are not always so.

Even from the negative point of view—freedom from things— the contemporary assumption that men never before enjoyed such freedom as they do now is open to question. Slavery, we are told, was the most evil and inhuman system of labour ever devised, yet the definition of slavery is basically this: to have a master and to be in no position to defy him, except by an act of exceptional daring, to be without property, and to be compelled to pass one's life in servile labour. In real terms, the opposite condition to slavery is self-employment; and to encourage self-employment, which is economically inefficient and politically anarchic, is the last thing that our industrial age can afford to do or that political collectivism can permit.

In the times of slavery, understood in the historical sense, a free man who scratched a bare living for himself was still regarded as incomparably superior to the slave, though the latter might be better fed and better clothed. Subjection to the laws and necessities of nature has always been regarded as a far nobler status than subjection to the will of other men; and, in the modern context, one might go further and suggest that a difference of quality also exists between the latter condition (which is still within the realm of personal relationships) and that of the man who is subject to the rules and regulations of a vast, impersonal organisation. As between the labourer and the white-collar worker (or jobholder) it may be said that the former still enjoys the greater freedom, since he is not compelled by social pressures to seek advancement within the organisation and has no need to maintain a 'middle-class' style of living; but we are promised that machines will soon take over most forms of unskilled labour. If this is so, the vast majority in the 'developed' countries will be jobholders and this will become the pattern to be imitated, so far as may be possible, in the 'developing' world. Maximum efficiency in the use of human material for the production of social wealth requires that no one should escape the net.

Since the same needs press both upon the socialist bloc and upon the 'capitalist' sector and both have much the same goal in view, the solutions to which they are driven look more and more alike. In a society in which everyone is, directly or indirectly, an employee of the State, there can be no escape for the man who does not conform to what is required of him; there is nowhere else to go. At present—and one must be thankful for small mercies—it is still possible in the 'West' for a man to walk out of his job and go to work for a rival establishment; but it would be rash to suppose that this particular freedom will endure. A process of economic unification is taking place, and must take place if the machine is to function efficiently, whereby small businesses are absorbed by larger ones which, in their turn, find common interests which supersede their rivalry, while the State—in the 'public interest'— breathes down their necks. The number of possible employers shrinks, and doors close one by one; nor are there any more open spaces or lands beyond the sea to which a man might at least dream of escaping, as the slave of earlier times could escape over the mountains or in a small boat. He would need to satisfy the immigration authorities and to hold a work permit. Parallel with the increasing control now exercised by states within their borders, a situation has arisen in recent years which effectively imprisons people in the country of their birth. To regard this process with anything but dread, as the walls close in upon us, suggests an almost unnatural immunity from claustrophobia; even the smallest animals struggle a little when they feel themselves trapped.

It may be said that the jobholder is still in a very different position from that of the slave, since he does not risk death if he rebels or tries to escape. This point turns on an assessment of pressures and their subjective effectiveness. The threat of death is one possible pressure among others. The threat of poverty or of disgrace and humiliation is another; and there are men who prefer death to dishonour and the loss of all those things that seemed to make life worth living. There are more ways than one to skin a cat.

There would be little point in saying that ordinary people should have a stronger spirit of independence. We are dealing here with the facts of human living, not with ideals, since it is these facts which will determine the future of our kind. There are circumstances—and social pressures—in terms of which the breaking of a career and failure in a given profession are feared quite as much as death and torture were feared under other dispensations. Few men live only for the delight of existence—for love and friendship; sight and sound and touch—and still less for the joys of religion or in hope of the beatific vision. The majority, including those who have the power to determine our political and economic future, need some kind of professional achievement to stave off the sense of futility which haunts the modern world. Such achievement is necessarily measured in terms of a ladder which may, in itself, lead nowhere but which seems important to those who know nothing of any greater glory. To be threatened with the loss of one's place on the ladder is then a most powerful sanction. When men are to be made docile it is not the outward gravity of the sanctions that matters, but their subjective effectiveness.

To foster liberty means, for a start, to reduce the pressures which prevent the ordinary, less than heroic man from thinking and acting as a responsible being, one who carries his own burden and chooses for himself. Pressures are seldom noticed until they are fully applied (by which time it may be too late to resist). While the system under which we live is operated in a humane way and remains sufficiently elastic still to permit some regard for the individual and his awkward needs, we think that we can safely ignore the reserve powers which are steadily building up in the armoury of the State, just as we ignore the nuclear potential of the 'super-powers', in the cheerful conviction that sensible people will never make use of the weapons either of oppression or of destruction which are now available. Such optimism betrays a singular ignorance of human nature. When we consider the many separate factors which point unmistakably in one direction and project the lines of their development only a little way into the future we have every reason to look to our defences. The slave with a kind, indulgent master might have little cause to fault the institution of slavery unless he considered the extent of his own dependence on that master's continuing good will. It is not a good thing to be defenceless, even when we see only kind faces around us.

A society of jobholders however is not merely one that lends itself most conveniently to regimentation; it is also a society in which the majority have little opportunity to satisfy their need to do and to make things that have their individual mark upon them. This need can be satisfied in the co-operative efforts of a small group, a tribe or a family, but not in the impersonal achievements of a vast organisation. Just as the labourer now makes only little bits of things, so the jobholder does only little bits of things.

The member of such an organisation, unless he occupies some quite special position, is never far from the sense of 'non-entity', and it is no coincidence that this term should be the very one that defines, in traditional doctrine, the character of the profane as opposed to the sacred realm (which is essentially the realm of being, of meaning and of acts that are real). He is not a cog in the machine—for machines are in serious trouble when a cog breaks—but something more dispensable, an interchangeable unit. He supplies a quantum of effort or of energy which could as well be supplied by almost anyone else. Those who know in their hearts that they are not really necessary—and are entirely replaceable—must inevitably be tempted to misrepresent the nature of their work and build up a false notion of its importance. A further alienation from truth takes place, a further loss of contact with reality. And one thing we can be sure of is that self-deception, whether on the level of the wind and the rain or on that of spiritual reality, must always come up against the real sooner or later, and that its destruction is very painful. 'Truth has come and deception has vanished away; deception is indeed by nature perishable.'*

* Qurān, 17:81.

59

Two other factors play their part in undermining the jobholder's inner security and therefore his capacity for defending his integrity. The first is the artificiality of the rewards which he receives for his work; there is no immediate or necessary connection between his monthly pay packet and what he has done or achieved. The relation between action and its reward has been obscured and may easily have been forgotten. For this man, unprepared by experience for the precarious nature of human life, there can only be a sense of outrage when he is brought into sharp and brutal contact with reality. He feels, as Thibon says, ' "That was due to me and I have not had it, so this is injustice !" '. It is all so unfair, and unfairness—he thinks—has no right to exist. Therefore reality does not have the right to be what it is, and everything is askew. 'The great fevers of revolt in our time proceed in large part from this narrow and materialistic sense of justice inherent in a society which has lost all communion with the elementary sources of life.'*

Secondly, there is no effective continuity between the generations in a society of jobholders. Whatever the achievements of the functionary, however good his position at the end of a lifetime of meritorious service, what he has achieved dies with him and a stranger steps into his shoes. His family has no role in his work; his children can play no part in helping him to maintain or build up something that they will eventually inherit. There are no crops to be sown and reaped, and he has nothing to hand onto them. The strongest of all family bonds—shared interest and participation in the work by which the family gains its livelihood—has been severed, so that parents and children have little in common beyond the biological link. As among the beasts, the children go out naked into the world and the aged die alone.

Before our eyes in the course of decades, not centuries, a new kind of world is coming into being, a world populated almost exclusively by dependants; but dependent upon whom and with what safeguards? Whether those who control the machinery of the State, the leaders in one country or another, have seized power or been elected by a mass-electorate which votes only on immediate, bread-and-butter issues, and whether they are motivated by self-interest or by good intentions, one thing is sure : they are themselves controlled by forces of change which they do not understand

* *Retour au Réel:* Gustave Thibon (Lardanchet), p. 19.

and, in obeying these forces, they are restrained neither by immutable principles nor by the weight of custom and tradition. The brakes have been taken off; and there is nothing to suggest that these people know where they are going.

There are valid precedents for thinking of the forces of change as directed by something rather different to blind chance; in other words, for 'personifying' them. Our ancestors would not have hesitated to speak of satanic forces, believing as they did that man must serve either God or the devil.

No doubt such phraseology seems too naive in the contemporary context—although one might remember the saying that the devil works best when he works disguised—but, whatever the terms used, the facts are plain enough. We are being hustled willy-nilly in a certain direction, far from all the landmarks to which humanity has been accustomed; and, if we do not know what it is we are going *to*, we can at least see what it is we are going *from* and judge thereby the loss we have suffered.

# 3

## LIBERTY AND OBEDIENCE

How far does a wise child go in pursuit of a butterfly when the terrain is treacherous? How far should any of us go in pursuit of what we want? Modern political theories offer so many good things at the end of the road—social justice, prosperity, security— and the hunter's instinct is aroused. One does not always notice the point at which the quarry changes shape, as all relative and contingent goods are liable to do, and becomes a siren luring us into very dangerous places.

Rationalism is by nature incautious and it operates in terms of very simple, unambiguous alternatives: if something is good, then its true nature has been identified once and for all and we should grasp it without hesitation (roses have no thorns in this scheme of things), regardless of irrational 'taboos' and regardless of timid people who dread change. There are no longer any markers to tell us when we are entering the danger area, for the traditional and customary restraints which formerly set a limit to the possibilities of straying have been removed. And yet the habit of expecting to be stopped if we go too far still endures. It is difficult to adjust to the fact that there is no longer anyone to tell us where and when to stop.

The good things of this world reflect the ambiguity inherent in the human condition itself. They are mixed blessings and, in dealing with them, our judgment needs to be as sound as that of a healthy belly which knows when it has had enough. What most endangers us is the indiscriminate and unrestrained pursuit of things which, taken in small measure, may be thoroughly desirable but, in excess, poison the system. 'It's only a matter of degree' is a phrase that should inspire fear and suspicion. The difference between an ordered society and a totalitarian one is a matter of degree. The difference between farmyard and animal factory is a matter of degree, as is that between hand-loom and conveyor belt or, for that matter, between a pleasurable sensation and agonising pain. In most cases the progression from one extreme to the other is gradual, a smooth curve on which are posted no warning signs to tell us when a good thing is about to become an evil one or to indicate the point of no return. Powers of discrimination and a capacity for choice such as were never before required are now essential to our survival as responsible beings.

The rationalist takes things one by one, and he can always point to the single phenomenon—a new technological development or a new law passed to deal with a specific problem—and ask whether there is anything sinister in this. Sound judgment however takes a wider view. It is essential to place present events in some kind of historical context and, despite the impossibility of seeing ahead with any certainty, to calculate future probabilities in terms of the tendencies apparent here and now. In judging a single incident, perhaps trivial in itself, we should ask two questions : is this incident fairly typical of our times and therefore likely to be repeated, and, if so, what will happen should it repeat itself over and over again in the course of the next few years? Each such incident must, therefore, be placed in series if we are to make at least an educated guess as to the direction in which it points.

One cannot consider the period of history which forms the background to these 'incidents' without taking into account the totalitarian political systems which came into being between 1917 and the outbreak of the Second World War. The masses were seized by new masters, fascist or socialist, and responded so readily to their heady theories that free elections would almost certainly have given them majorities which any 'democratic' leader might envy. The rigid distinction commonly made between Fascism and Socialism is, to say the least, of doubtful validity. Mussolini, after all, started his career as a fairly orthodox socialist, and his fascist ideology was to a great extent inspired by Marx's errant disciple, Georges Sorel. Hitler—who once proclaimed, 'I am a fanatical socialist!'—chose to regard his party as a socialist one and detested capitalism even while he made use of individual capitalists.

Totalitarianism and collectivism are still what they are, no matter what the local variations in the gimcrack theories by which they seek to justify their existence. Hitler's New Order, ruled by a golden-haired race of supermen, was neither more nor less absurd than the Marxist–Leninist dream of a heaven on earth in which the historical process comes to an abrupt end and everyone is eternally nice to everyone else. What these ideologies have in common far outweighs their differences, and one thing they most obviously have in common is hatred of the 'old order' and bitter opposition to everything that can be described as 'traditional'. They represent a blind movement of change, understood in its most malignant and destructive sense. The only possible relationship that can exist between them and religion (as the quintessence of all that has come down to us from the past) is one of mortal combat.

It would be pointless to debate whether Hitler, considered as a man, was more 'evil' than Lenin or Stalin : these were creatures thrown up, so to speak, from the depths ; they were what they were and had their part to play in the historical process. But his influence has been of very particular significance over the past thirty years in its effect upon political theory and popular thought. His shadow still darkens a whole area of debate, and it has been almost impossible to oppose left-wing ideas without being accused of 'fascist'—therefore Hitlerite—inclinations ; he has taken the place of the devil in contemporary mythology and therefore everything that he touched or is presumed to have thought is, by definition, diabolical.

An absurd and yet very effective equation has been drawn up : Hitler was a man of the 'Right', therefore everything that savours of 'rightist' philosophy and every attempt to defend the old order in one country or another is tainted with his wickedness. This indeed is his posthumous triumph, for no man could have hated the old order more bitterly. He was as much an apostle of change and just as much a product of anti-traditional theories as Lenin.

Quite apart however from the special place which Hitler occupies in contemporary demonology, the Nazi example of totalitarianism may be said to have a greater relevance to our situation than the Soviet one. For obvious historical reasons the Russians have been regarded by Western Europeans as a people apart, outside the mainstream of civilisation as it has been understood in the past two-and-a-half centuries. Nobody could be surprised at anything they did : 'they are not like us'. The Germans, on the other hand, are our kind of people. This, no doubt, is why the events which took place under the Nazi regime came as such a traumatic shock ; they could not be shrugged aside as the aberrations of an alien race, and Europe was brought face-to-face with an aspect of its own nature.

The Nazi concentration camps were not, as some would like to think, a kind of throw-back to the 'dark ages'; on the contrary, they were a very modern phenomenon, and the senseless brutality that sometimes took place in them has little significance compared with the purposeful exploitation of human material which was their primary function. They belong to our age, whether we like it or not, and what was done in Belsen and Buchenwald, Auschwitz and Sachsenhausen is not yet ready to be filed away in the archives.

There are many points of view from which their relevance to our age—and to our future—cannot be ignored. Of these, two seem particularly significant: the first relates to the nature of the obedience, both on the part of the civil servants who administered the camps and on that of the inmates, which made the system possible; the second to the morality in terms of which this obedience was justified.

A senior official of one of the camps had, as a motto on his letter-heads, 'There is only one thing that is valid: Orders.' And indeed, when everything else has gone, 'orders' remain. Rudolf Hoess sometime Commandant of Auschwitz and an efficient and con-scientious man, tells us in his autobiography that his father was 'a determined opponent of the Reich Government and its policy', yet always reminded his friends that 'however strong one's opposi-tion might be, the laws and decrees of the State had to be obeyed unconditionally.' Many good men elsewhere in the civilised world would have nodded their approval and might still do so; and yet one is bound to wonder whether, had Papa Hoess been a less exemplary father, his son would have been the man he was.

The peripheral features of religion show a remarkable tendency to survive for long periods after the centre has gone out of sight. Christians who have lost their faith may still observe certain rules of Christian morality; Muslims who no longer pray may still avoid pork and wine, and one finds 'primitive' tribes observing the taboos long after they have forgotten the doctrine which gave validity to these taboos. In the same way, a kind of conditioned reflex responsive to the word of authority remains active long after the very idea of legitimate authority (that is to say, an author-ity which merely administers what is believed to be a God-given order) has been completely lost; indeed, this reflex may become all the more powerfully established as a last defence against social chaos. In Germany during the Nazi period the sense of a categorical imperative to obey the men who give commands persisted even when authority was vested in creatures who seemed uniquely destined to deface human dignity and therefore to bring the very notion of human fitness for command into disrepute. Hoess says— and there is no reason to doubt him—that no SS officer would have contemplated raising a hand against Himmler even in his most secret thoughts: 'as Reichsführer SS, his person was inviolable'; his basic orders were 'sacred' and 'brooked no consideration, no argument, no interpretation.'*

These are—or should be—startling words: 'inviolable', 'sacred'. The Sun King, the divine Emperor, is inviolable and the sacred surrounds him as a numinous cloud; but this man was from the dregs of humankind. It is only quite recently that the majority of people have been deprived of belief in an ordered universe which is related to other, unseen realms of order in a total harmony. Once this belief has been destroyed and there appears to be no true order inherent in the very nature of things it is not difficult to conclude that only 'orders' will keep chaos at bay, no matter who gives them.

'See,' says the Qurān, 'in the creations of the heavens and the earth, the differences of night and day, and the ships which run upon the sea . . . and in the ordinance of the winds and the clouds, obedient between heaven and earth, are signs for those who are aware.'† Human obedience, in common with the obedience of all natural things to natural laws, reflects a Norm in which all have their roots and from which they derive their significance; but, when there is no true authority to act as a magnet, it seizes upon whatever comes within its range, and man's enormous capacity for obeying God and thereby integrating himself into a universal order is perverted into an instrument of enslavement.

In the concentration camps it was not only the officials and the guards who were bound by 'orders'; their victims also suffered the power of this spell. Whether we consider the ordinary inmates or such special prisoners as the doctors who did monstrous work 'because they had no alternative', our feelings tend to be ambiguous. On the one hand, we may very reasonably feel that we

* *Commandant of Auschwitz:* Rudolf Hoess (Pan Books), p. 162.
† Qurān, II:164.

ourselves, under such pressures as they suffered, would have done as they did; on the other, we are troubled by the suspicion that this is not the whole story. Individual rebellion against the camp authorities meant almost certain death, and yet quite ordinary men have faced an equal certainty of death in battle and, under many different circumstances throughout the ages, people have given their lives to save their fellows or for a cause in which they believed. However strong the instinct of self-preservation may be, it is astonishing how many have defied it, whether for a principle or, quite simply, in a rage.

Natural passions might have been expected to reinforce the urge to revolt. Quite apart from brutality and overwork, the prisoners suffered constant public humiliation of the most extreme kind. Homicidal rage would have been a natural reaction. Moreover, for those who were unlucky in the work to which they were assigned or who were in poor health, the chances of survival were negligible, and under such circumstances death might have seemed more palatable if a man could take one of his persecutors with him. And yet so few, so very few, did in fact revolt. The case is remembered of a beautiful Jewish woman who, stripped naked before the guards, seized an officer's revolver from its holster and shot him dead; but most were spellbound by 'orders' and obeyed the only authority that existed in their world.

It takes two sides to make a tyranny: the tyrant and the tyrannised. Plato maintained that slaves deserved their condition, in that those who were not of servile nature would prefer death to enslavement. There are circumstances under which a man of noble character finds his life of little account and is proud to cast it away.

According to Plotinus, 'Bad men rule by the feebleness of the ruled, and this is just'; and it is commonly said that people get the government they deserve. If responsibility has any real meaning and if human beings have a special dignity by virtue of their fitness for responsibility, then it is irresponsible not only to do ill under pressure but also to suffer ill passively. A harsh doctrine indeed, and certainly not a popular one; but it would be foolish to suppose that it is an easy thing to be a man.

How often one hears the decent citizen of our time, functionary or official, say with becoming modesty: 'I didn't make the rules; it's not for me to question my orders!' Perhaps at some other time, in some other place, one might applaud his sense of duty; but too much has happened in the past forty years, we have seen too much of what dutiful obedience may involve, and we have lost our innocence. Not to be frightened by statements of this kind, not to wonder how this good man would have behaved under the orders of the Reichsführer SS, one needs to be either very complacent or very optimistic.

Until he has been put to the test, no man can be trusted not to do monstrous things under the orders of an authority which he either fears or respects. Wives do not recognise their husbands nor children their fathers when this particular note is struck, and our friend goes away from us into a land of obedience where there is no more choice, no more responsibility, no more manhood.

In the United States in the early 'sixties an experiment was carried out which, surprisingly, surprised its sponsors. Volunteers were invited to take part in tests supposedly concerned with the effects of punishment on learning ability. The 'learner' (in fact an actor coached for his part) was strapped to his seat with an electrode fastened to his wrist; the volunteer 'teacher' sat in an 'experimental room' before a shock generator with a bank of switches ranging from 15 to 450 volts. Each time the 'learner' made a mistake or refused to answer a question the 'teacher' was instructed to give him a shock of increased intensity. The 'learner's' protests grew more strident until, at 285 volts, he screamed in agony; meanwhile the calm voice of authority overrode the teacher's hesitations: 'It is absolutely essential that you continue . . . You have no other choice, you must go on !'

'To our consternation,' says Professor Milgram, who set up the experiment, 'even the strongest protests from the victim did not prevent many subjects from administering the harshest punishment ordered by the experimenter,' and he comments that 'ordinary people simply doing their jobs without any particular hostility on their part can become agents in a terrible destructive process.'* The 'teachers' saw themselves as not being responsible for their own actions, but merely as the agents of an external authority: 'I wouldn't have done it myself; I was just doing what I was told' was the usual explanation offered in interviews held after the experiment. To rebut the suggestion that those who shocked the victim at the most severe level must have been from the 'sadistic

* *Obedience to Authority:* Stanley Milgram (Harper & Row, Inc).

fringe of society', Professor Milgram points out that two-thirds of
the participants fell into the category of 'obedient' subjects, and
they represented 'ordinary people drawn from working, mana-
gerial and professional classes'. An appeal had been made to their
'better natures', their sense of duty and respect for authority; no
other pressures were brought to bear.

Some such sense of duty, in addition to the fear of losing their
livelihood and suffering disgrace, motivates the obedience to
authority of those in whose hands our lives and welfare rest. What
the public sees, particularly through the media, is Government, a
regime, a President or Prime Minister; but the closer one ap-
proaches to the centres of power the more aware one becomes of
the role played by the instrument of government, the Civil Service.
The most powerful ruler in the world could sit in his office mouth-
ing orders until his voice failed; without humble and obedient
servants to execute his orders he would be talking to himself.

In those countries which permit strike action, powerful industrial groups are in a position to cause considerable incon-
venience, but there is only one group which could really 'bring a
country to its knees', abolish Government on the instant or
paralyse even the most ruthless dictator merely by turning a deaf
ear to what is said. The increasing complexity of industrial
societies and their dependence upon a vast administrative machine
which is, in fact, composed entirely of human beings—each with
a capacity for choice—has placed an astonishing power in the
hands of civil servants. When evil men occupy the seats of titular
power in one country or another they do so only by courtesy of
good men, who obey them without question, giving so much—the
best they have to give—to purposes which they do not think it
their right or duty to assess. Naked evil as such can seldom operate
in our world. It must wear a dress acceptable to the morality of the
period, for men are only successfully misled if they believe that
they are following the path of virtue.

'I myself derive no real satisfaction from my labours unless I
have completed a good job of work thoroughly.' This might be
any conscientious civil servant speaking. In fact it is the late Rudolf
Hoess expressing his view of the human function. Given his
liking for platitudes, he might well have added that, if a job is
worth doing at all, it is worth doing well, and presumably he died
with a sense of achievement. Many lesser men today, making their

small contribution to the world's 'progress', enjoy a similar sense of achievement.

Before putting too much reliance upon the ordinary, decent man's moral sense to protect us against the degeneration of human society into inhuman shape there are three points which should be borne in mind. First, the moral man (in the commonly accepted sense of the term) is in most cases disciplined and obedient, conforming to current standards in the belief that his conformity contributes to the wellbeing of his society. Secondly, defiance of a tyrannical government is likely to provoke savage reprisals not only against the rebel himself but also against his family and neighbours, so that 'innocent' people suffer. Thirdly, a man who is sexually restrained, honest in money matters and respectful of by-laws may still be capable of great wickedness when he meets a situation for which his moral rules do not provide.

In a stable and relatively unchanging society which lives within sight of eternal principles—within sight of the 'mountain' of which we spoke earlier—such morality may be the main support of ordered human living; but somewhere along the line, as religion and the sense of the Absolute faded into the lengthening shadows, the solid citizen's moral sense was left by the wayside to be picked up by the agents of darkness.

Moreover opposition to the State's authority—however unmistakably evil this may be—cannot always take 'moral' forms, particularly under present conditions. As the technology at the disposal of governments becomes more sophisticated the opportunities for the rebel to raise his voice in the market-place diminish, and a time is surely approaching when resistance will be possible only through cheating, subterfuge and sabotage. It is easier to be a public martyr than to do sly and underhand things in a good cause.

To return for a moment to the case of the civil servant, which is central to this issue, there are circumstances—and it is not necessary to name the countries in which such circumstances already exist or in which they might exist in the future—under which an official who defies his masters simply disappears, either killed or else removed to a safe place where his voice will not be heard. But what of his colleague who happens to lose vital papers at the critical moment, who innocently misinterprets his orders and misunderstands his instructions, who addresses letters to the wrong persons and despatches prisoners to the wrong destination?

He will lose his chances of promotion; but he will survive to throw more spanners in the works.

The issue is a complex one, the dilemma almost insoluble for those who depend upon current theories or passing fashions in morality to provide them with guidance. A heavy burden of decision is placed squarely on the shoulders of the individual, for although it is customary to speak of evil political regimes maintaining themselves in power through the 'passive' acceptance with which people submit to their rule, the fact is that no modern regime can survive for long without active and, indeed, conscientious cooperation on the part of a large and fairly representative section of the population.

In these circumstances many sensible people will take refuge in the principle of legality, convinced that they cannot go far wrong so long as they obey the law.

One is often told that respect for the law is the very foundation of civilised living and that, without this, there can only be disorder, injustice and the triumph of the strong over the weak. This is no doubt true enough within certain limits; but we can no longer say it without stopping to ask who makes the laws and what are the principles upon which they are based. That is the price we pay for having broken free from the shelter of religion and the restraints of custom. Nothing can be taken for granted any longer; and the conservatively minded people who would like to see the law obeyed without question seem to have forgotten the Nuremberg Laws and to be unaware of the nature of 'socialist legality' in the countries of the socialist bloc; moreover they are harking back to a period when the actual number of laws to be obeyed was a tiny fraction of those which now encompass us and when vast areas of human living which are now rigidly controlled were free and open. There must clearly be a limit to the sheer quantity of laws—and therefore of restrictions—which can or should be tolerated. Beyond this limit, legality in the traditional sense no longer has any meaning.

Behind the law, as we now understand it, is the ruler or the ruling oligarchy. This was not always so. There was a time when law was assumed to be the application of universal principles to the human situation at a particular moment and under particular circumstances. As such it enjoyed something of the respect accorded to these principles. Today it is, for the most part, the expression of Mr X or General Y's wishes, and there is no particular call to respect their wishes. The fact that some legislative assembly or parliament may have put its rubber stamp on the legislation does not really alter the situation.

To point this out is not to advocate anarchy, but only to suggest that, while fictions serve a useful purpose (and modern democratic societies are dependent upon a variety of fictions), truth will out in the end and sensible people prepare themselves for the day when this happens. Secular societies in the West are still to a considerable extent living 'on capital'. Their laws no longer have the backing either of religion or of ancient custom but still benefit from the respect habitually accorded to laws which did have such backing, either 'vertically' (relating them to the sacred, the transcendent) or 'horizontally' (relating them to centuries of traditional practice). The notion that they are somehow legitimised as expressions of the 'will of the People' is a fiction that may have its usefulness but soon wears thin.

For the moment—and for our comfort—we in the 'West' may be thankful that these laws are for the most part obeyed or at least considered to merit obedience; but such is the momentum of change in the second half of the twentieth century that a society may be transformed in a very short time, even without revolution, and extreme vigilance is required. Here, precisely, is one of those 'contingent goods' mentioned earlier, good today and bad tomorrow, changing shape almost overnight—as the German people discovered to their cost some years ago. The Germans had been so much admired for their sense of order and discipline and for their efficiency, but these were the very qualities which made the phenomenon of Hitlerism possible. Given the speed with which events are moving, no nation dare suppose itself safe from the good servants of evil who pride themselves on doing their job and doing it well. Under such circumstances: Happy the man who lives in a slovenly and incompetent land where civil servants can be bribed to betray their trust and the bungling administration is incapable of putting any plan into effect!

As it is, the pressures—political, social and, above all, economic—are growing in number and in weight; nowhere is there a land which can bask in the sunshine and let the cruel world go by. Measures deemed necessary to deal with these pressures come increasingly to resemble those adopted as a means of survival in time of war; the greater the threat, the less tolerance there can be for anything that interferes with the 'war effort', that is to say with the marshalling and exploitation of all available resources, not least of human resources.

The concentration camps were designed, not as places of punishment (for punishment is either a religious or a sentimental concept and has no place among the techniques of efficiency), but to serve three purposes: to act as powerhouses of labour at the service of the State, to keep out of circulation people who might have interfered with the smooth functioning of the State machinery, and, finally, as centres for the extermination of those who did not appear to fit into the monolithic structure of the State.

If we understand by sadism a lust for inflicting pain, then, by all accounts, there was no higher proportion of sadists and bullies among the camp guards than would be found among prison guards anywhere. Bettelheim remarked that it was very rare for a guard to give up five minutes of his free time to torment the prisoners.

It was simply a question of applying scientific techniques to break the human will and grind down the human person into exploitable shape; in other words to make him 'useful'. From kicks and blows to obscene tortures, everything was designed to make the machine function. A group of prisoners working with a stone-breaking machine in a camp quarry worked very much harder after one of their number had been fed into the stone-breaker.

People come in such awkward shapes and sizes that it is not always easy to beat them into uniformity. This is a problem with which socialism has always had to cope, and the National Socialists borrowed most of their techniques from the more experienced Marxist Socialists of the Russian Empire. These techniques were inevitably crude and involved the use of pain, terror and humiliation. But such methods are not altogether satisfactory and tend to provoke troublesome reactions. The Russian Revolution itself provoked a civil war which very nearly nipped it in the bud, and cruelty may in the long run twist society into shapes quite different to those intended by its perpetrators. It is better, from the collectivist point of view, to manipulate people by appeals to their 'better nature' and by persuasion. The end result is the same.

The key-word here is co-operation. After describing the ways in which every attempt by a prisoner in the camps to protect his personality from being completely destroyed or, for that matter, to help his friends involved co-operating with the system and therefore contributing to its efficient functioning, Bettelheim concludes: 'Within so tight a system as the concentration camp any defence that stayed within the frame of reference of the system promoted the goals of the system, not those of the defence. It seems that an institution like the concentration camp permits of no really successful defence—the only way not to submit to it in some measure would have been to destroy it.'*

The same could be said of a collectivist system gradually imposed by the democratic vote, which may in practice mean the vote of thirty percent or so of the electorate, and in such a case so-called moral sanctions can be brought to bear on those who resist its imposition. The Will of the People—grotesquely clothed in all the majesty of the divine Will—may then have been expressed by a few thoughtless voters who marked their crosses on a ballot paper in favour of someone who promised them a better house or cheaper food; and those who defy this will must be either mad or bad.

At least in the Russian Revolution the issues were clear-cut. No one could imagine that Lenin represented the Russian people or that he had any other aim but to impose his ideology by force. Nazi Germany, by its atrocities and by Hitler's self-advertisement, demonstrated its true character for all the world to see. It is in the urbane societies of the West, with their tame populations made gentle by decades of prosperity, that deception flourishes and issues are muffled under layers of liberalism and apparent good will. If these societies are drawn into the collectivist net, it will not be kicking and screaming, but anaesthetised in a soft institutional bed.

By whatever means—cruel or kind—'so tight a system' comes into existence, it cannot be resisted within its own 'frame of reference'. As in so many human situations, the more a man struggles to free himself the more surely he is trapped. An exit from such vicious circles is to be found only in a different dimension, in terms of a different frame of reference.

The worldly dimension, however, though it may be inwardly

* Bruno Bettelheim, op. cit. p. 235.

transcended, is not thereby annihilated; and on this level there are two quite different kinds of co-operation. The first involves total surrender; the victim is persuaded to accept the world's frame of reference, its principles, measurements and standards, and the 'camp'—or whatever other enclosed space he inhabits—becomes the prisoner's only reality. Bettelheim remarked upon the fact that old prisoners tended to identify with the SS, not only in goals and values, but even in appearance, trying to make their prison garb look as much as possible like an SS uniform. They wanted to look 'smart', they said, and to look smart meant to look as much like their gaolers as they could.

There is however a different kind of cooperation, and this may be described as tactical. The tree that bends before the wind survives; let the wind fall for a few moments, and it straightens itself. But, for this, rootedness is essential; and, men being what they are, physical rootedness is not enough (although it provides a good foundation). Only that which is supernaturally based can stand firm against the principalities and powers of this world, and only the man who is inwardly established in a different dimension to that in which the wind carries all before it has any hope of retaining the core of integrity and independence which is alone fit to save him from destruction. Modern societies—or perhaps one should say the forces which drive them—are, in some sense, aware of this, which is why their citizens must be prevented (particularly through the education of the young) from catching sight of any other dimensions of being and why religion must be made a function of society, serving its ends. The exploitation of all available resources requires that men should be, as it were, melted down to fuel the process; and the inner core of integrity is resistant to fire.

For those who have caught sight at least of the outworks of heaven and of a different kind of order to the one unbelievers would like to impose universally, 'tactical' cooperation is often the only alternative to martyrdom.

Already in many countries the religious believer walks each day of his life in enemy territory. Such is the trend of opinion elsewhere that one must expect this situation to become increasingly common. In terms of the kind of societies now under construction and of the goals they set themselves, the man whose priorities conflict totally with theirs must inevitably be considered anti-social, a true Enemy of the People. God's spies therefore employ such disguises as suit their purpose. Not for them the clash of swords or the martyr's crown, but rather a quiet watchfulness and the readiness to act when action is opportune. They are engaged in the Holy War as surely as any warrior on the field of battle, but their role is to be 'subtle as serpents' and to preserve by cunning what can no longer be preserved by force.

The Nazi concentration camps—or Soviet labour camps—may be taken as an image of secular society precisely because, by their crudity, they provoke a moral shock such as their less cruel and more sophisticated equivalents will never provoke among people who cannot recognise the devil unless he strikes them in the face. It is only too clear that, if ordinary men and women are prepared, under orders or in what they are persuaded is a good cause, to do the kind of things that have been done in the camps (as, on a lesser scale, in Professor Milgram's 'experiment'), then there is unlikely to be any limit to their readiness to pursue relative good far beyond the point at which it changes character, closing the ventilators which still permit men of true stature to breathe and, always in a good cause, helping to tighten the bonds put upon them by an earlier generation of administrators (who, in their innocence, never imagined that these bonds might one day be tightened), leaving it to their successors to continue the process to the point of strangulation.

It cannot be emphasised too often that those who scent danger must not let themselves be deceived into looking in the wrong direction. We are menaced less by brigands and ill-natured tyrants than by earnest men who only wish to act rightly and who face up bravely—too bravely sometimes—to the fact that the particular may have to be sacrificed to the general, the individual to the mass.

This sacrifice is made by degrees, and those who make it are convinced that, like most sensible people, they know where to stop. A small increase in control of the citizen by the benevolent State, the closing of a loophole through which a few bad characters were gaining an unfair advantage; such measures are easily justified and meet with approval. People who object to them must surely be very selfish (as some are, for one does not need to be a saint to be alarmed when the trap is closing), and decent people submit, if not happily, at least in the assurance that they are behaving responsibly. It is mostly by their better natures that the malign fisherman hooks his victims.

Increases in population are also a matter of degree. How many is too many? It is debatable how many hungry people will burden this planet by the end of the century, but already the numbers are far beyond any figure compatible either with freedom of movement or with the protection of the earth we tread, its contents and its carpeting of trees and foliage, its marvellous ornaments. We are already a ravaging horde, and countless things of beauty, irreplaceable and infinitely precious, are being destroyed day by day. Proud individuals, families and communities are being absorbed into the multitude, joining the ranks of the dispossessed, and in our great cities they learn to live as units of uncertain identity, jostling—not meeting. Their neighbour is the man they brush against in the crowd; and there are altogether too many of these neighbours for anyone to feel neighbourly. It would take all the breath a man has even to say 'Good morning!' to each one, let alone 'Who are you?', 'Where do you come from?', 'How do you fit into my world?'.

The horror of these cities, inviting destruction as all horrors do, is the isolation of each man or woman among so many people, touching only as dummies in a shop-window touch one another. There is a limit to the number of human contacts to which we can respond; when the demand made upon us is excessive we retire into a subjective shell and are thereby diminished; and when a man is faced with a situation which requires of him more than his resources of head and heart can supply, while being assured at the same time that there is no God upon whom he might call for strength or for a superhuman degree of charity, then he is grist for any mill.

Meanwhile populations increase, and they increase chiefly in countries which have no lingering tradition of political freedom (since their traditions of freedom were of a different kind and have been destroyed by the invasion of modern ideas). The problems which face any government which has to administer such vast numbers challenge ingenuity and efficiency to breaking point. Regulations which would suffice for the control of relatively small numbers will no longer serve when millions are to be governed, and the problems become so complex that everyone must do exactly as he is told if the machine is to function at all.

Science may hold out some prospect of feeding the hungry multitudes by wringing the great globe itself like a sponge and squeezing from it every last drop of nourishment it can provide, but if this is to be done the logistic problems are staggering and the planners can operate only in terms of statistics, never of human beings in their unclassifiable variety. There is no agreement as to precisely when the supply of metals, fossil fuels, timber and other resources will run out, but no one can doubt that they are being rapidly exhausted. The process of squeezing out the final few drops will not be a pretty one and, meanwhile, diminishing resources will have to be divided among more people, including vast populations in the so-called developing countries who have been sustained for years past only by 'rising expectations'. Dispossessed of the traditional ways of life which had formerly sustained them, they have been left with nothing but their expectations and are unlikely to take kindly to disappointment.

If certain basic liberties—hard to preserve at the best of times—are essential to man's survival as something more than an intelligent locust, then this will have to be asserted in new ways and with greater force than ever before. It will have to be justified in terms of an implacable order of priorities. Nothing will be achieved by talking of 'inalienable' human rights when these rights must be set in the balance against the 'right' of the multitudes to eat.

The time may come when the preservation even of a minimal area of personal freedom costs lives; when men, women and children who might still be fed if the machines were allowed to function without impediment will die if such impediments are permitted. We will always fudge issues while we can, but there are decisions and acts of choice which cannot be postponed indefinitely. 'Liberty costs lives!' could well be a slogan inciting the unfree to tear down the last bulwarks which divide human society from the antheap, but it is also a statement of fact. Schoolchildren are told that, in the past, liberty was always paid for in blood, but the lesson is never properly related to the present; the clear implication that liberty cannot survive without the payment of this blood fee is never brought out. Such harsh dilemmas compel us to face facts and make a choice, just as the concentration camp prisoner was forced to make a choice. But perhaps this is what men are for: choosing.

It could be said, with some justification, that the choice has already been made so far as the majority is concerned. Here and now in those few countries in which a considerable (though fast diminishing) degree of personal freedom is still preserved, liberty is cherished only in so far as it costs nothing. Required to sacrifice prosperity or comfort, social justice or 'fair shares', good government or efficient administration in return for retaining a real measure of freedom, most of our contemporaries do not so much make a choice as refuse to recognise that any choice has to be made. The decision goes by default. This is surely among the most dangerous consequences of a way of thinking, a climate of opinion, which may be defined as progressive, idealistic or optimistic according to taste, but which is rooted in the refusal to recognise or to understand the limitations inherent in the human condition.

The belief that liberty can exist without the abuse of liberty or that the sheep can be let loose without the wolves being loosed belongs to the same order of thinking. If men are permitted to exercise the liberty without which they are called 'men' only by courtesy and in terms of biological definition, then the worst among them can be controlled only by harsh and perhaps brutal methods. The gallows-tree stands high over a society of free men. The more obedient we are and the more effectively emasculated, the gentler our rulers can show themselves in the exercise of their authority, until we have a society so docile that there is no further need for police or prisons, let alone for the gallows, and the occasional black sheep is dealt with in a hospital for the mentally ill.

To many people that would seem an ideal environment in which to live out their lives—or to sleep their lives away—their chief ambition being to travel the course from birth to death as painlessly as possible. Their preference is a natural expression of the inertia which is one aspect of human nature. There is something in us which will always choose the lowest place, given the choice. But, quite apart from the fact that we must all one day awaken from our dreams into other dimensions in which the lie shrivels, the fiction is destroyed and all deceptions are swept away, this world itself is not by nature a safe pen in which the weak might slumber unmolested. Once conditioned to such docility, the good sheep are not left to pasture innocently, for there are forces abroad which are ready to seize and manipulate them, carrying them into

79

regions where their poor substance is broken and their bleating goes unheard.

The immediate justification however, on the strictly 'daylight' level, for making men usable and then making use of them lies in the pressure of circumstances which require the exploitation of all available materials. It is too easily forgotten that the world is all of one piece—the earth we tread, the crops we grow, the animals upon which we feed and our own selves—and exploitation is like a forest fire which does not distinguish between a tree, a house and those who live in the house. We can already see, if we are prepared to look, what the full scientific use of the animals which provide us with meat, milk and eggs involves. There are some who are sickened by the sight and others who accept it as an unfortunate necessity, but subjective reactions are of only limited interest; we would be better advised to consider where the process is supposed to stop.

The common belief at this present moment in history is that human creatures belong to an animal species which, by a quite fortuitous process, has developed certain very special skills. This species is considered to have an inherent right to exploit all 'lower' forms of life for its own advantage; but there can be no hard and fast distinction between one kind of animal and another. It is all a 'matter of degree'. For the time being residual feelings of respect for the human state, as though it were qualitatively different to animality, still endures. There is no reason to suppose that we shall continue indefinitely to make this sentimental distinction.

The parallels between our 'animal factories' and the concentration or labour camps are uncomfortably close. In a different context, the treatment accorded to 'primitive' tribes in Asia, Africa or South America suggests that the term 'human' is considered to be fully applicable only to those among the two-legged who are skilled in technology and properly imbued with modern ideas. Hitler's Master Race is still alive and well, but its identity is now defined in terms of modernism rather than of race.

Many established liberties were given up quite willingly during the war, not least in Britain, while in the Russian Empire the enslavement of the whole population under Stalin was justified on the grounds that the Empire was under threat from the capitalist world even when the guns were silent. In Germany itself, the concentration camps and the 'final solution of the Jewish problem' were supposed to serve a war effort; and on every side man's natural tendency to struggle against bondage was neutralised by a kind of moral pressure. The sacrifice of freedom, at least in the democratic context, is felt to be tolerable when it is temporary and related to a specific emergency. Once the sacrifice is made, the habit of freedom—which takes a long time to grow and establish itself—is very easily lost, and we are not likely to see again the leisurely conditions under which it develops. To be rooted in the structure of everyday life, liberties need to grow and flower in times of peace.

In the past, the British showed a particularly firm regard for the liberty of the subject and an almost unique distrust of the power of the central authority. It is no coincidence that they were the only people in Europe who had lived free from the pressures of war for many centuries. Wars happened over the sea, where armies marched to and fro across the great land-mass, killing, burning and looting; but for the British, untroubled by the presence of violence in town and village or the brutality of armed men in their homes, war meant the death of professional soldiers and sailors—a very different matter. Across the Atlantic men who had deliberately cut themselves loose from the maelstrom set up their great libertarian experiment in full awareness that only their geographical situation made this possible.

The constant threat not so much of sudden death, for that comes in peace or war, but of the total disruption of normal patterns of living—the proximity of the jungle—and the breaking of ancient habits makes certain liberties appear as luxuries and shatters the framework within which they could be taken for granted. Under war conditions or their equivalent everything goes into the melting pot, and priorities have to be rediscovered and reasserted.

Under present conditions there can be no privileged areas of peace, no hidden corners in which some group or nation might cultivate kindness outside the stream of 'progress' and its ruthless demands. If conditions of war—or at least of conflict and crisis—become permanent, then the surrender of liberties is irrevocable; and we can be sure the dangers and problems we shall face in the coming years will be no less demanding than was the Nazi threat. But in this case there will be no victory in sight, no light at the end of the tunnel. Even if rivalry between the 'blocs' were ended and even if population problems were solved by some massive catastrophe, the 'triumph of ironmongery' (as Frithjof Schuon has called it) would require a degree of organisation such as was formerly required only for survival in war.

'There is,' said Simone Weil, 'a certain relation to time which suits inert matter, and another sort of relation which suits thinking beings. It is a mistake to confuse the two.'* The adaptation of human beings to the requirements of machinery may take many different forms : we can regard the 'dark satanic mills' as a thing of the past, although the modern factory with its army of slaves performing tasks that provide no human satisfaction is quite satanic enough, but the compulsion to adapt human nature to the requirements of ironmongery is likely to take more subtle and sophisticated forms in the future. Quite apart from the fact that there has been no occasion, since the beginning of the industrial revolution, on which a technological advance has been set aside by a clear act of choice, most people would now feel that we are obliged to grasp every available instrument and to drive technological possibilities to their limit in the hope of satisfying the needs of the multitude.

Whether such advances take the form of more complex technology, producing goods in greater quantity and at a faster rate, or of devices for the more efficient organisation of society, they make the scientific or 'rational' use of human resources more necessary ; they make 'planning' essential. To achieve its objectives, such planning requires human units which can be fitted into the blueprint, doing what they are expected to do and consuming what they are expected to consume. This calls for the progressive narrowing of the individual's field of choice and an effective interchangeability as between units.

If the mass of people are to be interchangeable, they must be equal. Since they are not by nature equal, they must be made as nearly so as possible, and in practice this means reducing those who possess certain awkward features of superiority to the level of the amorphous mass. It is difficult not to see some merit in the Marxist attribution of the beliefs and ideals current in a particular age to economic factors, at least when this analysis is applied to the present age (its historical applications are more questionable, since non-material factors intervened more decisively in the past).

* *The Need for Roots:* Simone Weil, p. 57.

Contemporary egalitarianism has assumed a moralistic veneer, a flavour of righteousness and even the *cachet* of being in accordance with Christian ideals, a point which seems to have escaped the greatest minds of Christendom in the ages of faith. The fact remains that it accords very well with what are seen as the needs of our time and with the requirements of inhuman technology. The machines ask for faceless attendants, and earnest men who never doubt their own superiority (which alone qualifies them to preach to the silly mob) extol the virtues of equality.

It is easy enough to release among great numbers of people certain negative emotions which are kept out of sight so long as they are thought to be shameful but come quite naturally to the surface when the normal human order is undermined and men are left isolated in their lonely mortality, without hope of heaven or knowledge of community.

Naked emotions, however mean or savage, are forgivable as between human beings—for who among us dare cast the first stone?—but they become less so when dressed up in borrowed finery; envy parading behind the mask of Justice is an ugly brute. The 'Crabs in a barrel' mentality has become a significant feature of our age. In the West Indies, when land crabs are to be kept overnight before being boiled alive, they are placed in a wooden barrel. Some try to scramble up the sides of the barrel, and a few of them have at least a chance of escaping; but the housewife has nothing to fear—as soon as one crab climbs a little above its companions they pull it down. Next morning the pot is filled and all are boiled together. Mercifully, crabs have no voice with which to proclaim their concern for social justice.

'Donkey say the world no level'—to use another Jamaicanism—and the burdened beast in daily contact with the earth knows very well that 'equality' is not in the nature of things. Contact with reality at any level reminds the isolated 'ego' that there is no fairness to be found anywhere unless it is prepared to look outside its own small shell and advance towards the open spaces of true Justice. No amount of 'social engineering' will even out the world's unfairness as seen by the individual who refuses to emerge from his confinement, but the attempt to impose a pattern of uniformity and to prevent natural advantages or factors of superiority from asserting themselves, however unrealistic this attempt may be, is paid for in real coinage. No means has ever been found of reconciling liberty with social justice or of evading the obligation to make a choice between them. One of the more eminent among the founding fathers of the United States, Alexander Hamilton, said that inequalities of property would exist for as long as liberty existed, such inequalities being the unavoidable result of liberty itself, and he has yet to be proved wrong. They can only be prevented (or, where they already exist, abolished) by methods which are intolerable to those who care for liberty, and even today, if we seek a perfect example of 'fair shares for all', we will find it, not in the latest Peoples' Republic, but in prison institutions the world over.

The social frameworks of the past, in which each man had his recognised position, had already degenerated in Europe long before the French Revolution ushered in a new age, but to condemn a principle because certain of its manifestations have suffered the process of decay to which all things are prone is neither wise nor objective.

Gustave Thibon, saved by his peasant background from the illusions either of the bourgeoisie or of the proletariat, maintained that such frameworks functioned as protective shells and believed that the human personality developed more freely and with greater individuality (taking this term in its positive sense) within their shelter than in any amorphous society. To the contemporary mind, mention of social hierarchies calls up a vision of the impoverished and enslaved masses created by nineteenth century industrialism and of ruthless mine-owners and the like; but that was, precisely, a society in which traditional frameworks were being broken down in the industrial interest so that the machines might be fed. Whatever we may think of the more ancient social patterns, one thing is certain: they stood in the way of industrialism and of the methodical exploitation of human material, and they were destroyed for this reason. There was no revelation of a new and higher morality, no dawning of an age of reason after a long night of superstition; only the command from our ironmongery, 'Feed me!' and the quick response, 'We obey!'.

It rather seems as though machines require of us an egalitarian and fluid social structure, whereas men, left to their own devices, had found that quite a different kind of structure best served their needs. The acceptance of the inequalities inherent in the framework depended, no doubt, upon a faith or a certainty (as the case might be) which placed this network of pre-determined social relationships in a far wider context. Terrestrial man was principally concerned with his extra-terrestrial destiny and saw his life as an episode which could never be judged in isolation. From this he derived a contentment which the modern age despises. The avowed aim of revolutionaries and of many national leaders in the newly independent countries has been to destroy this contentment and to make unacceptable what was formerly accepted; a curious ambition, perhaps, for men of unquestionable integrity to set themselves. They believed, of course, that a more rational contentment would be achieved when the old, millennial order had been replaced by a new system devised by some solitary theorist in his study or in the Reading Room of the British Museum; they were contemptuous of 'pie in the sky' and proposed, instead, 'pie' on earth for our remote descendants at some indefinite time in the unforeseeable future.

Meanwhile, far from abolishing inequalities, egalitarianism has, at least for the time being, exposed them more ruthlessly than ever before. There are, no doubt, many people who feel no compulsion to enter the 'rat race' and prefer to cultivate a modest garden, but the pressures which compel participation are becoming increasingly powerful and it is, in any case, the racers—and not the gardeners—who shape the kind of world in which we shall all have to live.

The law of the jungle, now euphemistically described as 'equality of opportunity', has replaced the human artifice which was designed to exclude it, and a man's position, whether in capitalist or socialist countries, is determined by the practical talents with which he happens to have been endowed (as, under different conditions, he might have been endowed with inherited wealth) or, quite simply, by his strength and his cunning. The Marxist regards this as an intermediate stage and looks forward to the true egalitarianism of a communist society; but the fact that the Soviet Union, sixty years after the Revolution, does not even pretend to be appreciably closer to achieving communism suggests that intermediate stages can last, in human terms, for a very long time. One may be forgiven for wondering if this particular egg will ever hatch. In the meantime, those societies in which the old hierarchies have been destroyed are inevitably dominated by the power struggle, and failure to hold one's own in this struggle is taken as an indication of irremediable inferiority.

There were no such failures in the ancient hierarchical societies. Within the social context, men were not expected to move out of the position in which destiny had placed them at birth and the majority could get on with the business of living free from the compulsions of ambition (since no structure of this kind is completely rigid, those who nonetheless felt a compulsion to move upwards frequently found the means of doing so). But in the religious context, which seemed of infinitely greater importance, no bounds or limits were set even for the humblest of men, and in this case success did not depend upon wealth or talents, ruthlessness or luck.

The poorest man and the least educated could hope to attain to a state of vision and, indeed, of *being* compared with which all the king's gold and women were trash. No human soul, whatever the circumstances of his birth and whatever his handicaps, could be denied the opportunity of coming as close to the supreme prize as love and longing might take him; and this was a high place in which there was room for all comers.

The pursuit of relative good, mistaken for an absolute, has carried us a long way from the ancient patterns and from the social stability which is now so quaintly dismissed as a condition of 'stagnation' (as though our present frenetic agitation were an indication of clarity and lucidity). Deriving on the one hand from a naive hope of building heaven on earth and, on the other, from envy on the part of those who—deprived of any true dream of heaven—cannot bear to see others enjoy what escapes their own grasp, egalitarianism has created atomised societies which provide no defence against the reduction of human beings to the status of human material. Castle walls have crumbled and the swarming people of the flatlands are left unprotected; and yet none of this has happened without our consent and, in many cases, our busy and conscientious cooperation. It is we who change, not the conditions which define the possibilities of human living, and those who choose to look the other way when decisions are to be made and who obey the laws of men as though they were the laws of God have no real grounds for complaint.

It could be said that they have lost the animal's alert and watchful cunning without having achieved the vigilance of man's estate. If their worldly business occupies them to the exclusion of the 'remembrance of God', it diverts them also from paying attention to dangers which surround them on the earthly level; they are, in Muslim terms, *ghāfilūn* twice over, careless not only of their ultimate good but also of their present safety.

It is worth recalling yet again the saying of Plotinus that bad men rule through the feebleness of the ruled and that this is just. Liberty in the political realm is a privilege of the strong and the watchful. In periods of stability weakness may go unscathed, but in changing times, when everything is in the melting pot, no one can afford to walk unarmed or to be unobservant of the undergrowth. Peace is elsewhere. In this place and at this time we are all frontiersmen.

# 4

## MAN IN SOCIETY

Liberty in the social and political realm necessarily shares in the contingent character of all those relative goods which we overrate or underrate according to the current climate of opinion. In this realm there are no 'absolutes': everything is a question of balance and discrimination between the relatively important and the relatively unimportant. But there are circumstances in which the protection of some relative good becomes, as it were, the pre-condition for preserving something that is good in an absolute and timeless sense. The relative then takes its colouring from the principle which it protects.

Men were certainly not 'free', in the sense in which freedom is now understood, in the ancient traditional societies, theocratic or tribal. Their lives were conditioned from the cradle to the grave by patterns of belief and of behaviour which had been laid down either from the beginning of time or else from the moment when a divine Revelation (reaching the earth through a Prophet, a chosen Messenger) provided a whole sector of humanity with the informa-tion they required for their living and for their dying. In these circumstances they needed no other liberty: 'The Truth shall make you free'.

This point may be illustrated in terms of the following image: suppose the world to be a vast expanse spread out beneath the divine Sun, but with a heavy canopy of cloud over many areas. The sun's rays will strike the earth at certain specific points, creating by their inherent power patterns which preserve the quality of radiance even when clouds pass over. Those who live at one such point, having access to the light, do not need to move from where they are; but those in darkness will die there, chilled to the marrow, unless they are free to move on and seek the light in solitary pilgrimage.

The liberty with which we are concerned might therefore be

defined as freedom of movement within areas of darkness; the greater the darkness, the higher the priority assigned to such liberty. We have not yet become accustomed—as we now must—to the fact that under conditions of swift and radical change, involving the breakdown of the ancient structures created for our protection, priorities are no more stable than the circumstances to which they relate.

Confusion arises because we have turned our backs upon the very notion of absolute principles which determine the placing of all relative good and relative evil in an unalterable scale of value. It no longer seems possible to assess the legitimacy or otherwise of any particular political authority or social pattern; people know only what they 'like' and what they 'dislike'—the agreeable and the disagreeable—and this provides a notoriously uncertain standard of judgment. Without some notion of legitimacy it is impossible to make valid judgments in the political realm or, for example, to determine when obedience to authority is a virtue and when it is a sin.

Since, until so recently, men's ideas were determined by religion, it is only in the religious context that we can expect to find a definition of legitimacy as it has been understood through the ages. In this context it can be related to a very simple principle: no man worships another of his kind, no man bows down before another of his kind, no man gives unquestioning obedience to another of his kind. There is only one Divinity, one Master, one Ruler; and such is the nobility of our human estate that we can accept no other.

Such is the principle. Its applications, in the opaque and ambiguous situation of fallen man, are of an almost incalculable variety. We do not live in the light of heaven or in intimate contact with absolute principles, but in the midst of reflections and the reflections of reflections. Throughout recorded history men have in fact obeyed others of their kind, bowed down before them and, on occasion, worshipped them. But, in so doing, they have submitted, not to the man as such in his human poverty and imperfection, but to the Divinity which—by his function—he represents and symbolises in the tattered dress of his transient identity. It might be said that the traditional ruler was transparent (or assumed to be so) and that, through him, his subjects glimpsed the true object of their worship and their obedience. The notion of an earth entirely cut off from heaven or of a bubble isolated by its opaqueness from everything outside would have been unimaginable to them.

An example may be taken from a culture which has commonly been regarded as 'irreligious', as indeed it must appear if we confine ourselves strictly to the perspective of Semitic monotheism. In ancient China all authority flowed from the Emperor and his realm was known as the Middle Kingdom, being situated at the centre of the earth and therefore directly beneath the light of heaven. But who was this Emperor? A man of no consequence, except for one thing; he had received the Mandate of Heaven; he was an open channel between what is above and what is beneath and, as such, he maintained the world in existence by his mere presence, as does the sun by its simple shining. In ceremonial dress, he was clothed in symbols which were like so many messages from heaven to earth; his actions and even his gestures were regulated by rites which conveyed a heaven-sent pattern to all his people, and the celestial Empire was preserved by his ritual circumambulation of the *Ming Tang*, which was an image of the entire universe.

Bordering that Empire, in Tibet, the Dalai Lama was the channel through which the grace of the Boddhisattva Chenrezig flowed out to all his people, while around him the great monasteries were set like fires—domestic hearths of divinity—at which mountain travellers in that bare land warmed themselves. Their destruction by the Communists was like the encroachment of a new ice age.

The Japanese Emperor's authority, on the other hand, was hereditary and rested upon his descent through Jimmu Tenno from the solar goddess, Amaterasu-Omikami, and his title was 'The Sublime Gate' (*Mikado*): a gate, a door, a way-in, a way-out. In other words, he was the opening in the wall, but for which the Japanese race would have suffocated in this narrow world. In quite another setting (such is the richness of human possibility) the divinity of the Pharaoh was not doubted in ancient Egypt; and even the Romans understood that their sometimes clownish Emperors must be 'deified 'if they were to merit obedience—for who but a slave would obey a merely human master? Elsewhere and in every racial setting, tribal Chieftains decked in heavenly symbols which showed the nature of their authority and its source wore the cloaks or head-dress of majesty and so brought life to their people, fruitfulness to the fields and order out of chaos.

In the Indo-European world, where society was organised into a hierarchy of castes, there was a division of powers, but the temporal authority operated only by virtue of a legitimacy conferred upon it from above. The Hindu *kshatriya*, the kingly man, would have been a creature raging in darkness had he not received the gift of light through the *brahmin* caste, just as the moon is illuminated by the sun. On the European side of the fence, the Emperor was crowned by the Pope, the Vicar of Christ, but for which his commands would have been meaningless; and no warrior would have taken the field without priestly blessing. Such societies as these were like vast irrigation systems: grace was poured out upon the spiritual authority and, by descending steps, flowed down to the knight, the merchant and the common man. It is always the same story, whatever the cultural variations. An opening above—a breach or window in the carapace,—the influx of light, and then a man or men or a caste existing only to disseminate this light without which the people would be blind as worms.

Any one of these sacred societies—each of them unique—might seem narrow and partial if it is considered in isolation. Each developed certain human possibilities to the exclusion of others which have an equal right to flower in the light of day. But this is what limitation means, and life in the human form is synonymous with limitation. Each saw its own social and moral pattern as reflecting a heavenly order or a God-given Norm and found in this belief the justification and support for its way of life; but the traditional doctrines do not admit of the possibility of any single, definitive and entirely adequate reflection of this Norm on the level of space and time; it is reflected only in fragmentary forms and therefore in a diversity of what appear to be mutually contradictory systems.

Wholeness is expressed through variety and in manifestations which, although they may appear to compete, are in truth complementary. However narrow they might seem, none was in fact a closed system; they were comparable to the divergent 'perspectives' of those who observe the mountain from different points of view. At the same time, while no single society could ever incarnate the Norm in its totality or exhaust its possibilities, the individual man—making use of a limited perspective as his starting point—contained the capability of advancing until he achieved knowledge of the mountain as it is, in all its plenitude. The traditional wisdom to which we are heirs recognises this knowledge, vision or state of being as true and unqualified liberty, far beyond the realm of contingency and the limited freedom attainable within the bounds of the contingent.

Even within these bounds, however, there was usually a readiness to accept certain 'eccentrics' as entitled to exemption from the local norms of human behaviour, and many of these societies permitted the periodic destruction of their framework through a reversal of the normal order of things. Such a reversal might take place at the New Year, when the old world had come to an end and the new world was yet to be born, and conventions were turned topsy-turvy as a reminder that all human values are relative, just as the medieval Court Jester reminded the men of power that their power was only local and their glory transient. All things were then cast back, as it were, into the primordial times before social frameworks were made. There were other renewals which took place constantly : each birth, each marriage and each death represented a break in the normal time process, an end and a beginning, through which the fabric of creation was perpetually renewed.

Ours, in comparison, is a weary world, and the variety which compensates for the narrowness of any single human culture is fast disappearing from the face of the earth. Soon a man will run to some far corner and find there the same perspective, the same thoughts, the same environment. Seeking the unaccustomed which, in its subjective impact, can be like a vision of heaven, he will find sameness. The dissemination over the entire surface of the earth of a single civilisation, although this was inevitable as soon as the same industrial techniques and an identical climate of opinion became universal, reduces the human picture to monochrome. There are those who believe that a monochromatic humanity will, in effect, have lost its *raison d'être* and must therefore have reached the end of the road. Uniformity, they say, is not what we were made for ; and nothing that departs entirely from the purpose of its creation either can or should survive.

Such ideas are strange to the people of our time and seem far removed from what is thought of as 'common sense'. It is difficult even to find a true sceptic, that is to say someone who doubts doubt itself and therefore keeps an open mind when he is faced with what seems to him—in terms of his conditioning—improbable, if not impossible.

The fact remains that throughout the greater part of recorded history—and, no doubt, far beyond that limited area of knowledge —these were the ideas upon which men and women, shaped like ourselves both in body and in mind, based their understanding of the human situation and, in particular, of 'legitimacy' in the political realm. That they should have come to seem not merely 'irrational' but unthinkable is a measure of the strength of the countervailing force which, in traditional terms, belongs to the realm of darkness, decay and disintegration, and which has transformed human thinking in a very short space of time.

We cannot reverse the course of history or pretend to be other than we are ; but we do well to register the fact that better men than ourselves believed these things and, having done so, to look more critically than we commonly do at the assumptions taken for granted in our age.

It would be easier to do this if our view of the past were less partisan. Although historians may strive after objectivity, they are necessarily men of their time and men of a specific cultural heredity. Quite apart from the bias imposed by the Christian legacy, with its emphasis upon a once and once only divine Revelation, belief in progressive evolution (itself a kind of projection of the Christian hope onto a flat, two-dimensional surface) makes it extremely difficult for scholars to assess an ancient culture otherwise than in terms of this belief, while exploitation in the industrial interest during the past two centuries has soured our whole view of the past. Even if it were possible for him to be more objective—and less concerned with dates to the exclusion of timeless factors—the secular historian is necessarily concerned only with externals and the drama of events. The spiritual life of peoples—what one might figuratively call the extra-terrestrial dimension of their lives—largely escapes his attention, running as it does in channels quite different to those of politics, social conditions and all the events that make headlines for the historian as they do for the journalist. There is an open history and there is, as it were, a secret history; these two may move in opposite directions.

The story of Islam during the five centuries following the death of the Prophet provides an example of just such a contrast : outwardly, dissension and heroic conflict between noble but headstrong men in the midst of a religious and political expansion which carried the armies of the new Empire into France in the West and China in the East, followed by dynastic quarrels, division in the 'seamless garment' of the *dar-ul-Islam*, and all the sad disillusionments which are inseparable from the political realm ; inwardly, a quiet flowering of spirituality and profound commerce between heaven and earth against a background of sober and humane equilibrium achieved in societies in which every action and every relationship was shaped by the religion. This is a secret history which leaves behind it neither monuments nor scars. In the long run it is the only history that matters.

But in the ancient traditional societies these two strands of history were not separated: outward events made sense only in terms of their inward significance, trivial in themselves, yet significant in so far as they exteriorised spiritual truths; and in the political realm, which could not be isolated from the realm of meaning, the ruler was the man from outside our bubble, the herald of eternity in the shifting sands of time.

We shall not even begin to understand such societies unless we look for what lies under the shell of historical events. The contrast between their order of priorities and ours can scarcely be overstated. As a contemporary writer on Tibet, which was the last of the major traditional societies to be destroyed by the forces governing the modern world, has pointed out, the very things which seem to us most 'real' and most 'necessary' were, for the Tibetans, if not quite illusory, only of secondary importance, while the things which they, for their part, regarded as primary realities 'are for the majority of our people, including the highly educated—perhaps for them most of all—either all but non-existent or ascribable to a twilight realm of subjective imaginings'.*

How can any man whose mind is seized and possessed by the opinions and prejudices of our time ever hope to understand societies in which the order of human priorities was not merely different but totally reversed and, in our terms, 'upside-down'? Perhaps our present situation (and the illusion we have of intellectual clarity) might be illustrated by the lettering on a large packing-case seen on an English station platform a few years ago: 'In order to avoid confusion, the bottom is labelled top.' If this rather mysterious piece of information were taken seriously, it might help us to understand a great deal about the modern world.

The more ancient the traditional society, the more distorted is the view we are likely to have of it, indeed the historical evidence upon which to found any view at all is sparse, and it could be said that the more excellent a human society, the thinner the evidence it

* *The Way and the Mountain:* Marco Pallis (Peter Owen Ltd), p. 105.

leaves behind it in the historical record. 'Happenings' are, almost by definition, crimes or disasters, as every newspaper reader knows, and very little happened in these societies. The historian therefore tries to reconstruct them in terms of what is more familiar to him and this, inevitably, is decadence in one shape or another.

The tide which, according to the almost universal belief of our ancestors, leads inexorably towards the end of time and the closing of this human cycle may pause now and then—and there are always surface eddies which give the impression that the flow is advancing rather than receding—but it cannot be reversed. As in so many other contexts, modern ideas about the nature of time present an inverted image of ancient thought, rather as though everything were perceived through a convex lens ; for us the 'bottom' is always labelled 'top', and every descent is seen as an ascent.

This is not the place to consider in detail the traditional doctrine of cycles, in terms of which humanity was believed to pass through four great ages, drifting from the dawn-grandeur of the Golden Age, when the human creature spoke familiarly with his Creator, to the lengthening shadows of the Age of Iron. But no one can doubt that the ancient traditional societies—whether in the form of Hindu civilisation or of tribal cultures—have drifted downstream in the course of time and were (with rare exceptions, of which the North American Indians provide a possible example) already decadent before the impact of European conquest shattered their life-patterns. One symptom of this decadence was the fading into the remote distance of the very idea of a Supreme Being, the foreground being taken over by 'divine energies' or 'angelic powers' personified as 'gods' ; in other words, the descent into polytheism and idolatry.

Another symptom was the ever increasing division between the idea of divine Kingship and its earthly realisation, until the gap became so glaringly obvious that it could no longer be papered over and the very principle that all authority derives from above began to look like a fiction. The historian, considering this principle in the light of his progressive scenario, thinks at once of the degenerate examples immediately available to his inspection and assumes that matters have always been so, forgetting that the fiction—the degenerate form—exists only as the echo or parody of a truth.

The fact remains that a descent has taken place and that societies in which the presiding idea has faded almost out of sight are extremely vulnerable, requiring, not a wind of change, but a mere breeze to reduce the ancient and hallowed framework to dust. As in the familiar fairy tale, a child cries out that the King is naked and immediately the whole crowd is aware of the fact. No one any longer understands how they could have supposed that this forked radish, a man like themselves, was robed in splendour.

This is an inevitable process, but in Biblical terms it marks a kind of second 'Fall of Man'. By the first Fall he had been expelled from Paradise and, thereafter, had attempted to reproduce in the wilderness the conditions of the remembered Garden and to retain some of its habits. Eventually—since, after all, the wilderness is not the Garden and never can be—memory fades and practice decays until the last vestiges are swept away and we find ourselves on our own in falling darkness and increasing cold. At the same time, if the primal Fall was identified with the Knowledge of Good and Evil, the second implies the loss of this discriminative knowledge and the substitution for it of *ideas* of good and evil.

With this second fall humankind enters a new era, one in which there can no longer be any legitimate authority in the traditional sense. Wholly secular societies come into being.

Although there have been occasions on which the ancient, heaven-oriented society collapsed or was destroyed overnight, the process is usually more gradual, and there are cases in which certain traditional values—'habits of Paradise'—are honoured long after the social structure has changed beyond recognition. Such vestiges may survive for centuries after the metaphysical and religious ideas which validate them have been forgotten, like cut flowers preserved after the parent plant has died. The situation is therefore exceedingly complex and, when the channels between heaven and earth have been silted up, we make do with the bad as the only available alternative to the worse, groping for a sense of priorities in the midst of a chaos which changes shape as do clouds on a windy day.

Under these circumstances the preservation of what little can be salvaged from the wreck becomes immensely important. Ancient principles, no longer understood, come to be regarded as fictions, but even such fictions, if they preserve an order which still protects and nourishes men, leaving them free to discover individually the sources of splendour long after their society has lost sight of those sources, are not to be scorned. Poised between two poles—on the one hand the traditional societies in their pristine integrity and, on

96

the other, the totalitarian secular society from which every glimmer of light has been finally excluded—there lies a kind of neutral territory, ambiguous by nature, neither one thing nor the other, closed above but not yet open below to the invasion of demonic and dehumanising forces.

This is, almost by definition, a perilous situation, for nature is said to abhor a vacuum and, when images of a heavenly order are banished, images from quite another place are ready to break in. The world has become—to borrow C. S. Lewis's phrase—the 'silent planet', but such a closed system may at least provide a framework in which men are free to look upwards and to seek their salvation. Liberty to do so then takes its place at the head of any realistic order of priorities.

The 'neutral' society is necessarily disorderly, illogical in its structure, riddled with anomalies and, very possibly, tainted with corruption. Having lost the heavenly order and, as yet, escaped the deadly regimentation of the infernal host, it could hardly be otherwise. There are many worthy people who find this intolerable and would like to straighten the curves and iron out the bumps, creating, they hope, a more 'rational' society; but one does well to remember that disorder is not the direct opposite of order. The opposite of a heavenly order is its inverted image: an infernal one. Between these two lies the intermediate, neutral realm of confused disorder.

This may be denied in principle by those who place the peace and good order of society at the head of their priorities, but it is known well enough in practice. The 'lifer' in a high-security prison or the inmate of a Siberian labour-camp would quite rightly prefer freedom even under chaotic and grossly unfair social conditions to his present situation. A prisoner in his cell watching a bird's flight beyond the bars does not see any moral or intellectual problem in weighing the advantages of liberty against those of security. He is up against the reality of the human situation. But when a man is gradually, gently, lovingly imprisoned he neither sees nor seizes the moment of choice. True of man in society, this is true also in an infinitely wider context; for it is said that a moment comes for each of us in this brief life when we choose, for perpetuity, our domicile in heaven or in hell.

Order in the social realm is a relative good of great importance. We would all of us, no doubt, prefer to combine liberty with order in a reasonable balance rather than find ourselves obliged to choose between the two, and there is nothing wrong in wanting to enjoy simultaneously as many good things as can cohabit under the same roof. The problem arises when two or more of these good things are found, in practice, to be mutually irreconcilable, and it is in this situation that a scale of priorities must be established.

How, then, are we to distinguish—in the context of 'neutral' societies lacking any supernatural sanction—between the social order which offers a sound support for human living and one which threatens to suffocate the very qualities which make us distinctively human? First, surely, by facing the facts squarely and recognising that the feelings aroused by a sacred, traditional authority and the loyalty it evokes are inappropriate in relation to the secular State.

Since it is not in our interest to tear one another to pieces and since survival in this world requires at least a measure of cooperation, some kind of social framework has to be devised and some kind of central authority must exist. But in seeking support and protection from the State or from society as such we are dealing with a dangerous beast and have to be ever watchful that its protective embrace does not tighten into a bear-hug. The danger of being hugged to death is the price we pay for security, a fact recognised clearly enough by political thinkers in the late eighteenth as in the nineteenth century, but commonly overlooked in our more 'idealistic' times. The rights of the State over us and its claims upon us diminish in proportion to its loss of traditional legitimacy. When it no longer acknowledges any transcendent authority, it must become our servant, providing protection and certain amenities—a kind of glorified Water and Sewerage Authority.

At best, the secular State will provide a loose framework in which men and women can realise their possibilities or, as the Scots say, 'dree their own weird' and make their choice. Far from taking upon itself the responsibilities which previously rested on individual shoulders, it will leave them where they belong and strive to create conditions under which the exercise of personal responsibility is encouraged and, so far as possible, facilitated.

Towards the end of the last war, both Gustave Thibon and his former protegée, Simone Weil, set themselves to draw up the outlines of the kind of society that should be built in France when peace came. Both were realists—anti-Utopians—and both understood the importance of binding social obligations to the normal impulses of men and women, not as they should be, but as we find them.

'Cut off from self-interest,' wrote Thibon, 'virtue loses the weight by which it is incarnated; nothing binds it any longer to the earth. But self-interest, in its turn, separated from virtue, loses the power of flight which is its deliverance; there is no longer anything to raise it to heaven. This is the divorce between the ideal and the real: on the one hand a verbal and inoperative morality, on the other an anarchic swarming of unbalanced egoisms which devour one another, with, as an inevitable result, the degradation of individuals and the dissolution of societies.'* He knew only too well how distant were the societies which he saw around him from this sober and realistic pattern of living. The Christian of the Middle Ages, he said, knew but one real enemy: individual sin. 'Today we have to do battle against a more universal and tenacious evil, against a disorder that has infiltrated into our bodies, our customs, our institutions, mixed with the very air we breathe.'

Society petrifies and the atmosphere is poisoned unless it has in its midst men who, by their very presence, let in a breath of fresh air; men who exercise a responsibility rooted in values deeper and more universal than any which can take shape within the matrix of the world's business, more central and more nearly absolute than those of morality. Frameworks, outside the sacred realm, are always makeshifts; they are vivified and validated by men who, while they live their everyday lives within these bounds, have their hearts elsewhere. Such men do not make their appearance by command of the Government or because the planners have done their job well; they belong to the realm of the wayward and the unpredictable (for so it is that the extra-terrestrial, the spiritual, appears to us), and society must contain wide areas of freedom to accommodate them.

On a lower level—and a purely contingent one this time—the air circulates more freely if there is space for privileged groups, able to pursue unproductive and seemingly frivolous occupations, to explore by-ways which are closed to the busy majority, to indulge in fantasies and play with dreams, to mock those who take their social role seriously and to defy practicality; people, in other words, who introduce an element of variety into closed societies which would otherwise degenerate into total uniformity, and who suggest alternative perspectives. The citizens of a secular society, ground

* *Retour au Réel:* Gustave Thibon (Lardanchet), p. 161.

down by economic pressures, constantly reject 'inessentials' (understood in an exclusively material sense) and narrow their field of attention, like cattle concerned only with the patch of grass immediately ahead. Then, since they are not in fact cattle, the air becomes fetid unless their world is ventilated by men and women who are not of their kind.

It is no doubt inevitable that the 'neutral' society should tend towards uniformity, as though dragged downwards by the force of gravity. Variety in the human realm reflects the inexhaustible richness inherent in the light of heaven, and once this light is excluded a process of impoverishment sets in. Variety, which is not subject to numbering since it is expressed in unique entities, is increasingly replaced by sheer quantity, a quantity without significance or value since the units of which it is composed are interchangeable.

It was once a grave matter to destroy a man, for he was irreplaceable in his uniqueness; the destruction of a unit of the multitude is clearly unimportant, a fact which the great collectivist societies of our century have quite logically recognised. Equally logically, having lost the very concept of individual uniqueness and of the value which resides in this man or that woman made 'in the image of God', they have been compelled to seek value elsewhere and have found it in the collectivity as such, in the 'masses' or the 'people'; and from this point on the sacrifice of the individual to the collectivity can always be justified.

The neutral society is, as it were, poised over this abyss and drawn towards it, existing only as a transitional stage between the integral, traditional society living in the light of heaven (however narrow the lens through which that light is filtered) and the totalitarian collectivity which is, in a certain sense, its reversed image or parody.

It is not surprising that we should have a profound, albeit unconscious, nostalgia for the unity of the traditional societies and therefore be willing enough to seek social homogeneity at a lower level, if necessary a sub-human level—the homogeneity of the herd or the ant-heap. The nostalgia for unity finds at least a kind of satisfaction in societies in which the individual is completely absorbed into the mass, a mass that lives only to labour and to spawn. One need not quarrel with those who claim that people are happier so, particularly if they are better fed, better housed and better clothed; but quarrel one must with the implication that happiness on this level is all that matters. Here, as in many other contexts, believer and unbeliever part company, and there is no common ground upon which dialogue—or even argument—might be possible. These are, indeed, mortal enemies, engaged in a fight to the death.

Those who understand how important it is that such small areas of freedom as remain unenclosed in the modern world should be defended at all costs and for as long as defence is humanly possible need not be dismayed by the fact that they are probably fighting a losing battle. Temporary good is always worth defending because nothing under the sun lasts for long and nothing is final, except for one thing: the choice which this individual man or woman makes when the battle lines are drawn up. It is not for earthly victory or for the 'future of humanity' that we fight, but for our own justification. We play our parts on a very small stage set in a vast amphitheatre, and although—having done the little that is in our power—we may fall, defeated and overwhelmed, we can be sure that powers infinitely greater than any at our command will break in upon the 'silent planet' when the time is ripe and that the forces which seemed invincible will show themselves to have been no more substantial than the vapours of night when the sun rises.

It is not, therefore, our business to enquire for how long the sand-castles we build will last, or to reject joy because—sooner or later—sorrow will intervene, or, for that matter, to suppose ourselves so grand that we can only defend a city which will endure for ever. Our business is with the present moment, choosing the brief good which reflects an everlasting Good, and with the preservation of what is worth preserving for the time being. But we can never hope to do this on a basis of wishful thinking or sentimental illusions. Just as constant attentiveness to God is the foundation of all religious practice, so a sober realism—attentive to facts—is the foundation of effective action in the world. The defender must study the weaknesses of the city he defends and know the condition of its ramparts.

The people of the relatively free 'neutral' societies which still survive in the modern world slumber upon their freedoms, chiefly concerned with economic pressures and with the revamping of their social frameworks in terms of current theories of 'progress' and 'equality'. They believe that democratic forms of government in some way guarantee the preservation of liberty and that all the other safeguards once thought necessary can be carelessly discarded so long as free elections are allowed to take place at regular intervals. This is, to say the least of it, a very dubious proposition, assuming, as it must, that a majority of the electorate at any given time is more concerned with the preservation of individual liberty than with bread-and-butter problems. But there is a certain historical irony in the fact that the very circumstances which make it essential that people should have some real and effective control over their own affairs tend to make such control almost impossible.

In the traditional societies, which changed so little from one century to the next, the individual was protected by immemorial customs and by a social pattern which was thought to be inalterable. His rulers were equally bound by custom, their power strictly limited, and they too were unlikely to dream of innovation. There was no need for 'democracy' as it is now understood; and yet, in so many of these societies, democracy did exist in a very practical form as, for example, in the African tribal system. Even in these collectivist times this principle may be seen at work in a few tiny communities here or there. The Western Samoans, on attaining independence, chose their own ancient *matai* system in preference to parliamentary government, a system under which the franchise is confined to the Chiefs of the landholding clans, Chiefs who are themselves elected by all their clan fellows, including the women and the children. Such cases as this exist only on the margin of our juggernaut world (with its cargo of false deities), but they illustrate certain possibilities which are still viable.

In the conditions of swift change under which we now live neither rulers nor ruled are either bound or protected by any serious consideration beyond current fashions in opinion. Decisions are taken and new laws introduced which may transform the individual's life in a very short space of time, so that he and his family and his work can be fitted into the latest scheme for collective development. He needs as never before to have a hand on the levers of power or, at the very least, to be in a position to obstruct the rash and hasty manipulation of these levers; and yet, because of the complexity of modern civilisation and the organisational problems posed by industrial societies, government cannot operate effectively unless it is free from such interference and obstruction.

In this context, Thibon noted an important distinction between 'platonic' power and real power, 'platonic' liberties and real liberties or, in other words, between the theoretic and the effective. The voting ticket, he said, 'has flowered on the tomb of the communal and corporative liberties.' Universal adult suffrage has been substituted for a network of local privileges and communal freedoms; for who, it is asked, needs such privileges and liberties when he enjoys the right to vote?

The 'masses' as such can never possess or wield power. When the cake of power is divided between the units which make up the mass one is left with crumbs invisible to the naked eye. What people need is not a theoretic 'sovereignty', but real power on a small scale and real protection against those who operate on a big scale—the kind of power that can be handled and that feels good and solid in the hand, not the kind that exists only in terms of statistics and electoral majorities. But to possess this they would have to emerge from the 'mass' and become people again, jealously guarding their obstructive (and 'unfair', because unequally distributed) liberties. No modern State would tolerate such an untidy situation, and one is therefore compelled to ask whether we can afford the modern State, not merely as it is now but as it is likely to be a few years or a few decades from now.

It is not difficult to understand why this question is seldom asked. Liberty, as it was understood in the decades preceding the First World War, is not highly regarded now even in Western Europe, and this is partly due to the social changes which have taken place in recent years. Industrialism, as we have seen, created a new class of people fitted to its needs : a displaced and dispossessed proletariat. Liberties cherished by the ruling class could mean little more to them than did the liberties of the Athenian citizen to his slaves.

Nowhere is this more clearly illustrated than in the British experience. As the breeding-ground of the Industrial Revolution, Britain suffered the side-effects of early industrial development more acutely and more profoundly than any other country. When the nineteenth century Prime Minister Disraeli wrote of the 'two nations' he was not employing a figure of speech but identifying a fact of life. These two nations had so little in common that they might have been taken for different races. There was a ruling class, with well-defined characteristics which are still sometimes thought to represent the 'British character', and there was the labouring or slave class, more or less invisible throughout most of the nineteenth century, with totally different characteristics. Events in the middle years of the present century have, in effect, produced a complete reversal of roles, and it is inevitable—since such habits cannot be shaken off in the course of a few decades—that the class now in control should retain something of the slave-mentality.

In Britain and elsewhere in Europe (where the contrast was less acute owing to the survival of large agricultural, pre-industrial communities) the enfranchisement of the masses and the triumph of trade unionism have placed political and social power in the hands of those who have no tradition of individualism and independence, qualities which were ground out of them (and their fathers and grandfathers before them) in the factories and which they necessarily associate with their former masters and with the whole scenario of industrial exploitation. These circumstances fostered a collectivist mentality. Individual gestures of independence came to be seen as the betrayal of the common cause. In the trade unions' struggle for power there could be no tolerance for the man who broke ranks.

It would therefore be foolish to expect the masses (or their leaders) in Western Europe to resist the trend of the times or to be ready to sacrifice their newly acquired prosperity for the sake of liberties they have never enjoyed and have never learned to value. To say this is not to make a moral judgment but to register a fact. A man is enslaved and ill-treated. In due course he is, if not genuinely freed (for freedom is not a gift but a condition for which one must be fit), presented with the keys of political power. How could one expect that he would emerge as a man without a past?

The notion that universal adult suffrage in some way guarantees the liberty of the individual is without foundation. Democracy and the 'free society' may happen to coincide; they are certainly not synonymous terms. No one doubts that government with the consent of most of the governed is preferable to government without this consent; having said this one has not really said very much, and there is great danger in the complacent assumption that nothing more needs to be said.

This was not an assumption made by the American Founding Fathers when they drew up the Constitution of the United States. However great the errors of the eighteenth century political philosophers from the religious point of view, they understood the nature of power a great deal better than their successors. In North America the men who had the unprecedented task of setting up a new kind of society in a 'new world' understood very well that distrust plays a vital and healthy role in the political realm. What they most distrusted was the concentration of power in any single sector.

Quite unlike the revolutionaries either of France or of Russia, who were primarily concerned to turn their societies upside down and replace one form of unfettered power with another, the Americans distrusted not only the 'insolence of the despot', but also the 'insolence of the commonalty' or, to express this in contemporary terminology, the will of the people. It was almost as though they possessed an intuitive awareness that, with the disappearance of traditional authority, the first priority of the coming age would be limitation of the power of the secular State. The Constitution was designed to fetter power, in whatever quarter it might erupt, in the expectation that it would always be abused if unrestrained and that what they owed to future citizens of their country was protection from this abuse.

No such protection exists in those democracies which make a pseudo-absolute of the 'sovereignty of the people' (or of the people's representatives in a parliamentary assembly). As was suggested earlier, relative principles and values belong to the order of variable priorities and present us with a mortal threat when they are treated as 'absolutes' and one or another of them is given unqualified priority. The American Constitution, in effect, limits the 'sovereignty of the people' in terms of Constitutional Law, just as it limits the power of the Chief Executive and of the Congress.

The British example is again instructive in this context. It is almost as though the introduction of universal adult suffrage, combined with the sweeping aside of the checks and balances which previously existed—the Sovereign's effective power of veto and the blocking role of an hereditary Second Chamber—had stifled real political debate except on the extreme Left, so that a nation which produced some of the most notable political thinkers in Europe and mounted the first modern revolution, under Cromwell and his fellow regicides (a term which indicates the killing of a principle as much as of a person), is now notorious for its people's indifference to political philosophy and for the pragmatism of its governments.

At the same time, a concern for the liberty of the subject which was once regarded by other Europeans as little short of fanatical has been eroded in favour of something quite different, an obsession with 'fairness' understood in a strictly quantitative sense, together with an intense resentment of privilege in any form and a fanatical rejection of the fact that some human beings are, by nature and by destiny, superior to others. Vigilance in the cause of liberty has been replaced by watchfulness of the neighbour who might steal a march on us or jump the queue. This too is inevitable and has its origins in the slave-barracks. Free men are not concerned with fairness. They accept inequality. But slaves starve if one man seizes more than his fair share of the crusts available. They must keep a jealous eye on one another merely to survive and they must stand patiently in the queue because that is what the system demands.

Equally inevitably, a reasonable principle—the principle that governments should be guided by the wishes of the greater part of the population they govern and should act for the common good—has been pursued beyond reason and has led to a situation in which a notional majority of the electorate (which may in fact be a minority) is presumed to empower government to act without restraint.

This might not matter so much if modern governments exercised only such functions as were considered their proper business a century or more ago, but in our time government is omnipresent, fingering every aspect of human life and assuming a vast array of new responsibilities on the principle that human beings cannot be trusted to look after themselves or their companions; moreover, it has adopted a fundamentally revolutionary role, arrogating to itself the right to change the very structure of society.

In earlier times, men and women who were opposed to the ruling ideology of their period might stand aside and go their way, grumbling but uninvolved. They are now compelled, not only to accept what is done in the name of a fictional majority, but to participate and to contribute to it by their labour, like condemned men forced to dig their own graves.

The enforced involvement of every citizen in the aims and activities of their society seems to be inseparable from any political system which claims to execute the will of the people, in whatever fashion this mysterious will may have been ascertained. It is significant that military conscription was introduced for the first time by the Revolutionary Government in France, fighting the first 'People's War'. From this it was only a short step to the invention of another new principle, nationalism (in the contemporary sense of the term), which would in due course encourage men to commit, in the name of their nation, crimes which even the most vile among them would have hesitated to commit for his own sake.

This packaging of humanity into separate national enclosures has a neatness about it which appeals to the modern age and has followed a predictable course from the days of free movement to this present time in which people are effectively imprisoned within arbitrary frontiers, if not by the building of walls or the laying of barbed wire, then by a system of passports, currency restrictions and work permits binding them to a particular area much as serfs were once bound to their Lord's demesne. Marshalled in this fashion into camps, with barriers set up, they are the more easily managed, and the doctrine of 'national sovereignty', supposedly handed down with the Tablets of the Law, assists the process. Anyone or any group who seize power in a particular camp may do as they please. As in Cambodia in 1976, they may slaughter a million of their own people without anyone raising a finger to interfere. In the community of nations the Good Samaritan has no role to play, but the Pharisees are full of virtue.

Involvement in the society in which we are effectively imprisoned is also enforced by systems of direct taxation which would have been regarded as intolerable only a few years ago. Taxation in one form or another has been with us for a very long time, but here, as in other contexts, something that is in itself necessary takes on an entirely new colouring when pushed beyond a certain point. Apart from the indirect taxes (allowing room for personal choice) which enabled governments to function in the past, the Muslim *zakat* offers the best example of a direct levy designed to provide for the poor and to enforce the community's responsibility for those of its members who cannot fend for themselves or take care of their dependents; but there is a world of difference between such classic levies or tithes—forming part of a body of religious obligations —and modern income-tax, designed on the one hand to transfer responsibilities from the individual, the family or the community to the State and, on the other, to alter relationships within society.

If one considers the direction in which this points, the outcome must be obvious. The region in which individual choice is allowed to operate—the possibilities of variety created by differences of choice—are systematically narrowed. We come soon enough to a society in which the small proportion of his earnings that a man is allowed to spend freely is no more than 'pocket money' which will cover certain luxuries; the necessities of life—and many things which earlier ages would never have thought of as necessities—being provided by the State, while the possibility of anyone achieving financial independence, whatever the sacrifices he may be prepared to make, is completely removed. There is therefore a reversion to the childhood situation: security, but without choice or responsibility and without the opportunity to demonstrate either the good or the evil which characterises us. The world is then no longer a stage upon which people show what they are made of, but an asylum in which they are 'cared for' while they await the day when, stripped, unsheltered and alone, they will come to judgment.

There are those who would say that some such system is necessary and unavoidable in a complex and highly developed industrial society, and—in so far as advanced industrialism and liberty cannot exist under the same roof—they have a case. But the point of quite particular significance is the way in which this system has come to be taken for granted in the course of a few decades as though, like the wind and the rain, it were a phenomenon of nature. People have forgotten that in the last century brave men were prepared to go to prison as a matter of principle rather than pay this tax, and the few who now manage to evade it are commonly regarded, not as champions of liberty, but as scoundrels.

It is taken for granted that taxation should be levied as much for political and ideological purposes as for fiscal ones, so that the man who pays a large proportion of his income in taxation is not primarily contributing to his country's needs, but is making a sacrifice in the service of an idea to which he may be totally opposed. This is an entirely new and unprecedented situation. The fact that it goes virtually unchallenged is both strange and sinister, compelling us to ask yet again how many things which would at present seem intolerable to us might be accepted without question within a few decades or even sooner.

President Nyerere, the darling of Western liberals, remarked recently that: 'Many people would prefer to be left alone; we are not going to leave them alone'. His words might be echoed by the leaders of almost any modern State and express definitively the way in which benevolent governments see their role and their unquestioning faith that they have a right to draw every single individual into the process of change, convinced that only the mad or the wicked would want to stand out against this 'progress'.

We have travelled a very long way in the short time since Thoreau, the author of 'Walden', wrote : 'That government is best which governs least.' It is no longer necessary, as it was in the days of open and unashamed tyranny, to impose control in the teeth of hatred and opposition ; this can now be done in the name of social morality and the public good. Secularism, the profane realm, has become both so all-embracing and so overweaning that the religious man might willingly stand aside and cultivate his modest garden in a quiet place. This is barely possible anywhere and may soon be impossible everywhere. In a certain sense his situation is comparable to that of the early Christians, who asked only to be left free to pursue the way of salvation, but who were dragged out of their hiding places and martyred—since their very existence challenged the totalitarianism of pagan Rome—until, having no alternative, they destroyed the society which had tried to destroy them.

One does not look for a repetition of this miracle. In these 'latter days' when the world's religions are, at least in the corporate sense, advanced in age and far from the historic sources of their respective Revelations, when Christianity slumbers on its world-transforming truths and the hurricane force of Islam is long exhausted, no religion as such is likely to stand firm against the claims of the secular State and its pagan ideals.

Unavoidably—for nothing under the sun is exempt from time— the Word of God, when it is fleshed in the forms of this world and in human institutions, suffers an ageing process ; but, because it is what it is, individuals may still reach the living marrow of these old bones and, through this contact, be reborn into the primal age of their religious traditions. This may not appear as a major factor on the stage of world events, but it still represents a threat to societies which have turned their backs on God and on the trans-cendent dimension which would make nonsense of all their claims, and for this reason if for no other they are bound to hate religion, attacking it ruthlessly in the Socialist bloc and, elsewhere, either seducing it to purely social purposes or smothering it in worldliness. They have taken on a formidable opponent.

There is a kind of balance, a law of compensation, inherent in the nature of things. Precisely because ours is the age of the masses and of the collectivity, it is also the age of the individual. When all else slips and slides away, only this man or this woman—the minority

of one—can stand firm. It is, of course, an absurdity to suggest that
the average person should do so, setting himself up in proud and
solitary opposition to the multitude and pitting his judgment
against theirs ; but then it is quite impossible to tell who is 'average'
and who is not until the chips are down. Only dire necessity separates
the men from the boys.

Even so, the humble man will ask : What fits me to make so
momentous a decision?

In the first place, there is no one else to make it. In other times
men were encompassed in guidance and, indeed, in certainties. We
have chosen to live otherwise ; to 'think for ourselves' as the common
phrase has it, and to 'stand on our own feet' without the support of
immemorial custom, an unchanging morality, wise priests, a
religious framework, 'divine' rulers. We cannot now complain that
the responsibility placed upon us us too heavy to be borne ; and so
one says to this questioning man—There is no one else to do it :
only you. This is what we wanted, freedom from old hierarchies
and old dogmas, and our prayer has been answered. This man is
on his own.

Secondly, the convictions of the multitude are not so much true
convictions as mental and emotional habits, conditioned by a climate
of opinion which has no foundation beyond the sands of time. They
are the beliefs of non-believers and the thoughts of non-thinkers,
the parrot cries of a generation malformed by secular education and
mismoulded by an entirely profane human environment. It does
not really require undue pride or intellectual arrogance on the part
of those who have anchored their thought in a timeless and universal
wisdom to stand out against these pseudo-convictions. To say this
is not to denigrate modern man as such, at least in terms of his
potentialities, but to identify an unprecedented factor in his condition : unlike his fellows in any other period, he is bombarded from
infancy to old age, and through each day from morning to night,
with the ideas current at this moment in time. And yet this hubub
of propaganda can still be neutralised, as the roar of traffic is
neutralised for a man attentive to the business in hand, if he will but
listen to those other voices and attend to beliefs which are still filled
with a power which silences all such chatter.

The leaders of opinion in this age say that we are created chiefly
for the purpose of scratching one another's backs (being 'useful to
our society') ; monkeys do as much for each other. When the Muslim

says that we are created to pray, not to work, he is simply marking the distinction between man and beast and identifying the primary human duty. Axiomatic in traditional thinking is the idea that the animal creation is imprisoned in time; man is not.

There are many today who see more clearly than they know and who would stand firm against the trend of the times if they were not hamstrung by self-doubt. They are unsure of their own motives, as they are of their own wisdom, browbeaten by the superficial 'common sense' of the age and intimidated by its humanitarian pretentions. They should be aware that this humanitarianism is the cheapest virtue available; it costs absolutely nothing to express liberal and humanitarian opinions, requires no sacrifices and wins social approval. Put into practice, these opinions encourage the State to take over responsibility for the poor, the weak and the unfortunate; once this has been achieved the virtuous man is justified in feeling indignant when a friend or relative turns to him for help, since they should have gone to the authorities and filled out the appropriate forms. It is time to call the bluff of those who suggest that anyone who opposes the fashionable ideology of 'social responsibility' is showing a lack of concern for his neighbour, if not 'Hitlerite' tendencies.

No doubt Yeats had something of the sort in mind when he wrote:

'The best lack all conviction, while the worst
Are full of passionate intensity.'

For this reason, if no other, it is more than ever important to proclaim the abnormality of the modern age and to unmask its pretensions, assuring such doubters that it is not they but their world which is sick and that the gift of health obliges them to assume their responsibilities, not by rushing into action in company with the professional busybodies, but by being themselves and by achieving an integrity which rings true when struck by events. We do not need to seek occasions for action; they come to us, welcome or unwelcome, and their coming is a sufficient sign that they are our business.

Since it is in the Western sector of humanity that the modern age came to birth, it is here if anywhere that the single man is required to stand firm and question the ideologies of his time. Elsewhere in the world, these ideologies are too novel and therefore too exciting to be doubted, and in any case they have the smell of success about them; they have the big bombs, the dams and the dam-busters. But we are old in such ways and should by now be unimpressed by the superstitions of progress, just as we are virtually immune to certain diseases which, when first introduced into other regions of the world, decimated whole populations.

Moreover the Westerner is well placed to show courage and take risks. In material terms, he is supremely privileged, secure and comfortable. His 'poor' are rich by Asian or African standards, his belly is so regularly and amply filled that he forgets even to be thankful for the miracle of nourishment; few of his children die in infancy and he himself has every prospect of living long enough to repent of his sins. His anxieties relate, not to the necessities of subsistence, but to luxuries and playthings. One can scarcely say 'noblesse oblige', for not even his best friends would call this man noble, but he should at least acknowledge his exceptional good fortune and the obligations which fortune imposes. Having no excuse for the anxieties which drag a man's mind down to the exigencies of survival, he is free to develop and use the specifically human capacities he has been given and to seek Truth with unimpeded purpose.

But good fortune is not confined to the level of material subsistence. There is a more universal privilege which we all enjoy regardless of our worldly situation, a privilege which motivates all human praise and all gratitude. We have been born, not as beasts of the field or the jungle, but as men and women capable of looking beyond the exigencies of animal survival and of knowing, both above and within all passing contingencies, the Absolute which is both transcendent and present in the depths of our own being. The means of salvation or of liberation are at hand on every side—for, seen aright, there is no positive thing on this earth that cannot be a means of salvation, a channel of grace, a reflection of reality—illuminated by the divine messengers, the prophets, who have told us where to look and what to do.

From the moment of our birth into this human state—a state 'hard to obtain', as the Hindus say; immeasurably privileged in comparison with the animal, vegetable and mineral states—the Gates of Heaven are open. Capability implies obligation, and all that has been said of human societies in the modern age might be summarised in a few words: whatever obstructs or inhibits this capability is damnable and merits destruction; whatever fosters it is blessed and has all the rights.

While, having been placed here, we are entitled to feel natural concern over everyday problems on our own behalf and on that of our kindred and our neighbours, this concern exists against a background of thankfulness for good fortune which transient difficulties and misfortunes cannot wholly obscure. A sense of proportion is a human duty because it is something of which human beings are capable. There is really no common measure between time and eternity or between, on the one hand, the light and shade of this life and, on the other, the joy which is the very substance from which reality is woven. All that has been said of the social realm and of the dangers which press upon us must be situated in this context, given its fair measure of concern and no more.

A man is all or he is nothing : either a unique mode of the knowledge of God or a mote of dust among milliards of others. Outside of religion and of the truths communicated to us through Revelation, he is of no importance, and the Nazi or Communist view—or that of any other ideology which totally subordinates the individual to the collectivity—has logic on its side, as against the feeble sentimentalities of those who imagine that human lives or human feelings matter in the context of contemporary secularism. The least deserving of mercy when the swords are unsheathed is the humanist who supposes he can cherish humanity while excluding religion. He, in a sense, is the judge who orders the execution; and the Lenins, Hitlers, Stalins or Maos of our world—and other bewildered peasants or petit bourgeois intoxicated with Utopian theory—are merely the executioners.

While the clouds come down upon us and the storm rages, we build our sandcastles because they are good in their small way and some are beautiful, and because they reflect the patterns of another place, a more enduring realm, projected into these fragile turrets and outworks; but every man or woman born contains the possibility of being something infinitely more than a short-lived creature of this short-lived earth, just as a seed contains in virtuality a great tree. What we can be we must be, or fail utterly. That, in its stark simplicity, is our situation.

# 5
## MAN AS VICEROY

Once upon a time (but not so very long ago) a European beggar wandered into an Arab cafe in Blida. One of the Muslims there handed him a coin. 'Do you think God will take note of such alms-giving?' his companion asked him. 'You never know,' he told them, 'who may be concealed under the appearance of a poor man.'

Such prudence would be natural to a Muslim brought up to believe that the Friends of God come and go as they will, disguised now in rags, now in riches, with power to change utterly—when it is God's will—the nature of a situation or the pattern of a life. You never know. Each man's 'inner secret' is, they say, known only to God, and each man is to be treated with respect not only because the neighbour is worthy of respect but because he may be quite other than he seems and lightning may lie dormant in his hands.

Sometimes these hands are peacefully clasped, their power showing itself only to save or to heal. So the tale is told of a certain disciple who pestered his spiritual Master to teach him the Great Name, the secret Name of God that is said to be known only to those who are closest to Him and to carry with it an overwhelming force. Wearied by these constant demands, the Master told his disciple to spend the morning at the city gate and report scrupulously everything he saw. There was little to report. 'I saw the people go in and out. An old man passed with his donkey laden with firewood. A soldier came after him, beat him and seized both his donkey and the wood.' The Master asked him what he would have done to the soldier if he had known the Great Name. 'I should certainly have demanded his death!' 'Well,' said the Master, 'I must tell you that this old woodcutter who allowed himself to be maltreated without complaint is none other than he who long ago taught me the Name.'

But the lightning is not necessarily controlled by the Friend or Beloved of God, upon whom it rests with the gentleness of Spring sunshine. So the Muslims tell another tale to illustrate the fact that power as well as mercy inhere in the great ones who walk secretly among us. It is said that the eleventh-century Persian saint, Abu Sa'id, lived for a certain period in great luxury, feasting much and entertaining himself with music and dancing. Those who might have recognised his sanctity under the more conventional disguise of poverty were not sharp enough to see through such a mask as this and were duly scandalised. One of them, a certain Amir, pressed harshly for the settlement of a debt. The saint said nothing, did nothing, but the Amir's faithful hunting dogs went mad soon after, turned upon their master and tore him to pieces. God, they say, is not mocked; and those who mock his friends may create within the natural world such a whirlpool of disorder that they are themselves destroyed.

This is where our human ideas of justice and fairness, serviceable enough for certain purposes, are broken upon contact with a wider scheme of things. The Christian world has known, through many centuries, the legend of that 'innocent' bystander who, when Christ passed with his Cross, called out: 'Get on with you! Go faster!' and was therefore condemned to roam the earth until the Day of Judgment, homeless and rejected by all men. How was he to know that this scourged criminal was the Christ? How can we expect the average man to be so constantly on the alert that he is ready for the moment when Reality breaks through the carapace of time like lightning from heaven? But our incapacities are not, though we like to think them so, the measure of all things; and when the harmless little man who lives decently enough in the familiar shadows of the normal world finds himself suddenly in the full blaze of sunlight, he stumbles against the adamantine rock and is broken.

The People of the Book, as the Muslims call those who follow the Bible, were always aware of the presence in the midst of the crowd of individuals who might look like everyone else but who carried with them a breath of air from another place. Both Christian and Jewish legends tell of these mysterious strangers, passing unnoticed except by the few who were sufficiently alert to recognise them for what they were, but the pre-Christian legends of Europe—Germanic as well as Greek—tell the same tale in their stories of the gods disguised as poor wayfarers, strange visitors to the king's palace or the peasant's hut, bearing with them a message or a warning, the solution to a riddle or the secret of some hidden treasure. The same theme appears in Hindu and Buddhist mythology and, indeed, in the myths of almost every ancient people. The Wanderer is everywhere.

But the worlds in which the Wanderer was observed or made his presence known were worlds which, according to the modern view, vastly overestimated man's importance in the scheme of things, attributing to him a supernatural destiny beyond the brief span of his life on earth and supposing him fit for salvation or damnation. Ideas of Heaven and Hell (or, in Eastern terms, of transmigration through superior or inferior cycles of existence) spelt out the importance of human acts and the nature of human responsibilities in terms immediately comprehensible even to the simplest man. What he did in his small corner had a significance beyond the furthest frontiers of time and place, it shook the highest spheres, bringing down on his head either manna from heaven or fire. The human world, touched at so many points by the supernatural or the magical, its windows wide open, its limits undefined, was—in the proper sense of the term—awe-inspiring.

Awe and respect are closely linked. A purely 'social' morality, one based upon the practical interests of the community and upon the fact that misbehaviour on a wide scale represents a threat to the community's existence, lacks the dimension of awe and must eventually dispense with the idea of respect for the person (not just as a good man or a useful one, but as a man). If the idea of respect has so far survived, at least for purposes of lip-service (the Nazis still found it necessary to justify or misrepresent their actions in terms of an older morality, as do the Communists) this is because the immense shadow of the religious point of view still haunts even the most irreligious of our contemporary societies. It is only fairly recently that God 'died'.

But if the idea of respect for the person does still survive it has been reduced more and more to the social level and devalued. The word itself has taken on slightly comic undertones and has lost contact with the element of fear that once nourished it, fear of the unknown, fear of the vast regions that may extend behind an ordinary face. Losing respect for someone tends more and more to imply that one thinks less well of his character; it means that a judgment has been revised or reversed in the light of some particular action. And this is not the direction in which the roots of respect are to be found.

The limits of judgment become ill-defined if not forgotten in an age which considers man only in his social context. These limits are strict, for it is said that few sins are as grave as the 'sin of Pharoah' whereby mortal man attempts to usurp the ultimate Judgment Seat and so, whether he understands the meaning of his act or not, calls himself God. No man can say what another man is worth, for this would require a knowledge of values so infinitely distant from the social realm that it can find human expression only in silence. Respect is rooted in the knowledge that this silence absorbs and annihilates any words that we can speak.

If this were the beginning and the end of the matter, there would be no need to consider where the limits of human judgment lie. Silence may surround us and penetrate everywhere—it is, after all, a reflection of our own inadequacy—but we have voices and must use them. At every turn in our life in the world—particularly where our livelihood is concerned—we have to judge our fellows in terms of their usefulness for a particular task, their personal attitude to ourselves and their probable future line of conduct. We have to 'place' them in the immediate, given context ; and we may not have the time or the patience to give much thought to what they are outside this context. But we are also tempted, most of us, to inflate this practical, *ad hoc* judgment to the dimensions of an absolute one. We are tempted, in fact, to imagine that this momentary situation in the context of which we have made our judgment is of more than passing significance. And, in this sense, the 'sin of Pharaoh' is the commonest of sins.

We are still in danger of grave error if we deny the right of human love to eclipse judgment—without, of course, making judgment invalid in its own, limited context. A love that is blind to the facts of a particular character still takes a certain precedence by virtue of the nobility of its origin. The silly girl who loves a criminal and ignores the facts which stare her in the face, the foolish man who loves a whore and supposes her chaste, still know more than they think they know—and far more than they are thought to know. Lust itself, understood in the conventional sense, may open windows which are closed to sober judgment and reveal, however briefly (the 'sin' being in the brevity), a truth that was always there and always will be. And Muslims tell the tale of a woman saint of fabulous beauty who was followed one evening by a young stranger hoping for a night of pleasure. She led him by devious ways to the meeting place of her companions on the *sufi* Path and told them : 'Here is a true lover. Pour out for him the wine of True Love !'

Whatever tends towards the unification of what was formerly separated and brings a glimmer of light—the light of understanding, of fellow feeling, of attention—into what was formerly a place of darkness carries with it some faint stamp of nobility. When love is based upon 'illusion', some apparently ludicrous mistake regarding the character of the beloved, we still have to face the fact that the lover spoke the right language even if he did so for the wrong reasons. And sometimes it is enough that a man should speak the right language—we need not be too concerned with his reasoning.

If moral ideas are to exist at all as a basis for judgment, they can only be based either upon a supernatural pattern (which must necessarily conflict sometimes with the interests of the community) or upon social considerations. Once social considerations come to be regarded as the only practical ones, the legitimate judgments we make of a man's usefulness here and now tend to usurp a quality of absoluteness. Any group which provides shelter and nourishment for men has certain rights of self-protection, and these are likely to include the right to kill a man whose actions are totally incompatible with the group's well-being and safety. But this is still a matter of judgment within a given context and related only to that context, a judgment which may be correct here and now but might be quite wrong under different circumstances and at another time, nor can it pretend to be a judgment upon the man as such. It is when we try to change someone, to reform (or 're-form') him and make him fit for our own particular social matrix that we overstep the mark.

Society may have the right to inflict many kinds of punishment in its own defence, but there is one right it does not have and this is to deprive a human being of his ultimate dignity, treating him as inferior in essence and nature, and arrogating to itself the task of making something 'better' out of him. We live in an age in which the virtues of kindness tend to be rated above all others and in which the infliction of pain is—at least in certain Western countries—regarded as peculiarly obscene, but it is a pity that we cannot foster these virtues without losing sight of certain other considerations. For there is also an element of obscenity and insult implicit in the act of shutting up a grown man in a hideous though hygienic establishment in which he is treated as if he were a delinquent child.

The whip may be cruel compared with the model prison, but the whipped man recovers. The prisoner who suffers daily humiliation and deprivation of his manhood may never recover.

Society's right of self-defence against its enemies carries with it some obligation to treat these enemies as equals. In a different context (that of colonialism) the Jamaican author John Hearne has written perceptively of the rival merits—or demerits—of the kindly European as against other, less kindly colonising powers. 'Other conquerors had demanded the usual payments of money, forced labour and women; but the Europeans demanded perpetual acknowledgment of irremediable inferiority . . . They committed the unforgivable humiliation of turning the world into an enormous elementary school in which the white-skinned were the destined teachers and the dark-skinned could never, at their most responsible, be more than playground monitors. It is doubtful whether the most extreme example of savage plunder has ever been more destructive of human dignity than this weird combination of racial pride and social conscience.'

This attitude towards subject races was characteristic of the second half of the nineteenth century and the first half of the twentieth, and it derived to some extent (at least in its later development) from the theory of evolution and from the technological cleverness which appeared to prove the European's evolutionary superiority. But if we drop the word 'racial', then it can be said that a weird combination of pride and social conscience lies at the root of the modern attitude to those who are considered either inferior or unfortunate. In many cases—though not always explicitly—the idea of 'inferiority' has been substituted for that of 'wickedness'. Whereas wickedness often inspires a kind of awe, inferiority does not, and it is obviously easier to treat the inferior man kindly than the wicked one. In this sense, 'anti-social elements', as they are now described in a number of countries, are better off under the new dispensation. It is perhaps ungrateful of such 'elements' to feel that they would rather be treated as rogues than as foolish children.

To say that certain types of criminal behave like children or have the mentalities of children is a very loose figure of speech. One need only place such a man beside a real child to be aware of this. And only a society that has begun to see itself as absolute and as encompassing the horizon—rather than as an island of safety in a menacing and mysterious sea—could assume so readily that those who do not fit into its scheme of things must be less than men.

At the same time, by the substitution of ideas of reform and readjustment for the idea of punishment, society loses the chance of satisfying one of its darkest but most pressing needs. There are certain crimes (child-murder is one of them) which arouse in many people a horror and an anger that must find an outlet or fester inwardly. The normal outlet lies in the satisfaction of seeing the criminal suffer in his own body something of the horror that he has inflicted both upon his victims and upon his society, achieving thereby a kind of *catharsis*. But this involves treating him as a man, an equal, rather than as a sickly inferior. This need finds satisfaction, not in humiliating but in hurting him, and however savage it may seem (savage as grief) it does hark back to the ancient awareness that a really monstrous crime disturbs the equilibrium —and health—of the human community in such a way that order and balance can be restored only by a monstrous punishment. Two 'blacks' may not make a 'white', but they do on occasion balance and therefore annul each other in the harsh scales of natural life.

From another point of view, however, it is just as well that we have become kinder, for the imperfections of human 'justice' are no longer compensated by the inefficiency of the available means of catching and holding the criminal. It might be said that society has a right to punish only as long as its enemy has a chance to escape. In an age of escape-proof prisons and closed frontiers, the saving grace of incompetence no longer balances the pseudo-absolute operations of human judgment. On the day that the late Dr Crippen was arrested by the use of transatlantic radio we were, perhaps, deprived of the right to execute murderers. And now the passport— and a whole mass of restrictions on free journeying—have taken their place among the sinister paraphernalia of our age.

The claims of human society and of human 'justice', since they could never be absolute, have always derived their legitimacy from the fact that they were localised, their arm short though it might be strong. Their physical range was limited and there were always other places to which not only the criminal but also the victim, the odd-man-out, could take himself in voluntary exile. A man might disappear, and his society would not pursue him, could not pursue him. But when relative rights and relative justice become inexorable they lose thereby all legitimacy. From then on it is catch as catch can.

One of the most striking signs of the increasing power of society to engulf its members and to suffocate them is this closing of the frontiers to all but approved travellers, a power that is reinforced by increasingly efficient technological devices. The totalitarian society's chief requirement, if it aims at absolute dominance over the human being, is that he should not be free even to dream of escape. In the course of only a few years the last loopholes have been blocked and we are now close to the 'ideal' situation in which the only means of physical escape from a given social matrix will be either suicidal violence or suicide itself.

And yet, leaving to one side the case of those whose centre of awareness is open to quite another level of being—for this is not a matter of escape but of profound involvement in the fountain and origin of human affairs—there remains the escape-hatch of insanity, one that may be put to increasing use as the last physical frontiers are sealed to all but those who have no need or inclination to escape. And this could be one of the means whereby societies that have usurped the quality of absoluteness will destroy themselves without any need for a bolt from heaven to open them up. When men of good sense have gone too far in rationalising the social structure and in cementing its walls the time will have come for the madmen to take over.

As with the criminal, so with the lunatic. Although insanity, unlike criminality, does still inspire a certain fear and an inkling of strange seas washing against the shores of our island. This fear, however, has become separated from the sense of awe and is deplored, by the best authorities ; we should, so we are told, pity the insane in exactly the same way that we pity the physically sick. It is only the insane themselves who disagree with this view and they, of course, are mad. But insanity is not always purely negative in character. A man may have 'lost his wits' but, for good or ill, something else may have taken their place. He is seldom no more than a person from whom some part has been amputated in the sense in which a one-legged man is simply a man who has lost a leg. And when we treat him as such he feels obscurely but deeply insulted, even if we are quite unaware of our own impertinence. It is not surprising that so many of the doctors who work in mental asylums seem to their friends a little 'unbalanced' ; in a certain sense they have been in daily contact with other worlds of experience which have something of the same self-sufficient coherence that our world seems to possess.

In the Islamic world insanity has tended to evoke a certain awe and respect based, no doubt upon the Muslim's traditional prudence: 'You never know ...' But when the Quranic revelations descended upon the Prophet Muhammad they pressed upon his physical body with an almost intolerable weight and Muslims have been particularly aware of the tremendous strength required if one is to stand and survive under the touch of the divine hand. They expect to find among the insane some who, for all their excellence, were not strong enough to bear this touch and whose worldly personalities became disordered under its weight. In this context, moving among such principalities and powers as may have consumed or possessed the inmates of a madhouse—or perhaps under the shadow of a more absolute and transcendent presence—the psychiatrist who does not walk warily is a true babe in the woods.

And here we are not far from the roots of true charity understood, not as a supernatural virtue, but as the rugged element in prudent self-interest which, in Thibon's view, provides fertile soil for the seminal action of grace. In terms of social morality, charity is replaced by 'social justice' and by the ideal of an egalitarianism which is expected to make it obsolete; but, in terms of realism, charity begins with the awareness of our ignorance as to whom it is we face when we face our neighbour or a stranger, a poor man, a thief ... When royalty slips in the mud every hand is held out to help; and this same fear of offending one who might hold our fate in his hands dictated the prudent charity of other times—unless it was translated to a more universal level and ignorance was replaced by the knowledge of an implicit omnipresent royalty.

'Tell all the truth,' wrote the American poetess, Emily Dickinson, 'but tell it slant.' Outside the field of mathematics there are sound reasons for speaking, if not in riddles, at least by means of implication and allusion, parable and even hyperbole, rather than in bald statements which, taken too literally, lead to the petrification of meaning. Neither the facilities of human speech nor the contours of the human mentality lend themselves readily to the expression of truths which lie beyond the sphere of day-to-day affairs. But there are points at which the direct statement, however liable it may be to misunderstanding, becomes unavoidable. Any discussion of man's real identity leads to such a point.

What is man in terms of the doctrines by which men have lived through all ages? He is, according to the Christians, made in the very Image of God. For the Muslims, he is the Viceroy placed by a transcendent Master in and over creation. For the Hindus his inmost core is one with the eternal and infinite Brahman, beside which there exist only dreams and shadows : 'That art thou !' And for numberless 'primitive' peoples he is the central being who, unlike anything else in the creation that surrounds him, has the power to journey to and fro as message-bearer between heaven and earth. We—humankind—have until now thought him the one alone of all that enjoy the light of day who can speak, by permission of his Lord, with the voice of ultimate authority.

This is the idea that lies at the root of all prayer and all priesthood. This is what men have lived by since the ages which preceded the 'dawn of history' even as history itself precedes today's newspaper. Man is either Viceroy or else he is an animal that claims special rights by virtue of its cunning and the devouring efficiency of teeth sharpened by technological instruments, an animal whose time is up. If he is such an animal, then he has no rights—he is no more nor less than meat—and elephants and lions, rabbits and mice must in some dim recess of their being rejoice to see the usurper develop the means of his own total destruction. But if he is Viceroy, then all decay and all trouble in the created world that surrounds him is in some measure to be laid to his count.

There is no getting around this choice, any more than the man with the gun can be evaded by retreat into a dream world. If the human creature is what he now thinks himself to be, then every acre of ground he takes from the other beasts is stolen property, and each time he kills an animal one of his kind should be slaughtered to keep the scales even. But if he is truly what, until recently, he thought he was, then he bears on his infirm back the burden of creation, a stumbling staggering creature—a nobleman who has taken to drink and exhausted himself with whores—unless he calls upon a supernatural source of strength. Even then there is no guarantee that his back will not break, for his earthly existence is indeed brittle.

In purely human terms the idea of this poor creature as Viceroy of God is no less absurd than the notion that he is created in the

Divine Image. Yet the gulf which separates the ordinary man—
this man of small stature—from the latent nobility of the human
state may be bridged by the Arabic phrase, *ka'annaka* ('as if
you . . .'). Perfect virtue, excellence (*ihsan*), said the Prophet
Muhammad, is 'that you should worship God as if you saw him;
for if you see him not, yet he sees you.'

What matters is the intention to fulfil—or to try to fulfil—our
proper function. The incapacity to do so unaided is universal; but
our intention is expressed in the effort to act 'as if' we were what in
truth and in essence we are. The rest is a matter of grace—for how
could a Viceroy fulfil his function without the mandate and the
support of the King? He cannot appoint himself (the self-appointed
ruler is by definition a rebel and a tyrant). He does not derive his
authority from himself nor does the exercise of this authority
depend upon his own strength. He is appointed by another, his
authority derives from another and he is but the shadow of that
other. Yet what a shadow this is!

The complete fulfilment of the human function belongs, no
doubt, to Adam before the fall, to the Golden Age, and we in our
shabby place cannot afford to be perfectionists or to suppose that
what cannot be done well should not be done at all. The essential
distinction is between those who recognise this virtuality in man
and those who are blind to it. The possibility expressed in the words
'as if' is indeed the glory which surrounds and plays upon the human
form. This is why the prudent man is convinced that 'you never
know . . .' For the very pavements await the coming of the Wanderer. 'The saint has himself become prayer, the meeting place of
earth and Heaven; and thus he contains the universe, and the
universe prays with him.'*

If man stands above the web of 'eating and being eaten', above
natural process, this is not on account of his inventive genius, his
intellectual superiority to the monkeys or his capacity to generalise
about the nature of interstellar space, nor does it depend upon his
power to travel faster than a horse. His eminence derives from his
unique responsibility for coping with the burden of creation. As
long as he has one-tenth of a part of this awareness of his task, he is
still a man, and perhaps a hundredth part will do, but at some point,

* *Spiritual Perspectives and Human Facts:* Frithjof Schuon (Faber &
Faber), p. 213.

eventually, the dilution becomes excessive until at last he is no more than one of the lesser beasts among those which crop the grass or devour their kindred.

The relationship of human beings to the animal world, as it is documented in history and anthropology, is immensely complex, but beyond the Christian sector attitudes have tended to crystallise around two opposite poles, with many variations in between. On the one hand there is the refusal to make use of animals except for domestic purposes, hence vegetarianism and the religious ban on the wearing of anything made from animal skins. Against this we have the ritual of hunting tribes, aimed at 'reconciling' the animal soul to its fate, and the Muslim and Jewish 'sacrifice' of the animal that is to lend its flesh to the fostering of human strength (strength to participate in a work of redemption which includes the animal creation). Closely related to both these poles we find the belief (present also in the annals of early Christianity) that carnivorous beasts become gentle as lambs in the presence of a holy man. But never at either pole or anywhere along the line that joins them do we find the suggestion that man has absolute rights over the animals, to do with them as he pleases. 'There is not an animal on the earth, nor a flying creature soaring on two wings, but they are peoples like unto you,' says the Qurān.

A stern insistence upon courtesy to the living creatures that share our world with us is common to the most diverse religious traditions. If a cobra comes into your garden, says a Muslim book of spiritual instruction, you may order it to leave at once. If it returns you should give it a second warning. And if it returns for the third time you are free to kill it.

To treat such counsels as whimsical is to miss the point completely and to fall into the common contemporary error of dismissing half the truth that comes our way as belonging to the realm of fairy tales and ignoring the rest as 'metaphysical'—and therefore incomprehensible. The point of this particular story is that man by virtue of his 'central', viceregal position enjoys certain special privileges but does not enjoy the right to abuse these privileges. And the courtesy which it recommends is a courtesy based on awe and respect for all that lives. Also, no doubt, upon a certain sense of equality (to which countless traditional tales bear witness), not the same equality as that between man and man, but a relative equality nonetheless (those same traditional tales cite plenty of examples of the divinity manifesting itself through an animal). Formerly the world was thought to be made up of men and beasts ; today it is a 'human' world in which coal and oil and edible animals are counted among exploitable riches which exist only for our use.

But this respect and this courtesy have nothing to do with a sentimentality which focuses upon the 'doggy' qualities of certain petted creatures, a sentimentality which is only the reverse side of a picture which includes our animal factories and the inventive medical experiments carried out on animals. The question that has to be asked is not whether these farming techniques or these experiments involve suffering (a matter upon which there may be legitimate differences of opinion) but whether we have any inherent right to do such things ; in other words, it is a basic principle that is at stake. On this point the traditional doctrines are unanimous. This is a misuse of the living creatures which share our world, an offence against creation and therefore against God. If we are determined to find ways of prolonging our earthly lives beyond their natural term, we would do better to experiment upon ourselves rather than involve non-human 'peoples' in our greed for longevity. Moreover this reduction of the whole issue to a simple question of cruelty carries with it certain sinister political implications, suggesting, as it does, that no political system is evil unless it involves force and cruelty.

There is, in any case, a profoundly threatening significance in the precautions with which the men of earlier times surrounded themselves in their dealings with the animal creation ; the implication that abuse of these creatures must lead to our own destruction and that whatever we do to them will, by a simple process of cause-and-effect, have to be done to us in one way or another. It was not for nothing that the North American hunter underwent the most elaborate rituals of purification before taking upon himself the huge responsibility of killing animals—his 'brothers' and his 'sisters'—so that, clothed and fed, his people might carry on their work of mediation between heaven and earth, a redemptive function which encompassed all creatures that draw breath.

By a most curious irony, it is only since men came to see themselves as no more than clever animals, without any 'central' role or any supernatural privileges, that they have started to treat the animal creation as totally alien and totally without rights. What is this, however, but a symptom of disintegration and of the descent into infernal regions of greed and unawareness, and of a savagery which shuts out the divine Mercy, exposing us to all the fury which reflects, on the level of our earthly existence, the divine Wrath?

Meanwhile, as always, the world is full of mirrors and the animal creation shows us our own reflection. It is perhaps an ogrish reflection, though this is not much noticed nowadays. For if the people of our time are fearful of shadows and worry over trifles, it is also true that they are strangely unafraid when fear might seem more justified. They have no inkling of what the Muslims call *haybah*—'fear of the Tremendous'. Only little things alarm them. Terrified of material insecurity, quick to conform to the norms of their society and watchful of their pension rights, they stand up like titans to tempt Providence and to commit outrages that could hardly be expected—in any world which made any kind of sense— to go unpunished. But real titans know what they are doing, what they risk; whereas we whine indignantly about the nuclear bomb or bacteriological warfare as though these things threatened us by accident, the fault of a few naughty politicians.

One of the earliest of the Muslim *sufi* Masters told his disciples, 'When I commit a fault, I am made aware of it by my donkey's temper,' and the Islamic tradition is full of stories to illustrate the manner in which the animals hold up a mirror to man and reflect in their behaviour the success or failure of his manhood, as also the fear they have of all who are deeply involved in a 'worldliness' that ultimately threatens them. So Dermenghem tells of a student of Fes so poor that he lived in a cave and his single robe was in tatters. A gazelle used to come every night and sleep beside him in his cave and all the dogs in the neighbourhood rejoiced when he passed. But one day his mother made a collection among his fellow students and, unknown to him, sewed a bag of money into his robe. That evening, when he climbed back to his cave, the dogs ran snapping and barking at his heels and, when he reached it, the gazelle fled from him. Late in the night, sleepless and troubled, he found the bag of money and flung it far from him. Before dawn the gazelle returned and next morning when he went down the hill, the dogs danced for joy.*

And it is said that the Companions once asked the Messenger of God, 'Shall we be rewarded for good done to animals?' 'There will

---

* *Le Culte des Saints dans l'Islam Maghrébin:* Emile Dermenghem.

be a reward,' he said, 'for whoever quenches the thirst of any creature endowed with a living heart.'

But matters would still be comparatively simple if the inmost core of responsibility reached outwards no further than the circle of living beings and stopped there. It does not stop there. At the heart of the most diverse religious traditions lies the doctrine that vice-regal responsibility encompasses our environment as a whole and that the distinction between animate and inanimate is not final, that wood and stone and the very soil itself are within the circle of man's power to redeem or to abuse. If Christianity has sometimes neglected this side of the matter, as Islam and Judaism have not, this is because the attention of Christians has been so focused upon a single act of universal Redemption that the call to 'imitate' Christ has often been understood only in a limited moral sense.

In order to fulfil our function we must make some use of our environment for food, for clothing, for the instrument of our trade and, indeed, for the actual deployment of the possibilities which lie within us, but the enjoyment of the good things available to us is conditional—'For the earth is the Lord's', say the Christians, and it is not as owners that we make use of it. The fear of demons (inhabiting inanimate matter or haunting the dark corners of the world) which has been found so widely among 'primitive' peoples and dismissed by anthropologists as animism or the personification of natural forces, is a vestigial trace of the once universal knowledge that all things have a claim upon us, a claim which, if it is ignored, must bring certain consequences in its train. It is not demons but consequences that haunt the dark forest, as they do the madman's dreams; and the praise of poverty found at some point in all religions has a more than personal, moral significance, implying as it does that man is to be parsimonious in the use he makes of his natural environment and is not free to treat it as children treat a bag of sweets.

Obligations, however, carry privileges with them and man has the unique function of being able to take the inanimate into his hands and make it beautiful. This, one might say, is the exercise of his redemptive power—to bring into the light of day the meaning that is only implicit in brute matter and to give form to what was until then no more than a dark, inchoate longing for the miracle of form. Here, most of all, the clumsy two-legged one can call himself King of the Castle, bestowing nobility where he will; and here is the contradiction to all fear and all parsimony, if only a man were big enough to get a grip on the very globe itself and bring out its meaning.

All sacred art is rooted in the certainty that the artist, by virtue of his 'central' role and by the skill with which he fulfils his role, acts as a channel through which the patterns of heaven enlighten the material of our earthly environment. And the forms and canons of a particular artistic tradition exist to express meaning in exactly the same way that the words of a particular language exist, not merely as pleasing sounds, but as tools with which to say something. The making of things that are themselves meaningful in terms of a specific artistic language and the incorporation of these things into a human realm that is saturated with meaning is in essence a 'vice-regal' function; and in this case matter has been twice blessed, first by becoming a vehicle of meaning and then by participation in the ritual and religious life whereby the human community maintains contact with the source of meaning itself.

Here then we have two concepts, two attitudes, between which there can be no reconciliation: on the one hand, a world which is material for the creation of beauty; on the other, a world which is fodder for the human animal and grist for his mills. And here also we are reminded of the distinction made earlier between that which is drawn out of the river of change for enduring use and that which is merely devoured and excreted in the process of man's 'meta-bolism with nature'. In terms of that reverence for the natural world which, like respect for the animal realm, was once normal to man beauty is never a luxury—it is a pre-condition of use.

'We of the nineteenth and twentieth centuries have the unenviable distinction of having created the first ugly civilisation in the long history of mankind. The industrial age has brought innumerable benefits, but it has created an environment for man that is visually little short of a nightmare.'* There are those who would say that this environment is itself the product of a nightmare—one in which man as such has lost his dignity and his heritage, reduced to the status of a dumb beast in a world without meaning and consumed by his own ravenous appetites.

The riches of the modern world are unearned riches, for it is only by fulfilling some small part of his viceregal function that man earns the right to make use of his environment. We see a caricature of this belief in the contemporary view that 'unearned incomes' are

* Sir John Rothenstein in *The Times*, 20th February 1965.

wicked and that we have a right only to what we earn by our mental
or physical labour (labour which is, by definition, a labour of
exploitation); whereas the ancient view was that man has earned
what he is able to assimilate spiritually, what he can love as well as
use and what he can raise from obscurity into the daylight of beauty
and significance. Whatever else he takes to himself is stolen
property.

Social morality, censorious of theft from our own kind, cannot
take account of responsibility to and for creation. At any and every
time conflicts must arise between the two moralities (though they
are in fact situated at different levels and must therefore be in some
measure complementary to each other), but when the very idea of a
duty beyond that which we owe to our neighbour is lost sight of or
dismissed as irrelevant to human needs, then social morality inflates
to fill the vacuum and, from being functional, becomes absolute. At
the same time it changes character, becoming more and more a
question of self-interest writ large. The beast that digs and forages
and consumes, blind to everything but its immediate needs, is then
no longer the individual man; it is the social collectivity as a whole,
making use of its power to appeal to the 'better natures' of its
component individuals (in terms of morality, altruism and other
high-sounding principles) the better to subordinate them to its
ultimately self-destroying purpose. For the short-sightedness of
self-interest is proverbial, and social morality, no longer dwarfed by
the vision of horizons wider than those of the 'human animal', must
eventually degenerate into the attitude of a parasite greedily unaware that it is destroying its host.

Such a situation as ours, in which the common assumptions of
this particular moment in time are imposed upon everyone by a
vast educational machine and on the television screens which
dominate almost every home, can be 'put in its place' only if it is set
in juxtaposition to some totally different situation based upon quite
other assumptions regarding the nature and destiny of man. Contemporary science fiction has been used on a number of occasions
to drive home the point that our world is not necessarily The World
and that our way of life is not the only way open to rational beings,
but it is not really necessary to reach out to the stars in order to make
comparisons. In the past two hundred years the European has
destroyed or corrupted a great number of ancient cultures which, if

we have the courage and the honesty to look into the mirror they provide, show us all that we need to know of ourselves.

No history has ever been written of this cultural holocaust (for the Communists are by no means alone in making history fit theory). A man might usefully make a lifetime study of the impact of Western civilisation upon some corner of Asia or Africa without exhausting the lessons to be drawn from it. But, for our present purpose, the most striking and the most illuminating examples lie in the very heartland of the modern world—in the encounter between the invading palefaced people and the 'Indians' of North America.

There were, at the time of the European invasion, some six hundred Indian nations or social groups in America north of the Rio Grande. Between them they brought to life—and lived out in body and soul—an astonishing variety of religious and social patterns, so that it might be said that if no other human beings had ever existed on the face of the earth the richness of human possibilities would still have had its flowering.

And yet there was a certain unity in the midst of this astonishing diversity, the factor of unity being the realisation or actualisation—under many different forms—of man's viceregal identity. Indeed it could be said that this factor of unity was itself the source out of which all this rich diversity flowed. A prophetic genius which was once, perhaps, the distinguishing quality of the human as against the animal creature survived in that strangely virgin land of forest and mountain, plain and desert, long after it had become—for other races—no more than a rumour voiced in myth and dubious history.

It was almost as though, for that small segment of humanity, the world was not yet a fallen world (although, from another point of view, the hardness of the Indian's life and his deep awareness of pain suggest that it was only by an act of supreme heroism that he preserved a flavour of the Golden Age in a darkened universe). In his relationship with the natural world and with the beasts around him and, above all, in his intimate awareness of the neighbourly powers of heaven, he was a living exemplar of human qualities scarcely dreamed of in our time. This is an exemplar that should have a particular appeal for an age which often makes a cult of the development of the human personality ; for the chief object of the Indian's art was himself.

This art, says Schuon, is 'concentrated, direct and bold', a framework for the human person. In the midst of an intensely perceived environment of landscape, of sky and stars, of natural elements and wild beasts, this man wore the garments of one who knows himself to be king of the great castle of creation: 'his majestic head-dresses (above all his great array of eagle feathers), his dress streaming with fringes and embroidered with solar symbols, the bright-patterned moccasins which seem designed to take away from the feet all heaviness and all uniformity, the feminine robes of an exquisite simplicity . . .'*

Man dresses the part his culture tells him he is called upon to play, but in traditional societies he dresses (or paints himself) also as a means of showing in visible form the true identity which is hidden within the bodily shell. If he dresses as a 'god', this is because he believes the 'god' inhabits his innermost being, and his costume is like a mask which expresses what is most enduring in him, covering the plasticity of flesh, which changes, ages from year to year (an image of becoming and of our incorporation in the flux of time), with a changeless image.

The North American Indian, says Schuon, had no intention of 'fixing' himself on this earth, where things crystallise or petrify in time if they do not evaporate: 'this explains his aversion to houses, especially stone ones, and also the absence of writing which, from his perspective, would "fix" and "kill" the sacred flow of the spirit . . . The red man's sanctuary is everywhere; and this is also why the earth should remain intact, virgin and sacred, as when it left the Divine Hands . . .'† For many of the nomadic tribes, the notion of putting plough or spade to the earth would have been exactly comparable to what desecration of the High Altar is for the Christian. In certain of his rites he humbled himself before the whole of creation, because all visible things were created before him and, being older than he, deserved respect; but, at the same time, man was pre-eminent because he alone was capable of knowing the 'Great Spirit' (*Wakan Tanka*, in Sioux terms). As Viceroy he knew and listened to his Master, and as Viceroy he respected and spoke to his province.

In order to discern the tragic nature of the white man's impact upon such a culture as this it is not essential to believe that the Indian's view of the world was correct, although this was the kind of view that humanity has taken through most of its history, and

* *Language of the Self:* Frithjof Schuon (Ganesh & Co), p. 222.
† Ibid, pp. 220-21.

even the most brash newcomer must surely hesitate before dismissing it out of hand. The one essential is that we should put aside for a moment the conviction that our way of living and thinking and acting is the only valid way and look with unprejudiced eyes upon this particular 'clash of cultures'.

But if one believes that the modern view stands in relation to the traditional beliefs of our kind as an aberration (or simply as a state of ignorance in the exact sense of the term), then what happened was not merely tragic, it was diabolical. The destruction of bridges which link heaven and earth, providing men with the means of fulfilling their viceregal function, is always a diabolical thing and may be expected to bring in its train the most hideous consequences for the world as a whole.

'The conscious, calculated, methodical, official and by no means anonymous destruction of the "red" race, its traditions and culture, in North America and partly also in South America, far from having been an unavoidable process—and as such possibly excusable in the name of natural laws, provided one does not oneself claim to have outgrown these laws thanks to "civilisation"—this destruction, it must be said, certainly remains one of the greatest crimes and most notable vandalisms of all human history.'* Since the presence in their midst of people who find meaning in the world is intolerable to those who think themselves the victims of a meaningless universe, the basic structure of the Indian's spiritual life had to be destroyed. 'First, in the Sioux country, the Army crushed the Sun Dance with armed force. Then the missionaries influenced the Bureau of Indian Affairs to impose regulations against not only the Sun Dance but all "pagan" ceremonies which, they believed, impeded the progress of the Indians towards Christian civilisation. The Interior Department framed a criminal code forbidding Indian religious practices . . . .'† But it was not as Christians, trying to impose one code of meaning upon another, that the white man descended upon the Indian. It was as a horde in which rapacity and the sterile superstitions of 'progress' had already destroyed the spiritual heritage which had been its own birthright.

These invaders differed from all others who, in one part of the world or another, had burst their frontiers in an access of superabundant energy, because they alone had achieved the capacity to

---

* *Light on the Ancient Worlds*: Frithjof Schuon (Perennial Books), p. 85.
† *Indians of the Americas*: John Collier (Mentor Books), p. 137.

look upon everything in creation as material for exploitation, seeing a tree only as timber, a lamb only as meat and a mountain only as the site for a quarry. This single-minded rapacity, now taken for granted as natural to man, was so strange to the Indians of the eighteenth and nineteenth centuries that the invaders might as well have come from another planet. Even their descendants hesitate to speak of the 'nameless thing' for which their languages offer no appropriate term—the combination of greed and fraud and perfidy which they encountered in their dealings with the white man. Nothing in their previous experience had forewarned them that men could be like that.

But rapacity breeds its own skills, and the invaders, though to Indian eyes they appeared ignorant, physically dirty, mostly drunken and, in general, both godless and lawless, carried dreadful weapons in their hands and enjoyed all the advantages which the unprincipled enjoy in their dealings with those for whom honour is paramount. The hordes spread out over a land of almost magical richness, untapped, unravaged, in which the very trees had been regarded as temple pillars and the earth itself too sacred to be trodden except by winged moccasins, and congratulated themselves upon pursuing so worthily their civilising mission.

For the victims of this mission there could only be, in the words of a former US Commissioner of Indian Affairs, 'sadness deeper than imagination can hold—sadness of men completely conscious, watching the universe being destroyed by a numberless and scorning foe . . .'* John Collier, who had a unique opportunity to know these people and who wrote of them, 'They had what the world has lost . . . . The ancient, lost reverence and passion for the earth and its web of life,' emphasises the quality of sadness rather than anger in the Indian's assessment of his dealings with the white man. Perhaps this sadness includes a certain pity for all of us, since humanity is ultimately indivisible.

It was on land long held sacred (and kept intact from human scarring) and from particles of matter once thought to be beads in the garment of the 'Great Spirit' that the first nuclear weapons were developed. And there, high over the land which had once been too holy to suffer the touch of spade or plough, the first of the 'mushroom clouds' spread its grim canopy.

* John Collier, op. cit., p. 104.

When the Westerner is asked in what period of history he would have chosen to be born, had the choice been offered him, he chooses —if he is sensible—the present day. He is a twentieth-century man with a twentieth-century face and twentieth-century emotions. Transported, just as he is, to some other period of time he would, no doubt, be thoroughly miserable. But when he assumes that the people of other times must have led lives of complete wretchedness because he, in their place, would be wretched, he is allowing subjectivism to run away with his judgment. He needs all that the modern world can offer in the way of richness and he could do with more of it, but this need is an aspect of his twentieth-century nature and he has no grounds for supposing that all men in all times have had the same needs.

The invalid must have comforts and delicacies for which the healthy man would have no use, and, if we are deprived of our real function in the universe, then we are indeed sick with the most debilitating and demoralising of diseases, that of uselessness. If the human creature is—as was generally supposed—designed for the use of God, as a channel of communication between the given world and all that lies beyond it, then he will find no satisfaction in serving other masters. The service of his fellow creatures or of the State or of some ideal—or else, as an alternative, a life given up to sexual excess or the search for excitement—can never be more than substitutes.

When time has worked its disillusionment, the exhausted 'do-gooder', the worn component of the State machine and the embittered idealist are not really so very different to the ageing rake who has pursued enjoyment throughout his life and has come now to the end of the road. The one thing necessary was missing. Within the narrow bounds of the profane or secular realm some lives may be marginally better than others, some marginally worse, but it does not matter very much. When people scuffle together in a dark room, from which every glimmer of light has been excluded, they may do as they will.

'We have the possibility,' wrote Simone Weil, 'of being mediators between God and the part of creation which is confided to us. Our consent is necessary, so that through us he should perceive his own creation.'* And she added, later in the same book, 'Every creature who has come to perfect obedience constitutes a singular mode,

* *La Pesanteur et la Grace:* Simone Weil (Plon), p. 46.

unique and irreplaceable, of the presence, knowledge and operation of God in the world.'*

When we are called upon to break down the obstructions raised by our own anxious and demanding selfhood this is not because unselfishness is a socially useful virtue, but solely that we may provide a clear channel through which grace descends and vivifies the things of this world and through which the achieved glories of the world may be, as it were, carried back to their source. Our immortality is as a window, not as a wall.

But men are not conceived to remain for ever embryos—or for ever children, adults or old men. Nor is a child to be considered simply as an undeveloped adult, or an aged man as an adult in decay. In our ultimate identity we are all that we have ever been together with all that we are yet to be, and if a man's life makes sense it does so as a whole, not in terms of this or that cross-section apparent at a given moment, but as it might be seen from beyond time. Now, said the Rabbi Baalshem on his death-bed, now I know why I was born!

The pattern of any given life can be seen only when it is completed. It is said that some few are so gifted that they can perceive the outlines of the whole from a small fragment of action—just as the decisive qualities of a man's character may sometimes show themselves in a mannerism or in the way he reacts to a particular crisis (for there is a sense in which the whole must be expressed in every part)—but this is outside the competence of ordinary human judgment, which generalises too readily from the fragmentary. People often don a mask, not to conceal the 'true' personality, but to disguise characteristics which they know are not really significant in terms of their true identity but by which they might be judged and assessed. In the same way that a profound maturing of the personality is often preceded by a period of great uneasiness and even of physical illness, so a man's best qualities may first show themselves in clumsy and inept forms, the personality as such taking its first awkward steps at a new level. There are human states which can be judged only in terms of what they will lead to in ten or twenty years' time, and this is particularly true of the young.

The freedom we require of society is the freedom to actualise what in truth we are. 'For Thou hast said, "Although I know thy secret, nevertheless declare it now in thine outward act".'† Just as

* *La Pesanteur et la Grâce:* Simone Weil (Plon), p. 55.
† *Mathnawi of Jalalu 'din Rumi* 1.60.

the artist is called upon not so much to impose meaning upon material objects as to bring into the light of day a significance already inherent in them, so man as such is called upon to show— within the limits of his earthly context—what his real name is ; for, says Rumi, 'that which is our end is really our Name with God.'*

If man is a 'central' being, a Viceroy, as the traditional doctrines of humanity maintain, then this is the starting point for his acts of self-revelation. But there are as many ways of exercising the vice-regal function as there are living men. 'Everyone,' says Martin Buber (quoting a Chassidic saying), 'should know and remember that his state is unique in the world and that no one ever lived who was exactly the same as he, for had there ever been anyone exactly the same as he there would have been no need for him to have existed ; but in reality each person is a new thing in the world, and he should make his individuality complete, for the coming of the Messiah is delayed through it not being complete.'†

And in this the Jews voice another belief that is implicit in the most diverse traditional teachings, the belief that the created world itself exists so that certain possibilities—a store of latent meaning— which can find outward expression only in the peculiar conditions of space and time may be demonstrated and exhausted, and that creation cannot come to its end (and final redemption) until all that can be said has been said and all that can be done has been done.

It is here that responsibility starts, acting upon the first of all the things we are given to act upon—our own most intimate individuality—and so working its way from the centre outwards towards the peripheral world. But when we consider a particular being's success or failure in expressing what he exists to express (so far as we can guess at it) we have to keep one essential fact in view : this achievement does not necessarily obey the laws of growth and maturity as we know them, and it may show itself in youth (or even in childhood), so that the rest of this particular life-span seems like a dusty anti-climax, or it may flower in old age, like a bloom on a dying plant, when all the useful powers of mind and body are falling into decay. Its timing is not by our calendars.

But any talk of 'individuality' carries with it, particularly in the modern context, certain grave dangers of misunderstanding. Too

* *Mathnawi of Jalalu 'din Rumi* 1.1244.
† *Jewish Mysticism and the Legends of Baalshem:* Martin Buber (J. M. Dent), p. 29.

often it suggests a self-enclosed 'subject' set down in a predomi-
nantly hostile world of 'objects', and this 'subject' or person is
regarded as a bundle of thoughts and emotions, hereditary and
acquired characteristics, rolled into a ball that is then kicked and
buffeted by 'outside' circumstances. We cannot begin to understand
the traditional view of man unless we realise that these circumstances are themselves an aspect of the individuality insofar as they
are its destiny.

The ultimate subject, the innermost core of man's being, is not
perceived by the mind, the emotions or the senses. These are
objects of its awareness. There is no radical distinction to be made
between what a man is given in the way of mind, emotional make-up
and body on the one hand and, on the other, what he is given in the
way of outward circumstances and environment. Together they
form a significant whole and all are aspects of a particular individual
life.

The being between birth and death scrawls—in matter and in
events—a pattern which, taken as a whole, expresses his unique
identity. This man, So-and-So, is not a sealed personality moving
through an alien environment. He is the sum total of all that he
does and all that happens to him and all that comes within his range,
spread out (from our point of view) in time and space, but a single,
timeless fact in the mind of God. What we are and where we are
cannot ultimately be divided. And to accept our destiny is to accept
ourselves, recognising that what happens to us is as much a part of
our nature—in the widest sense—as the most intimate contours of
our own selfhood. It is sometimes said that the fatal bullet has its
victim's name upon it and fits no other flesh.

In the last resort, a man looks at the love or anger within himself
and says, So this is me. Looks at his withered hand or wounded
foot and says, So this is me. Looks at the woman he has married or
the garden he has planted and says, So this is me. Looks finally
upon his enemy and upon his death and says, So this is me. But in
saying this he bears witness to the fact that he is also incomparably
more than an itemised list of the elements which compose his
individuality and its inseparable field of action.

And in acknowledging so much that is a part of ourselves (since
our boundaries extend to the furthest horizons we can see from our
particular vantage point) we make an act of recognition which
actualises what was inherent in us from the start—almost as though

we existed only to discover what was always there—recognising our name-tag on everything that comes our way. But the part of us that is our destiny, streaming in upon us in the form of 'outside' events through the course of time, can be recognised as belonging to our own particular pattern only when it has happened. The religious man can say, 'Thy will be done!' as a statement of his intention to accept this will when it has been done and is apparent to him, but it is not our nature to be able to foresee the future except under the most unusual circumstances. In general, acceptance of destiny is acceptance of what has happened, not of what might happen (but might be prevented).

Islam, which is—in the highest degree—the religion of sub-mission to destiny, is also the religion of Holy War. And there are, for Islam, two aspects to this *Jihad*, the 'lesser' one being the war against all that makes for disunity and separation in our environ-ment, and the 'greater' being the war against all that makes for disunity and separation within ourselves. The nature of this war is illuminated by the fact that as soon as the battle—or a particular phase of the battle—is over, the outcome, whether victory or defeat, is to be accepted as God's will and as the only means whereby a particular message could find expression in human events.

Islam requires that men should fight with all the strength they have against what seems to them evil, hostile or destructive, but that in doing so they should keep always in mind the Quranic phrase which is heard so constantly in the conversation of Muslims —'But God knows best . . .' In other words, since it is in the nature of things that we should have some powers of judgment and dis-crimination, we must use these powers and act upon them, but our action always takes place in the half-light, provisional and liable to correction in terms of a total pattern of which we are unaware. When we fail, it is because success at that particular moment and in that particular context would have been a monstrous thing, con-trary to sense and opposed to what we are and always have been beyond our deployment in time.

The stars are in their places. Wind and weather, expressing the nature of the terrestrial world, have carved their meaning upon the mountains. And men 'who understand' (to use the phrase that occurs again and again in the Quran) set themselves to read the 'signs' that are given them in the natural world and in the events which come upon them, convinced that nothing can be ignored, nothing is irrelevant—not the chance word, not the unexpected encounter, not the fragmentary dream—and that the pattern which is their 'Name with God' is being revealed from moment to moment, as though by so many brush strokes.

But the fact that a man's efforts meet with failure can never be taken (as some have supposed) to imply that the effort should never have been made. That this effort should have been made was as necessary to the pattern as was its defeat—or its apparent defeat (since 'unsuccessful' action can have a profound influence upon events); nor does the fact that a particular cause may seem to have been totally defeated mean that it was 'wrong' and that the cause which triumphed was 'right'. Our powers of judgment do not extend far enough to assess the ultimate outcome of the efforts we make, and we cannot see the end of their repercussions in the course of time. Indeed, time itself—and our inability to look ahead into the future in the way we look back at the past—is the precondition of our particular kind of freedom as creatures existing here and now, and it is time that makes possible the exercise of viceregal responsibility.

The complaint that such conditional freedom permits no more than the acting out of a play already written and concluded is, like the argument between 'free will' and determinism, based upon a confusion of perspectives and of levels. Whatever the doctrinal differences—the differences of statement—between the world's religions, all acknowledge that the future is 'known to God', or already inherent within the ultimate matrix of Reality and that, in a certain sense, all that is to happen is already *there*. What matters from our point of view is that it is not yet *here*—and that we are not God. For us it has not yet happened. That is why we exist, our identity fragmented in space and time; and, as the fragments are gathered and the identity put together again, we are actualising here and now something that—in our given condition—we cannot know in any other way.

And because that part of our environment with which we come into contact in the course of our existence is itself an aspect of our ultimate identity, it can be said that the Viceroy's real field of action is always himself and that the only battle he fights is—in Muslim terms—the 'Greater Holy War', which is the battle for self-unification. But, because we are what we are, the practical distinction between 'subjective' and 'objective' remains a fact of experience and provides the framework within which we operate. And it is perfectly possible to operate in terms of this distinction without imagining that it has any validity beyond our particular locality.

What matters, perhaps, is the awareness that the conditions which govern this cockpit of ours are indeed local and relative and that we ourselves have a dual nature, at once subject to these conditions in our daily lives (through our mentality, our emotions and our senses) and at the same time transcending them at another level of our being. This awareness, although it took so many different forms and was often implicit rather than expressed, was once universal. Its loss has made invalids of us.

The people of other times knew suffering as we do and, so far as the limits of recorded history go, may have known more of it. But they did not have our acquaintance with meaningless suffering and its partner, despair, which adds an entirely new dimension to pain and misfortune. And if many of them accepted their destiny as something imposed by the nature of things rather than as an aspect of their own identity in the course of actualisation, their acceptance had its roots nonetheless in a traditional wisdom which gave purpose and meaning to acceptance. What are for us abstractions (or fairy tales) were, for them, realities. They could do without the luxuries and pastimes which we need to make our wretchedness momentarily tolerable.

In the context of a world that made sense, a sense that was bound to evaporate as soon as men no longer incorporated it in their daily lives and in all that they touched or had to do with, the viceregal function lay at the heart of all other human functions. If the world has changed, this only reflects the change in the idea we now have of our place in it. When the Viceroy lets go of the reins, all things run wild.

# 6

# KNOWLEDGE AND ITS
# COUNTERFEITS

Given the nature of the time process, it is not particularly surprising that the notion of man's viceregal function and dignity should have been forgotten. We are by nature forgetful, which is no doubt why the religion of Islam describes itself specifically as 'a reminder to mankind'. What is truly astonishing is that this notion should now appear nonsensical to the vast majority of people in the West and, indeed, to 'educated' people everywhere. The fact that a view of man's destiny which could be considered, until so recently, as something inherent in human thinking should be dismissed as a fairy tale would be incredible if it had not actually happened.

No wonder that many of those who hold to the traditional view believe the devil himself has bewitched our kind, putting to sleep the faculties through which we were formerly aware of realities beyond the field of sense-perception and making use of mirages to lead us into a waterless desert. This process culminates in a narrowing of horizons which Mircea Eliade and others have described in terms of 'provincialism'. We live and think and operate today within the dimensions of a wafer-thin cross-section of historical time, effectively isolated from the past as from the future.

Evolutionary theory, as it is commonly understood by non-specialists, has penetrated very deeply into the substratum of human thought. It shapes opinion and distorts judgment in almost every sphere, all the more effectively because it has become a kind of unconscious and therefore unquestioned bias. People readily assume that each generation is likely to be a little wiser (and possibly even a little better) than the preceding one; this assumption is inherent in the idea of progress as it is commonly understood. If that were so, then the beliefs and ideas of earlier generations might reasonably be dismissed as obsolete. Religion would be no more than a vestige of primitive thought, and Christ might be considered, at best, as a man ahead of his time, a signpost on the evolutionary path. This appears to have been the view of Teilhard de Chardin, that misled and misleading priest.

We make certain deductions from the facts available to our senses in this thin slice of time. It is assumed that the people of earlier ages tried to do the same, and since they did not deduce what we have deduced from these facts they must necessarily have been our inferiors. It is taken for granted that their beliefs were based, as ours are, upon the observation of physical phenomena. They were not very good observers and persistently drew the wrong conclusions from such facts as they did observe; they belonged, it is said, to a 'pre-logical' stage of human development.

This is, in the first place, a childish attitude. It is common enough for children to enjoy a sense of superiority over adults who cannot climb trees as they do or who make a mess of a jigsaw puzzle which presents no problem to an eight-year-old, and a child may reasonably wonder why a grown-up who can afford to buy ice-cream or chocolates every day of his life does not do so, just as we are puzzled that the ancients never developed effective techniques for the exploitation of the earth's riches. Grown-ups, however, have a different order of priorities.

This childish aspect of modernism is nothing if not naive in its view of the past. It takes for granted that if all we want is ice-cream or its equivalents, then this is all that people ever wanted. They did not know how to produce it quickly, hygienically and in quantity. We do. They were not clever enough to invent motor cars and aeroplanes. We are (without ever asking ourselves whether our journeys are really necessary). They thought the earth was the centre of the universe. We know better.

Arguments of this kind, however ludicrous they may seem, are at the root of a great deal of modern thinking, not, of course, among a sophisticated minority of scholars and intellectuals, but among ordinary people who have received the usual smattering of education and have been encouraged to believe that they know something worth knowing. What matters, from this point of view, is not the pure form of a particular theory but the form in which it has been popularised, processed through the educational machine and assimilated by the masses. Religious (or metaphysical) ideas, when they penetrate whole populations within a traditional environment, may adopt simplified and what might be described as 'picturesque' forms without thereby sacrificing either integrity or effectiveness, but secular and scientific notions soon become slipshod and inaccurate when they are popularised.

Most important of all, perhaps, modern thought is 'provincial' in so far as most people are confined within the narrow limits of faculties designed to deal only with our own small corner of creation and ill-adapted (as is our language itself) to anything beyond self-preservation and the getting of food. Our ideas of truth and indeed of all that *is* seldom go beyond the things which fit the contours of a mind as limited in its way as are our physical senses; and we are necessarily ignorant in the precise sense of the term, since it is obvious that the mind as such cannot comprehend—within its own terms of reference—what lies beyond this particular locality and the view visible from here.

The distinction between ignorance and agnosticism—a distinction which is often ignored in our time—is of great importance. The former is both natural and realistic; it knows itself and recognises its own impotence. To be human is, in the first place, to be ignorant and to accept the fact that there is a great deal we cannot know and, for that matter, a great deal we do not need to know. Idle curiosity is certainly a vice—a lust of the mind—whereas acknowledgement of the fact that we have no intrinsic right to receive answers to all our questions is an aspect of humility as it is of realism. It is said that St Augustine was asked: 'What was God doing before he created the world?' 'Preparing hell for those who ask unnecessary questions!'

Agnosticism however raises a personal incapacity to the dignity of a universal law. It amounts to the dogmatic assertion that what 'I' do not know cannot be known, and it limits the very concept of what is knowable to the little area of observation open to the unsanctified and unilluminated human mentality. The agnostic attitude derives from a refusal to admit that anyone can be or ever could have been our superior in this, the most important realm of all: the true knowledge of what there is to be known. Religion is now seen exclusively in terms of faith rather than of supernatural knowledge. In egalitarian terms, faith is acceptable; you may believe in fairies if you wish to. But the claim to a direct and certain knowledge of realities beyond the mind's normal compass excludes those who do not possess it and savours of presumption. The idea that a saint among the saints may have *known* God—not merely *believed* in him—suggests 'unfairness' and implies the superiority of some men to others. It puts us in our place.

Squatting in this place, this little pool, and hungry for certainties, people hold on with a kind of desperation to the current notion of what is (or is not) 'rational'; and yet, 'the rationalism of a frog at the bottom of a well consists in denying the existence of mountains; this is logic of a kind, perhaps, but it has nothing to do with reality.'* This rationalism is inextricably linked with the scientific point of view, which is advanced as the only logical interpretation of the world. Unfortunately nothing in this realm is as clear as it should be. The 'facts' with which science supplies us are of quite a different order to those registered by our physical senses. What the scientist says, in effect, is this: you may take my propositions as proved, provided you accept all the assumptions which appear self-evident at this time, so long as you agree that the objective world exactly fits the patterns inherent in human thinking (or vice versa), on the understanding that the simplest explanation of a given phenomenon must be the right one and assuming that the physical world is sealed off from interference from any other realm. This adds up to a formidable list of qualifications.

Contrary to popular belief, science does not offer us certainties in the way that our senses provide a kind of certainty on their own level. Scientific hypotheses are not facts, and before the scientist can even begin to construct his theories he must make a number of very sweeping assumptions which most people may agree to take for granted, since they are in accordance with the present climate of opinion, but which can never be proved.

He must assume the absolute, objective validity of his own mental processes and believe that the logic of these processes is a universal law to which everything that is or ever could be conforms. Common sense tells him that this is so, but common sense is a variable factor which changes from one age to another. He can never be certain that the images which his senses present to his mind are a true representation of realities which exist independently and objectively. Not unlike the man who interprets the outside world in terms of what is taking place in his own entrails, seeing a bright day when he feels well and finding the world a dark place when his system is choked with waste products, he may in fact be applying to observed

* *Logic and Transcendence:* Frithjof Schuon, p. 42.

data the laws which govern his own mentality, an instrument constructed for the practical business of living much as the entrails are constructed for the digestion of food. Since inner and outer, subjective and objective, are, in the last analysis, two sides of the same coin, he is likely to find that the protean physical world provides the answers he expects of it (these answers being implicit in the phrasing of his questions) and experiment will confirm the theories he has constructed without, in fact, taking him beyond the subjective realm.

However complex the instruments designed to extend the range of our senses, scientific exploration is always to some extent dealing with patterns inherent in the exploring mind and meeting the mirror images it has projected. Nature mocks and eludes us, seeming to fit herself into our mental categories because our minds are themselves embedded in her structure. We imagine ourselves standing—or floating—above the natural world, competent to survey it objectively, and the intervention of scientific instruments between our naked senses and the objects of observation heightens this illusion ; but a mentality which is part of the natural world can never escape and look down as a disembodied agent upon its own matrix. That element in man which does indeed transcend the natural world is in him but not of him, and the objectivity of its awareness is very different from the fictional objectivity exercised by one facet of nature in relation to another.

But while the scientist, in his increasingly private and abstract sphere, finds a marvellous concordance between his thinking process and the movement of a needle on a dial or the traces of radiation on a photographic plate, the ordinary man of our time faces a widening gulf between scientific theory and any kind of objective experience known to him.

No longer can men be told that the truth of things will be confirmed in their own intimate experience if only they will look and listen. The proofs and arguments of contemporary science are so abstract and so technical that they are no longer open to criticism by the non-specialist and cannot be tested against any kind of experience known to man as a living creature. Informed that the electron's position does not change with time, but does not remain the same, and that, although the electron is not at rest, it is not in motion, François Mauriac remarked : 'What this professor says is far more incredible than what we poor Christians believe !'. The theories employed by modern physics have not merely by-passed the contours of the rational mind; they have gone beyond the range of human imagination.

'In those never-never, through-the-looking-glass abodes,' says Professor Huston Smith, 'parallel lines meet, curves get you from star to star more quickly than do Euclid's straight lines, a particle will pass through alternative apertures simultaneously without dividing, time shrinks and expands, electrons . . . jump orbit without traversing the intervening distance, and particles fired in opposite directions, each at a speed approximating that of light, separate from each other no faster than the speed of light.'* After this no one has any excuse for finding obscurities or improbabilities in the higher reaches of theology and metaphysics. If the majority of people still imagine that the physical sciences relate in some way to their normal experience this can only be because they are living in the past, comfortably immured in the mechanistic science of the nineteenth century.

Although in no sense supernatural, contemporary scientific theories do not relate to the spectacle of nature as we know it in our daily lives, and their 'proofs' derive from experiments carried out under almost unimaginable conditions (at temperatures a fraction of a degree above absolute zero and so on) with the aid of immensely complex equipment. In factual terms—and a fact, after all, is something against which we expect to be able to stub our toes— this is a very remote and esoteric region. And it is partly because these theories, together with their proofs, are unverifiable in terms of human experience and because they originate in the extra-terrestrial conditions created in the secrecy of the laboratory that they have such power to bind and fascinate. Their glassy surface offers no purchase to the mind's sceptical probing.

A field of knowledge in which the ordinary person can participate only by believing what he is told by experts corresponds very well to the political field of the totalitarian State in which he participates only by doing what he is told to do by an anonymous *them*, while the notion that every new fact discovered by science adds to the universal store of human knowledge and that this quantitative accumulation is an unqualified good finds its echo in the belief that every technological advance contributes to the wellbeing of mankind.

* *Forgotten Truth:* Huston Smith (Harper & Row), pp. 105–6.

Speaking of the 'normal and providential limitation of the data of experience', Schuon remarks that, while no knowledge is bad in itself and in principle, many forms of knowledge may be harmful in practice 'because they do not correspond to man's hereditary habits and are imposed on him without his being spiritually prepared; the soul finds it hard to accommodate facts that nature has not offered to its experience, unless it is enlightened with metaphysical knowledge or with an impregnable sanctity.' The unenlightened and unsanctified personality, subjected to a barrage of facts and theories which contradict its own intimate experience of the world, is more likely to be maimed than nourished. Through their education and by means of books, newspapers and television, people's minds are now crammed with ill-assorted fragments of knowledge. Without any unifying principle, this adds up to little more than a pile of debris which is never effectively sorted or assessed. No wonder we choke on it and lose our bearings.

People have a longing for normality or, in other words, a need to be what they are meant to be. It would be strange were this not so, but the fact remains that, when the true norm has been forgotten, it is only too easy to go off into the wilds in pursuit of a substitute. Just as nostalgia for the integral traditional society, in which everything fits and everyone has his place under the light of heaven, can draw us fatally towards the totalitarian society, so nostalgia for true and certain knowledge induces us to embrace its counterfeits and to mistake an accumulation of facts for something that they can never be. Quantity, by whatever factors it may be multiplied, is never more than a finite number, a fragment. Though you pile fact upon fact until the heap of evidence seems to touch the sky, it is still nothing in comparison with totality, just as a distance of countless light-years still comes no closer to infinity than does a single centimeter.

A counterfeit coin is still a coin, though we mistake its nature and its value. Those who are deceived may blame it, but the coin is what it is, no more, no less. Scientific knowledge is what it is, neither absolutely true nor absolutely false, but always relative and contingent. Theories based upon the observation of happenings which occur again and again in a particular cross-section of time have their practical uses but can never be more than hypothetical; in so far as we take them for certainties, they are counterfeits.

To say this is not to suggest that observed facts and the general laws derived from them are without significance, but only to emphasise the fact that they belong to the realm of relativity— and therefore of uncertainty—and cannot under any circumstances emerge from this domain. They deal with phenomena in a particular theatre at a particular moment in time, but they can tell us nothing about the open, the universal, the total. They remain bound to a locality, since any given phenomenon may be 'explained' in a variety of ways and at various levels ; our preconceptions—and the prevailing climate of opinion—determine our choice of explanation.

At the same time, science can never allow for the ambiguity inherent in the natural world, an ambiguity which is brought out with particular clarity in the Hindu doctrine of *maya*, the divine art, the divine magic, the divinely willed 'illusion' which is, in a sense, all things to all men. The physical sciences deal exclusively with the slippery and deceptive realm of *maya* and therefore cannot in any way determine the nature of the Absolute or, indeed, pretend to take precedence over direct, immediate knowledge on the one hand or its objective counterpart, Revelation, on the other. But what can—and does—happen is that these relativities and probabilities are inflated until they fill the view and nothing else can be seen.

Facts and the theories derived from them lodge only in the mind, whereas the metaphysical truths which lay at the root of human belief in other times transcend the personality as such and are no more exclusively mental than emotional or sensory. They may be expressed in mental formulations—an idea or a statement—but they can never be enclosed within this formulation or in any way limited by our faculties. In the ancient traditional societies they were reflected, not merely in the theories whereby the mind organises its material, but also in myths and rituals, as they were in every aspect of common life—man's waking and his sleeping, his eating, his love-making, his fighting and his work. This was the basis of that unity of life which most of us would give all that we have to repossess. Fragmentation of the personality is the salient characteristic of 'modern' as against 'primitive' man, and the problems which now arise regarding man's role in society, patterns of sexual behaviour, or the distinction between creative work and servile labour are aspects of this fragmentation.

Since responsibility is necessarily a function of the whole man, those whose actions are regulated by only one part of their nature and who are at war with themselves find it easy to deny paternity when faced with the consequences of what they have done. The scientist whose pursuit of knowledge leads (indirectly, as it seems to him) to appalling consequences is aware that he never willed this outcome, very much as the man who rapes a young girl can say quite truly that he never meant to harm her. Scientists may suggest that the pursuit of knowledge for its own sake is natural to man, just as the rapist may feel that emotion, if it is powerful enough, contains its own justification; and both can take refuge in the excessive emphasis upon motives and conditioning which tends to isolate modern man from the great web of consequences which he actualises. The fact remains that consequences do follow acts, and they must belong to someone.

There exists a popular image, fostered by the media, of the dedicated scientist, working long hours in his laboratory—yet happy as a child at play—careless about money and naive in the ways of the world. Real scientists may not always be quite like this, but it is understandable if they adopt the required pose on occasion; like so many masks, it expresses a truth. When this 'innocent' is faced with the consequences of his obsessive pursuit of knowledge, unregulated by any principle beyond a kind of mental lust, the truth becomes shockingly apparent. With indecent haste, he seeks for scapegoats (wicked politicians or rapacious businessmen) who have bent his precious discoveries to their own evil purposes. He had, of course, taken it for granted that none but angels would make use of the knowledge he has wrung from his intercourse with the natural world.

It is not as though he had never been warned; and this is the most astonishing aspect of the scientist's claim to innocence. The very fact that he is able to carry on his pursuit of factual knowledge is the outcome, at least according to one of the basic lessons children learn at school, of a long battle against 'persecution', against 'obscurantism' and against 'superstition' or, in other words, against the massed weight of human opinion in earlier centuries. There is however another way of looking at the obstructions formerly placed in the way of scientific advance. A fence at the cliff's edge is an obstruction, certainly, but it has not been placed where it is without reason; and to suppose that the men who raised these obstructions were quite without intelligence or foresight is an impertinence which only reflects our own stupidity.

The battle against the physical sciences was waged with particular ferocity in Christendom at the end of the Middle Ages. The gestures of those who tried most desperately to halt the process make one think of dumb men attempting to prevent someone from striding cheerfully to perdition. The Inquisition, for example, did not have the right words, they could not have been expected to know the unknown or to see in detail where this new learning would lead, but a sound intuition alerted pious men to a fearful danger. In a fury of despair they would dig up a dead man's bones to condemn him, too late.

The investigation of the natural world 'in depth' and the pursuit of factual knowledge for its own sake were then regarded as dangerous and ultimately destructive activities. It is absurd to be surprised if these activities do turn out to be both dangerous and ultimately destructive.

In the Islamic sector of the world the sciences showed less inclination to go off at a tangent from the total truth and were not subjected to the same 'persecution'. The presiding idea which dominates every aspect of Islamic thought—the divine Unity, beside which nothing can be said to have more than a shadowy and contingent existence—was of such power that fragmentary ideas were unlikely to escape from its magnetic field.

Even so, the note of warning was sounded often enough and Ibn 'Arabi, perhaps the greatest of the medieval Muslim philosophers, compared scientific delving into the secrets of nature to incest, a prying under the Mother's skirts; and this is one way of characterising the desire of one facet of the natural world to know another in its most intimate contours. The penetration of nature by the fact-finding and analytic mind keeps time now with the rape of the earth we tread and with the exploitation of our fellow creatures. An incestuous conjunction of mind with matter engenders some monstrous offspring.

Our bodies (and there is a sense in which the whole world, the whole of nature, is our body) are clothing which lasts a little while and then falls apart. We have better things to do than pick obsessively at this clothing, placing its fragments under the microscope, making it our sole and absolute concern. Human dignity forbids such dreary obscenities.

It is not easy to stand out against the spirit of the age, nor is there any reason why it should be. It is right that people's minds should to some extent be closed to ideas which do not fit the framework of preconceptions which enables them to think and to act coherently ; a man whose mind was wide open to every notion that came his way would be paralysed by uncertainty and deafened by a cacophony of conflicting sounds. The fact remains that those who attempt to break down this protective wall of preconception start at an immense disadvantage when required to argue their case.

In the open societies of the West, free discussion and argument have great influence, particularly now that they are brought into almost every home by television. Where there exists a solid substratum of agreement—that is to say, whenever the debate is within the limits of the present climate of opinion—argument serves a practical purpose. If two men wish to travel to the same destination it is useful for them to argue over which is the best route to take ; but if their goals are quite different they are bound to be at cross-purposes. Where there is a radical disagreement over fundamentals, argument, in the commonly accepted sense of the term, brings confusion rather than clarity. What do the opponent of science and the scientist—or, to come to essentials, believer and unbeliever—have to say to each other?

Not that dialogue is impossible. One can envisage a debate, held in quietness and intimate privacy (with no possibility of playing to the gallery), in which a believer and an unbeliever explore one another's minds over a long period and, inspired by a common desire to understand, achieve communication. Confined to thirty minutes in a television studio, such debate can only be farcical. Time and patience are of the essence, not to mention divine grace, love and a kind of stillness deeply infused with the longing for truth. Those who stand poles apart should never attempt hasty dialogue, unless they confine themselves to discussing the state of the weather. 'Haste is from the devil,' say the Muslims, 'and slowness is from God' ; and the clocks must be stopped if these two men are to understand each other.

But time is too valuable (when awareness of the timeless has been lost) for clocks to be stopped, love is at best a bit-player in this drama, and stillness is incompatible with controversy. All that such hasty debates between believer and unbeliever offer us is a battle of wits and a contest in verbal skills ; and, since the former is out of tune with the spirit of his age, the rules of the game and the weapons are never of his choosing.

But perhaps there is no battle to be fought or won, for in most cases these antagonists have only the illusion of meeting and there is simply the spectacle—familiar in farce—of two men shadow-boxing on opposite sides of the stage, unaware that their blows never make contact. They are in different places. It is not enough to share a common language if there are no common assumptions to provide the basis for argument. Without any such basis each partici-pant feels that the other is 'missing the point', as indeed he is since the 'point' is the truth as seen from the place at which he has taken his stand and these men are too far apart to share the same view. Heirs of a fairly unified culture, we still take a certain uniformity of viewpoint for granted, but in the modern age it is quite possible for people living side-by-side in the same society to inhabit entirely different worlds.

Because such a situation is by nature painful, those who take their stand upon the religious interpretation of the universe, being a minority and respecting democratic procedures, go to extra-ordinary lengths to meet their scientifically-minded companions rather more than half-way, as though a man tall enough to look over the fence were to squat down—for the sake of keeping company with his children—and peer through the hole they have bored in the wood, pretending this is all that can be seen of the next-door garden.

If 'provincialism' is taken to indicate narrowness of viewpoint, then Eliade's phrase is particularly apt in relation to the contraction which has taken place over a long period and which was already well advanced among 'educated' people when Descartes first made awareness of his own thinking self the starting-point of all human knowledge, taking care to shut the doors and windows before sinking into the cavern of mental self-awareness.

In appearance, the outer world has expanded as the inner has contracted. A small vaulted universe, lit by friendly lamps and haunted by familiar spirits, has opened out into the unimaginable vastness of space with its thin population of burning stars; on the other hand, inner space, a spiritual universe extending from nadir to Empyrean, has contracted to the dimensions of the skull-box. This process (reminiscent of the scientific theory of an 'expanding universe') might be visualised in terms of a child's bubble-blowing —an 'objective' world which swells in proportion to the life-breath pumped into it. But size, unless it has human significance, is nothing in relation to infinity. A distance of a thousand light-years is further than a man could walk; and having said this there is little more to be said about such distances. They are irrelevant to the business of being a man.

It is in this sense that man is 'the measure of all things'. As Viceroy, his concern is with the area given him as his particular and unique destiny; his only concern beyond this area is with an eternity subject neither to contraction nor expansion.

The vastness of 'inner space', with its many dimensions, permits contraries to co-exist; but the attempt to fit truths which belong to different levels and make sense in terms of different perspectives into one framework at one particular level (that of the laws which govern our mental processes in the context of everyday life) is an impossible task. It is also an unnecessary task, for we ourselves do not live on one level only. But this is what rationalism, with its two-dimensional scheme of things, tries to do, and this is why the scientific view cannot be questioned on its own ground or in terms of the proofs and arguments which it considers valid.

It might seem too easy—and yet it would be true enough—to say that rationalism is false simply because it is an '-ism'. It is false because of its pretensions to universality, its claim to include the whole of reality within its orbit, and because it excludes everything that cannot be fitted into its own particular and local categories; false, in other words, because it is a counterfeit, pretending to be something that it is not. Reason is one mode of knowledge among others, and rationalism is its 'Pharaonic sin' (whereby the partial and fragmentary usurps the place of wholeness).

Man is a rational being, but he is also something much more. Reason is one of his tools—not his definition. Its nature is to operate in terms of irreconcilable alternatives: this is black or white; this creature is either male or female; either this animal will eat me or I shall eat it, and so on. These alternatives are indeed real on the level of our sensory experience, and since this experience is a form of true knowledge the instruments by means of which it is perceived and organised cannot be entirely false—so long as they keep their place. But the man who imagines that he can interpret all that *is* in terms of rational categories might be compared to someone who supposes he can absorb and digest knowledge through his belly.

Those who are unable to understand that they add up to more

than the sum of their own instruments and who cannot accept the fact that the area of possible knowledge extends into moulds quite unrelated to the contours of the human mentality are prisoners in their own empirical and conditioned selfhood. Their speculation is a ball bounced against the walls of their cell.

The fact that there are aspects of truth which can never be formulated in logical terms is frustrating to the mind's lust for totality; the inconceivable is dismissed as being unknowable and therefore 'unreal'. Illusions are always conceivable, since they are rooted in our faculties and cannot exist without us; but truth does not need us and is independent of our faculties as it is of our powers of conceptualisation. God, in his essence, is said to be quite inconceivable in terms of the mind's language; but there is nothing inconceivable about a flying hippopotamus, however improbable such a creature may be. The mind comprehends facts and is at ease with fictions. It is not by its nature apt to grasp realities unless enlightened by an enabling power which comes from beyond its sphere.

To dismiss partial modes of knowledge simply because they are what they are is just as grave a fallacy as to mistake the partial for something total and all-embracing. If reality could not in some measure be represented in mental, emotional and physical terms it would not be reality; and if the mind had no contact with reality we would all be mad. What has been lost in a mind-fixated age is awareness that the mental representation is by nature limited and incomplete, as is the emotional state or the physical image. Truth is expressed in these different languages without being exhausted by anything we can think, feel or say about it.

There is a necessary tension in the religious and intellectual spheres between acceptance and rejection of the partial images through which mind, emotion and senses maintain their hold on reality. Most of us cannot do without our mental concepts, our anthropomorphic image of God and our physical symbols; and the hidden truth responds to our need because it has its origin in the fountain of the divine Mercy and also because it is by nature partially conceivable, a fit object for love, and present in the sights, sounds, odours, flavours and tactile qualities of the physical world. To reject such partial knowledge as is offered by our natural faculties is a kind of self-mutilation; but to suppose that truth in its totality can be encompassed by these faculties is idolatry.

The inveterate human tendency to idolatry (worship of the reflection to the exclusion of that which is reflected) is, in the Muslim view, the most dangerous and the most universal of sins. The Islamic Revelation broke in upon a culture which had petrified into gross forms of idolatry; this was a moment in time when the breaking of images and the release of the spirit of truth from a stony prison was most necessary. But quite outside the historical circumstances which, providentially, determine the accent and emphasis of a particular religion, this Revelation had the function of redressing the balance between those who would bind the truth in mental formulae, emotional fixations and physical images, and those who insist upon its transcendence above all that we are capable of thinking or feeling or doing.

Without supernatural wisdom and without the humility which recognises the subordination of the reasoning process to that wisdom, it is impossible for human minds to keep a just balance between transcendence and immanence, reconciling the notion of God as totally 'other' (in Quranic terms, 'having no likeness whatsoever') with the idea of God as intimately present everywhere ('closer to man than his jugular vein'); but it is still a useful exercise to set such contrary ideas side-by-side within the mind's narrow cabin (as do the Zen Buddhists by means of their paradoxical *koans*), until we begin to sense, far beyond our human reach, the existence of a point at which the contraries meet.

When two concepts, each capsulated in accordance with our mental needs, appear at once irreconcilable—as, for example, do the notions of predestination and free will—and yet necessary if our existence is to make any kind of sense, then we can only reach out towards that incomprehensible point. It is beyond the range of our bread-and-butter faculties, but this does not in any sense indicate that it is absent from the world or unrelated to the human person in his totality. On the contrary, the belief—normal to mankind—that there is a meaning inherent in everything that exists and everything that happens must necessarily imply the omnipresence of that point, that truth, that centre.

Such beliefs as this are commonly classified as 'mystical'. They can then be treated, not with the hostility and resentment which so often accompanies the dismissal of 'organised religion', but with a gesture of respect to a gentle and poetic eccentricity, too remote from everyday life to represent a threat to our way of life. And yet there have been some good swordsmen among the mystics who, like David, have slain their ten-thousands.

In so far as the term has any precise meaning, mystics have no doubt followed their inward path in all places and all periods, triumphing over the obstacles presented by social chaos or social regimentation, sharing the vocation of the heroes and martyrs who stride over the turbulence or the petrifaction of their world with all the splendour of elephants rampaging through the bush. But the place they are going is the place we must all reach, and most people are not mystics, heroes or potential martyrs. They are not even elephants.

This is where the attempt to isolate mystical experience from the habitual stream of life in the sense in which, for example, musical experience may be isolated as something irrelevant to the lives of those who cannot share it, breaks down. The mystic is different from the rest only as the flyer is different from the walker, though both must hope to come to the city gate before nightfall. What he is talking about is also their business; but whereas he may find his way unaided by the society in which he happens to live, the common man, the quite unelephantine man, needs all the help he can get and has a right to expect this help from his society; and human societies, if they are to have any claim upon our loyalty beyond that of practical convenience, exist to beat a path through the bush for those who cannot fly or even trample.

What the traditional, God-centred societies offered their members was a life saturated with the awareness of realities beyond the reach of mind, feeling or sense in terms of their normal functioning and a whole system of bridges leading to mountain or hillock, as the case may be, but certainly leading outwards and upwards from the flatlands. The objects of sense were vivified by symbolism, emotion was universalised in ritual, and mental concepts were not self-sufficient propositions (limiting reality) but keys to supernatural knowledge.

In earlier times, says Thibon, 'men did not know the contours of the human and cosmic lock, but they possessed the key ... Modern thought as a whole no longer occupies itself at all with the nature or existence of this key. The only question posed before a closed door is to examine it most painstakingly, not to open it.'*
Or else we ignore the door altogether (mistaking it for a section of

* *Échelle de Jacob*: Gustave Thibon, p. 177.

an impenetrable wall) and set the key under a microscope, treating the instrument which lies in our hands as though it were an end in itself.

This could be a definition of idolatry: to worship a key instead of setting it to the lock. And here we come to the great divide which separates rationalism and all its offshoots from the traditional view of ideas, feelings and the phenomena of the material world as symbols and therefore as signs which, if properly used, point towards the timeless perfection which, in their flickering fashion, they signify. 'We shall show them Our signs on the horizon and within themselves, until it is clear to them that *this* is the Truth.'* For the Islamic Revelation embodied in the Qurān, all that we see and all that we find is of a superabundant richness, not on its own account, but because in its very existence it reflects the divine Qualities and reminds us of their source. A star, a bird on the wing, a forest or a river, and many lesser things ('Allāh disdains not to coin the similitude even of a gnat . . .') are facets of a universal Revelation.

But to live with things that are other than they seem, among signs that point away from themselves, amidst bridges that lead elsewhere and ladders of which only the lower rungs are visible is hard for those who hunger after narrow certainties. It is easier to settle down where we are and regard the sign as a work of art, the bridge as a piece of masonry and the ladder as a wooden frame, accepting appearances for what little they are worth and trying to forget that death will—so far as we are concerned—reduce all such works to nothingness.

'Primordial man sees the "more" in the "less",' says Frithjof Schuon. 'The infrahuman world in fact reflects the heavens and transmits in an existential language a divine message that is at once multiple and unique.'† Christianity, he points out, could not fail to react against the real 'paganism' of the cultural environment within which it crystallised as a world religion, but in so doing it also destroyed values which did not in the least deserve the reproach of 'paganism'; modern technology, he adds, 'is but an end product, no doubt very indirect, of a perspective which, after having banished the gods and genies from nature and, having rendered it

* Qurān, 41:53.
† *Images de l'Esprit* (Flammarion), pp. 15–16.

"profane", by this very fact finally made possible its "profanation" in the most brutal sense of this word.'

Paganism in the proper sense of the term is an idolatry applied to the natural world, but it is also, in most cases, the debris of a religion in the final stages of decay, when its adherents, like dogs, sniff at the pointed finger rather than going where the finger points ; idolatry, animism, fetishism and other such aberrations (assuming that they exist objectively, and not merely in the modern observer's mind) all bear witness to the fact that phenomena which were once adored as symbols of transcendent realities have come to be worshipped for their own sakes. There are many intermediate stages in this degenerative process, and it follows that one cannot always mark the dividing line between images which are adored for what they symbolise and those which are worshipped as 'gods'. In any religious context—and most of all in that of Hinduism—there will be some men who understand that the image points away from itself and others who mistake it for an independent reality (in which case it becomes a counterfeit). At a time when the sacred is all but banished from our world, we do well to be tolerant of 'superstition', so long as the intention behind it—a willingness to adore the holy—is sound.

A new divine Revelation, breaking in upon the rusty structure of the particular 'milieu' into which it is directed, is likely to sweep the ancient images aside. It has no need of them. It offers a real and effective alternative, a highroad in place of the little paths and bridges which people had been using (or misusing) for ages past. But when the highroad itself has begun to suffer the erosion of time and has narrowed, then the loss is felt. Once it is out of sight— so far as the majority of people are concerned—no true path is to be despised, no bridge scorned as 'naive' or 'childish'.

It is, in any case, one thing for the lightning stroke to destroy such supports and quite another for busy, opinionated little men to set themselves up as wreckers.

Islam and Christianity were both, at their inception, revolutionary religions and therefore destructive, at least in a relative sense. It happens to have been that sector of the world which was formerly Christian that has imposed its patterns of thought and behaviour almost universally, and ex-Christians are therefore the wreckers with whom we are chiefly concerned. The vast majority of Westerners who are not Christian believers in the full sense can

fairly be described as ex-Christians (or pseudo-Christians). Such
a heritage cannot easily be shaken off, and the fiercest opponents of
religion are often those who cannot forgive God for not being a
Christian (as they understand the term). The destructiveness
which was once no more than a side-effect of a great act of renewal
turns sour and vicious in men for whom the blazing certainty of
God's love and of Christ's redemptive sacrifice no longer have any
meaning. The rose in decay stinks.

It could be said that the world is nothing but a tissue of bridges
leading from here, where we find ourselves, to the 'other shore',
and in theory it is open to anyone to recognise sticks and stones
for what they really are and so to discover a Paradise which was
never finally lost. For him, no doubt, this world—so opaque, so
darkened in this winter season—is still transparent as it is said to
have been when it issued from the hand of God, and prison bars
are no more than candy-sticks that snap in a child's grip. Perhaps
there will always be such strangers, born out of their time, since
time is not absolute and must sometimes be mocked. But what
of the rest? The things we handle seem dark and heavy, the bars
are thick, and age wears us out. We have great need of crutches and
cannot be too proud to accept them wherever they are to be found.
With them, we may hope to hobble over such rickety bridges as
remain undestroyed.

What does a cripple feel, with fire or flood behind him and a
jostling crowd making for the only exit, if someone wantonly
knocks his crutch away and then destroys the bridge which led to
safety? Rage, surely; and if men knew what they have lost through
the arrogant destructiveness of the crutch-snatchers and bridge-
wreckers their rage would make the anger of warring armies and
revolutionary mobs seem kittenish.

The principal function of modern thought has been the wanton
destruction of 'superstition', a term which—though it may
properly be applied to little habits which have survived in isolation
from the doctrines which gave them meaning—has expanded to
include every kind of belief in the supernatural. Bridges, ladders
and, ultimately, the highroads provided by the great religions
have at least one thing in common: they are invisible to those in
whom this belief has been undermined.

It is difficult to measure wickedness and to define its degrees,
but those who set themselves to persuade their fellow men that the

world is nothing but a meaningless agglomeration of material particles (or the blind interaction of minute quanta of energy) totally separate from man's inner being and that there is no joy anywhere, no spiritual effort to be made, no eternal goal to be reached, have done a thing beside which no massacre of the innocents can stand comparison. Like the former Commandant of Auschwitz, these destroyers of bridges have been, for the most part, well-behaved, keeping their fingers off their neighbour's goods and their neighbour's wife; and this, as much as anything, makes current notions of morality seem infantile. If those who do the most harm go unpunished, how can we condemn mere thieves and murderers?

But if wickedness may often be defined in terms of a half-witted pursuit of relative good, then it can be said that much of this wrecking has been undertaken in the name of a fine ideal, the ideal of perfection. The idealist, the perfectionist, cannot tolerate what is grimy or flawed or broken. Lacking any sense of the sacred, lacking any courtesy towards creation and quite without modesty— a true 'savage'—he rages to destroy the imperfect wherever he finds it (and that is everywhere). Our world is, by definition, a grimy, flawed and broken place, subject to decay and riddled with death. If it were otherwise it would not be the world or—to put the matter another way—this universe of time and space would be indistinguishable from the timeless and central perfection of Paradise and would therefore lose its separate existence. The world may be rendered transparent, so that perfection is discerned behind its shapes and patterns, and it may be loved so that its very deformities become the objects of a redeeming compassion; but it cannot be fundamentally changed at its own level. We have the power only to substitute one evil for another, 'swopping black dog for monkey' (as the Jamaicans say) or leaping merrily out of the frying pan into the fire.

At the root of modern idealism, with its refusal to accept imperfection as something inherent in the human condition, there lies a bitter and perhaps satanic puritanism which, carried to its logical conclusion, would set fire to this world of ours and destroy it utterly.

'You can work miracles', said one of his companions to the Muslim saint, al-Hallaj; 'Can you bring me an apple from Heaven?' The saint raised his hand and, within the instant, held in it an apple which he offered to his friend. Biting into the fruit, the man observed with horror that there was a worm in it. 'That,' said al-Hallaj, 'is because, in passing from the eternal realm into the world of time, it has taken on something of the latter's corruptibility.'

This story has a bearing on contemporary attitudes to such traditional bridges as remain relatively intact in the modern world. Ignored or dismissed by the scientific view of reality, they are at the same time condemned for the rust which has settled on their outworks. They suffer the combined assault of rationalist and moralist. Even the man who has sufficient humility to acknowledge his own imperfections looks for a kind of primordial perfection in religious institutions and primordial purity in religious people. As a fallen being himself, he might be expected to know better.

Whatever 'passes from the eternal realm into the world of time' must take on some of the limitations inherent in this world and become subject to the laws which govern the context of its incarnation. The organisation and institutions in which a divine Revelation is fleshed cannot be immune to the process of decay, even though the grace which shines at the centre of its manifestation remains untainted. Since we are what we are and the world is what it is, this reservoir of grace is tapped only by those who are prepared to embrace the outer shell until, like the Prince who awakens the Sleeping Beauty, they find what was always there, awaiting them in the innermost room of the castle. From this point of view the imperfections of any organised religion as it appears to the outsider and the scandal created by some of its representatives might be compared to the trials which the mythological Hero must surmount before he reaches the goal of all desire.

There are many people in our time who, with an arrogance which masks the inadequacies of a superficial education, think it intolerable that plaster saints and household icons and desert tombs should serve as bridges to true knowledge and that a God who is said to be almighty should permit his grace and power to operate through such seemingly humble instruments. They forget that this same God is omnipresent and that men are therefore apt to find him where they can.

The divine Presence within things—in sticks and stones, in bits and pieces—implies their wholeness, but those who are themselves inwardly divided and fragmented cannot recognise this. In the idealist's alienation, his refusal to stoop to the small, imperfect things, there is a profound betrayal of man's viceregality; for the Viceroy is a bridge-builder, and these men know only how to destroy. Obsessed by their ideas of neatness, they take their scissors and snip away at existence like a child who, when he tries to make his cut-out figure perfectly symmetrical, cuts first on one side, then on the other, until there is nothing left. They seek mastery through a process of reduction, and all that does not fit is to be eliminated; but in the long run nothing fits their categories. Everything must go.

'The explanation of the world by a series of reductions has an aim in view: to rid the world of extra-mundane values. It is a systematic banalisation of the world undertaken for the purpose of conquering and mastering it. But the conquest of the world is not—in any case was not until half a century ago—the purpose of all human societies. It is an idiosyncrasy of Western man.'*

In the traditional view of human destiny, degeneration is an inevitable feature of time and history; but this process can take quite different forms, on the one hand active and aggressive, tending to violence and, on the other, passive, indolent and relatively peaceful. One cannot doubt that the first of these is the white man's sickness and we know how contagious it has proved to be; but the possibilities inherent in human nature do not differ fundamentally between one race and another, and it might be more accurate to say that the white man brought out in Asians and Africans qualities which were already present, only waiting to be awakened—witness the speed with which Western vices and ideologies have spread through the rest of the world and also the eagerness with which so many traditional peoples have exchanged their own craftsmanship for Western junk. This final destructive fever had to break out somewhere. Once it had come to the surface, no sector of our world was immune.

The grim ambition to subdue creation to our own narrow purposes—symptomatic of the search for a counterfeit Paradise—is now almost universal. Its inevitable frustration must surely lead to increasing violence, ultimately self-destructive. And yet all this is no more than the frenetic activity of ants around their little mound, busy and blind under an indifferent sun. When they are

---

* *The Two and the One:* Mircea Eliade (Harwell Press), pp. 156–7.

done and peace is over all, the sun will still be shining and the scattered fragments of existence will be re-assembled into the wholeness which is their only meaning: 'And say—Truth has come and illusion has vanished away; illusion is indeed by nature ephemeral.'*

* Qurān, 17:81.

# 7

## THE ONLY HERITAGE
## WE HAVE

The arrogance of the West in relation to other cultures is decently cloaked in our time, for this is an age of polite falsities; but it has not been outgrown. The fact that non-Europeans are expected to adopt Western patterns of government and 'post-Christian' morality (as enshrined in the Charter of the United Nations) is evidence of this. Condemnation of any departure from our own particular norms of behaviour—rooted as they are in European history—by Africans, Arabs or Asians is nowadays expressed more in terms of sorrow than of anger, but it is expressed nonetheless and bears witness to a complacency which has survived two World Wars and ignores the fact that our history is a quite unparalleled story of destruction and exploitation.

This complacency still blocks the way to any appreciation of what has been—and, to some extent, still is—the human norm elsewhere; and yet, without such understanding, it is impossible for the modern world to see itself either in context or with any degree of objectivity.

The distinguished historian of religion, Mircea Eliade, has suggested that for the past half-century Western scholars have approached the study of mythology from a completely different viewpoint to that of their nineteenth century predecessors. Unlike the Victorians, for whom the word 'myth' was equivalent to 'fiction', modern scholars—so he says—accept the myth in the terms in which it has been understood in the archaic societies, that is to say as a true story telling us something about the nature of the universe and man's place in it.

This may be true of certain rare scholars, but it is very far from being true of the general public or, for that matter, of the television pundits who play a dominant role in moulding public opinion. In this field, as in many others, the intellectual assumptions of ordinary people are still based upon the scientific thinking of fifty years ago; and if reputable scholars have now abandoned the notion that the great archaic myths are no more than an inept, pre-scientific attempt to account for the observed phenomena of nature, their views do not seem to have reached the writers of school text-books or penetrated the minds of the majority of educated people in the Western world.

A superficial study of the myths and rituals of 'primitive' peoples played a significant part in undermining the faith of Christians during the second half of the nineteenth century. First it was taken for granted that these other races were 'lower on the evolutionary scale' than Europeans (What, after all, had they invented? Where were their railway trains?) Secondly it was assumed by people who had completely lost the capacity for analogical and symbolical thinking that the myths by which these races lived were meant to be taken quite literally and represented no more than the first gropings of the rational animal towards a scientific explanation of the universe. On this basis, since it was impossible to miss the parallels between 'primitive religion' and the most 'advanced' of religions, Christianity, the question had to be asked whether the latter should not be classified as just one more pre-scientific effort to account for observed facts.

If these arguments were sound, then either one of two conclusions might be drawn from them. It could be assumed that religion is a phenomenon which evolves in step with human 'evolution', so long as it is constantly purged of its 'superstitious' and 'unscientific' elements and kept up-to-date; or else that religion as such, including Christianity, is no more than a vestige of the pre-scientific age, to be discarded together with all the other superstitions we have inherited from the times of ignorance.

Protestant sects, constantly on the defensive, have been only too ready to adopt the first of these conclusions in the mistaken notion that it offers their religion some hope of survival, and we have recently seen the hierarchy of the Catholic Church stumbling into this very pitfall. They imagine that Christianity might be allowed to survive on a modest scale if it can be shown to be useful to society, that is, to make men better citizens, more decent neighbours, more conscientious tax-payers; and they are ready to abandon everything that smacks of 'other-worldliness', of metaphysics or of ritualism. The more ground they give, the harder they are pressed by their enemies.

And yet there is only one question that either needs or deserves to be asked, and the answer to this question cannot depend upon any contingent factor or upon moral and social considerations. Religion is either true or false, reality or illusion. If it is true, then nothing more needs to be said and the question as to whether it makes men better citizens is irrelevant. If it were false, then it would be no less so if proved capable of transforming this world into a far more comfortable place. Our personal or social convenience has nothing to do with the issue, and far above all purely human considerations—beyond the need for consolation or the fear of damnation—this question is posed in stark simplicity. The answer we give to it determines the answers to all other conceivable questions; if affirmative, it is a total affirmation; if negative, an all-embracing negation.

There are occasions when poison and antidote are to be found in the same place. Faced with the confusion of perspectives which has been the inevitable result of the breakdown of those human and geographical barriers which formerly divided different cultures and different religious domains into so many separate worlds, there is no going back to the simplicity of a single, self-sufficient viewpoint. We are compelled to go forward to the recognition that perspectives never really clash, their orientation being always towards the same, unique centre. The knowledge of other doctrines, other ways to the centre, which has done so much to shake the faith of those who had believed their own truth to be the only one (as, in a sense, it was, since they needed no other to attain salvation) must now be used to revitalise all those relative truths which serve as bridges between our present existence and a realm beyond such relativities. One bridge is enough for any man. But first he must be convinced of its soundness. Under present circumstances this seems to depend upon having some general knowledge of the nature of bridges.

This knowledge can scarcely be effective unless it takes account of what is in fact the specifically human heritage (and the substance out of which all bridges have been built), the 'primordial tradition' or 'perennial philosophy'. This is the bedrock of all human awareness of what we are and where we are, and it might be said that all the doctrines which have kept us human through the ages and enabled us to make use of our heritage have been no more than divinely willed adaptations of this basic wisdom to the increasingly desperate needs of a fallen—and still falling—humanity.

The great acts of renewal, the Revelations from which are descended the world religions as we now know them, came about, not as milestones on the evolutionary way, but as medicines for a worsening sickness. They happened when (and wherever) the archaic wisdom was in so grave a condition of decay that a direct intervention from outside the normal context of human existence was required if men were not to lose all sense of their real nature and destiny. In the case of Hinduism, the acts of renewal never broke the continuity of the tradition, but gave it a new impetus. Christianity was able to maintain a close link with the Judaic tradition (hence the inclusion of the Old Testament in the Christian Bible). And Islam, although it came into being in what was virtually a spiritual vacuum, has always been perfectly explicit as to its role: the Prophet Muhammad was not an innovator, but a reminder of forgotten truths and the restorer of an ancient wisdom, pointing a way of return to the normal and universal religion of mankind and crowning, by his mission, the work of countless prophets and messengers who had maintained the link between God and man since the beginning of time.

Such interventions and renewals would have been unnecessary if it had been possible then (or now) for men to tap the full resources of the primordial traditions by remounting the stream of time and—as the People of the Book might say—bursting back into the Garden of Eden. But the direction of time is only too clearly indicated in everything around us, in the running down of clocks, in the ageing and decay of things and organisms and in the dissolution of patterns into their component fragments. This direction may be temporarily reversed (since creation is not a closed system) through the inbreak of That which *is* outside time, through Revelation or through the rituals of renewal practised by many 'archaic' peoples, but the possibility of returning once and for all to the place from which mankind set out does not exist within our frame of reference.

The lightning stroke of Revelation seizes upon wandering fragments and organises them into a pattern through which some quantum of meaning finds expression or some message is flashed upon the screen of existence. The pattern, however, must eventually be subjected to the normal processes of time and suffer the common fate of all things under the sun.

This is why we are denied access to the fullness of our heritage and surmise its existence from the bits and pieces, the echoes and the memories which are seen to lie all around us if only we are prepared to recognise them for what they are. These fragments, still to be found in the myths and rituals of the few 'primitive' peoples who have not yet been totally submerged in the stream of modernism, are immensely precious. They may have been warped by the passage of time, and those who still live by them may in many cases have forgotten their true meaning, but the fact remains that they exist, they are accessible to us and, like a charred but still just legible document, they provide confirmation of our viceregal identity.

The religions with which the Westerner is most closely acquainted—those of Semitic origin and, perhaps, Buddhism—are 'historical' in character, first in the quite simple sense that they do have a history strictly comparable to that of human institutions and temporal events, and secondly because the story of their achievements and of the vicissitudes they have suffered takes a significant place in their teaching. Time as we experience it in our daily lives is the background against which they are observed and understood.

The archaic doctrines, on the other hand, have no history. Their relationship to ordinary time has been that of rocks towards the sea which gradually erodes them. In this lies their strength, insofar as they recall conditions before the dawn of recorded history, and their weakness, in that they cannot serve as models in relation to which men of our time might organise their lives. They might in a certain sense be said to rest upon the fiction that nothing has changed, nothing has happened, since time began. They have survived precisely because events in time have been treated as meaningless unless they could be related back to the pre-temporal patterns of creation, reintegrated into these patterns and thus transcended so far as their historical actuality is concerned. Inwardly, at least, they have made time stand still.

A particular characteristic quality of all traditional societies, says Mircea Eliade, is their opposition to the 'ordinary' concept of time and their determination constantly to return, through ritual action, to the mythical moment of their origin, the 'Great Time'. Neither the objects of the exterior world nor human acts as such have any separate being or significance—they are *real* only as imitations of the universal, primordial gestures made by God or the gods at the moment of creation. Nothing is worth noticing or mentioning unless it has been bathed in the waters of its source.

It follows that, for the ancients as for 'primitive' peoples up to the present time, myth and history cannot be separated, historical events being valid, in their view, only to the extent that they illustrate mythical themes. The modern historian, concerned to discover what 'really' happened, has the unenviable task of trying to separate the two, but for the ancients it was the myth—the pre-temporal event—that was truly real, and happenings came about only because the reverberations of this event determined the patterns of time or—if we translate this into religious terms—'that it might be fulfilled which was spoken by the prophets'. On the one hand there is the view in terms of which the world could not under any circumstances be thought of as separated from its timeless source; on the other a view which takes this separation completely for granted.

In the personal life as in the wider context of world events archaic man has considered the actions of daily life to be *real* only if they fill out the contours of a pre-existent and harmonious mould. There are certain ways of hunting (or, in agricultural communities, of ploughing, sowing and reaping), certain ways of eating and making love and constructing artifacts which are in accordance with the heavenly precedents handed down in the myths and rituals of his people—'We must do what the gods did Then'—and all other ways are disorderly and ultimately unproductive. His thirst for the Real and his awareness that, if he commits himself to trivialities, he must himself become trivial and lose the quality of dignity, the quality of viceregality, dominates all his faculties. In the circumstances of our time, so far from our origins, it might be said that he is defeated before he even starts, that the stream of time now runs too fast and too fiercely to be resisted and that the echoes which still reach him from 'That Time' are too dim to be effectively obeyed. This may be so. But he lives on as a reminder and as a sign for those who are prepared to understand.

The fact that archaic man is a survivor from a period when the conditions of human life were quite different to what they now are makes it difficult for him to accept as natural misfortunes such as sickness, infertility or accidental death which do not seem to us at all mysterious in their origin. For him they indicate a disruption of the harmony and order which still appear to him as normal, since he retains, however dimly, some recollection of a time before these ills had become the common lot of our kind, and he therefore ascribes them to some disruptive act of witchcraft or to human failure. This is not really so remote from the religious point of view, which finds their cause in human sinfulness. For the 'primitive' as, in a certain sense, for the Christian, we live commonly under a curse, but the former—because he has chosen to ignore the changes which time has brought about—is still surprised by this fact and tries to pin the fault on someone in his immediate neighbourhood.

Still at home in the world, still trusting the environment (which we see as something to be subdued and conquered), he assumes its innocence and blames himself or others like himself for the ills to which his flesh is prone. He does not see the rhythms of nature as phenomena of time; the alternations of day and night and the changes of the lunar cycle and of the seasons are events which happened once and for all in That Time, and his own life is integrated into their pattern because he and they are aspects of a single timeless order.

And because time does not appear to him as a continuous, uninterrupted process, the changes which take place in the course of his life are in the nature of mutations. We know of only one 'rite of passage', the dreaded phenomenon of physical death, whereas the life of archaic man is scattered with deaths and rebirths—rites of naming, puberty, marriage and so on—each representing a harsh severance from the past and a total break with the habits and attachments of his former existence, so that he might be expected to re-emerge from the ritual moment into the light of common day with a new name and a new identity. In such a context physical death cannot have the quality of uniqueness that it has for us, but is simply the greatest and most cataclysmic of the 'rites of passage'. He does not need to think or talk in terms of a 'life after death' since he is accustomed to regard every ending as the necessary prelude to a new beginning. He himself, in this most intimate selfhood, is projected into the primordial moment when everything began, and every death, every break in continuity, coincides with the primal sacrifice out of which time and multiplicity were born into their fiery and self-consuming existence.

Rooted in a coherent world and free from the oppressive sense of meaninglessness which time and multiplicity induce when they are seen as self-subsisting, this man could scarcely be expected to ask the questions we ask or to search high and low for a significance which (in his experience) saturates both the common objects of sense and the ordinary events which compose a human lifespan. It is a fundamental assumption of all traditional doctrines, whether archaic or religious—however their outward forms may differ— that men have been provided not only with the mental, emotional and sensory equipment necessary for them to be able to cope with their worldly environment but also with answers to all the real questions that can be asked. The question which remains unanswered is the one which has been posed in the wrong terms.

These answers, however, are not of a kind to satisfy the questioning mind when it breaks loose from the personality as a whole and demands that everything should be translated into its own specific terms, nor can they be passed from hand to hand like coins. These answers are bonds of connection between the individual and all that is; but because they relate not to the partial but to the whole man it follows that the whole man must be apt to receive them if they are to mean anything to him. Division and turbulence, obscurity or falsity at any level of his being, will set barriers in the way of total understanding; for totality can only be comprehended by totality: 'It is not the eyes which grow blind. It is the hearts within the breasts that grow blind', says the Qurān.

Two quite different obstacles provide barriers to human understanding. The first (with which we are all well acquainted in our age) is the technical difficulty of matters which require special training and instruction combined with an active practical intelligence if they are to be grasped. In this case the barrier is there for all to see. No one supposes that he can master a book on nuclear physics merely because he is able to read.

The second obstacle is more subtle and perhaps more deceptive since it relates to the understanding of statements, symbols and stories which, on the surface, appear transparently simple and wide-open even to the most naive and least instructed intelligence. Like the tests which the traditional hero undergoes, but with a less obvious challenge, they try each man's capacity to plumb the depths of the truth offered to his understanding, but they also allow those of small capacity to think they have grasped all that there is to be grasped. In this sense they are, almost by definition, merciful, in that they give to each as much as he is able to receive. But there is always the danger that those who see only the concrete image, the outer husk, and—thinking themselves intelligent—assume that there is nothing more to be seen will dismiss such truths as being too trivial to merit their further attention.

Of this attitude, which is the common one of our time both towards the symbolic formulations of 'primitive' peoples and towards the religious scriptures, one might say as the Jamaicans do of a stupid man who supposes himself intelligent : 'Him is so ignorant that him don't know him don't know.' The symbolic and analogical modes of thought which were natural to our remote ancestors and are still natural to certain archaic peoples are regarded as primitive in the evolutionary sense of the term, that is, as lacking in something that has since been acquired in the way of understanding. People speak of 'pre-logical' modes of thought, implying that those who employed such modes were incapable of the full exercise of reason and therefore a little less than human.

There is, however, a totally different view that might be taken of such matters and of our modern incapacity to think in the concrete and synthetic terms of symbols and analogy. According to this view, the transformation of symbols into rational concepts and into the ABC of explicit doctrines is to be regarded, not as an evolutionary advance, but as a concession to man's diminishing aptitude for grasping any truth in its totality, its variety of aspects and its suprarational richness and density of meaning. It is the fool rather than the intelligent man who needs to have everything explained to him.

As Frithjof Schuon has pointed out on a number of occasions, the explicit doctrine is already inherent in the symbolic formulation. Its deployment in terms of discourse and argument adds nothing to it and can never exhaust its meaning. Indeed, when the majority of people have begun to take symbols literally so that it becomes necessary to state in conceptual form what was previously implicit, there is an unavoidable impoverishment of meaning in the process of fitting it to the rigid limitations of human language. In our time learned men find it necessary to write whole books to explain the significance of one symbol in all the variety of its implications. 'And if all the trees in the earth were pens and the sea, with seven more seas to help it, were ink, the words of God could not be exhausted.'*

Symbols are, in the first place, things. Our understanding of them depends upon our capacity for seeing the elements of our environment as they really are (or in terms of what they mean) rather than as they appear in terms of human appetite. And the essential truth, says Schuon, 'is that everything, each thing, each energy by the fact that it exists . . . represents a possible entry towards the Real.'† The process whereby the environment gradually congeals or loses its quality of transparency, until things are no more than objects which can either be put to practical use or else be kicked aside when they get in our way, is the same as the process whereby symbols are drained of meaning and reduced to the level either of poetic allegory or of 'primitive science'. For modern man, only the objects of sense appear unquestionably real, while everything else is either 'subjective' or 'abstract'. For archaic man, reality resides not in the object as such but in what it signifies; stripped of this significance it is a shadowy thing on the verge of non-existence.

We are free, being what we are, to regard such a view as false, but we only make fools of ourselves if we dismiss it without even troubling to ask what it is all about and without considering—if only for a moment—the possibility that we might be wrong. For this is the only heritage we have. Our human past has nothing else to offer us. And before we resign ourselves to abject poverty (comforted, no doubt, by the forlorn hope that science will eventually make us rich) we might do well to recall Pascal's question as to whether the heir to a fortune would ever think of dismissing his title-deeds as forgeries without troubling to examine them. Folly, however, is more often the symptom of a vice than of a lack of intelligence, and it is not uncommon for arrogance to induce a wilful blindness. If 'history is bunk' and our human past a tale of ignorance and superstition, then we might claim to be giants; but if we are the heirs of men who were nobler than us and knew more than we do, then we are pygmies and must bow our heads in shame.

* Qurān, 31:27.
† *Images de l'Esprit:* Frithjof Schuon, p. 100.

There is no virtue in the accumulation of factual knowledge for its own sake, but once men have wandered outside the normal limitations of the knowledge that is useful to them in terms of their spiritual and physical needs, then it becomes necessary, not to bring them back to the limited perspective (which is impossible since history cannot be reversed), but to balance the scraps of knowledge they have picked up as a dog picks up stray bones with an awareness of truths which set these scraps in their proper context.

What possible relevance can the habits of some ancient people or of an Australian aboriginal tribe have to the lives of people in modern Europe or America? None, until the latter have strayed outside their own world and begun to concern themselves with such things. But once this concern exists it may lead us to a region of false ideas which devastate our homeland—like deadly bacteria brought back from outer space—unless they can be rectified in terms of a perspective wider than any that is provided by a purely local viewpoint. If we insist upon knowing about things which are, from the practical point of view, none of our business, then we have to grow a few inches to accommodate this strange knowledge. Otherwise our capacity for comprehending the world, our world, as a whole that makes sense may burst at the seams.

The ordinary Christian of earlier times did not need to know that God has spoken in many languages and through a great variety of masks. The disturbing fact that the vessels in which this Speech is preserved are necessarily relative in character was irrelevant to his salvation, for he was securely lodged in a religious context that fulfilled his real needs, answered his questions and provided him with his bridge to eternity.

All that concerned him was to perfect and intensify his own way to God, making use of the entirely adequate doctrinal and ritual supports available to him. The knowledge that there existed alternative ways, equally effective for those to whose habits and patterns of thought they were adjusted, could not have helped him in this task. And if, through ignorance, he assumed that his own faith was the only truth and that such others as he might hear of through travellers' tales were necessarily false, this did no harm. It was when the geographical barriers came down and the Europeans—first Christian and, later, ex-Christian—fanned out over the globe that the situation changed radically.

'No blame can be attached to a person for attacking a foreign Tradition in the name of his own belief if it is done through ignorance purely and simply', says Schuon; 'when however this is not the case, the person will be guilty of a blasphemy, since by outraging the Divine Truth in an alien form he is merely profiting by an opportunity to offend God without having to trouble his own conscience. This is the real explanation of the gross and impure zeal displayed by those who, in the name of religious conviction, devote their lives to making sacred things appear odious . . .'* A study of certain aspects of Christian missionary endeavour suggests that there was indeed a 'gross and impure zeal' at work. This zeal has now been intensified in the service of the pseudo-religion of progress.

So long as a particular religion is contained and insulated in its own world (the frontiers of which have been determined by geographical or racial factors), the arguments and dogmas upon which the faith of the majority of believers is based can remain, in the precise sense of the term, parochial. Their narrowness and their vulnerability to any criticism founded upon a more sophisticated knowledge (or more rigorous logic) than is provided by the parish worthies does not matter so long as they are effective, that is to say, if they open windows onto the truly universal. They can only do this if they are—within the limits of certain terms of reference—adequate representations of the truth, but such representations do not need to be very subtle or very comprehensive so long as they serve to awaken that which is already present at the centre of man's being or, from another point of view, to open his heart to the action of Grace.

But religious dogmas are particularly vulnerable to those who, instead of using them as stepping-stones to a forgotten but still recoverable knowledge, sit down to examine and analyse their structure. Dogmatic doctrine cannot be more than an *aide-memoire*. It collapses when treated as though it were a scientific statement, for what it represents cannot be stated in the way that the laws which govern the movements of the planets or the formation of crystals are stated. The latter belong to our own level of existence and may be expressed in the language of our kind, whereas the truths towards which dogmas (like symbols) point

* *The Transcendent Unity of Religions:* Frithjof Schuon (Faber and Faber), p. 28.

the way are not reducible to any of the dimensions of relativity. They will not come down to us, except in the form of intimations—bait for the spirit not yet entirely submerged in the glassy depths. It is we who are required to go to that central place where they reside in their essential fullness. The certainty that we are able to do this is among the basic certainties upon which the religions, as well as the primordial doctrine, have built their castles. When this is lost sight of—and the innermost room of the castle is locked up—religion loses its *raison d'être* and falls into decay.

And of course we lose sight of this certainty. It gets buried under the debris of the centuries. But the innermost room is still there and the lock will still turn though the key may be rusty; for the reservoir of grace which is the luminous centre of every Revelation is timeless, immune from the process of decay which erodes its temporal outworks. God does not retreat: it is we who go away.

Our absence (carried downstream from our spiritual home) has been, according to traditional teaching, the occasion for the great religious Revelations which, if they could not outwardly and objectively restore the primordial harmony—for Paradise lost is not regained at the same level of existence—at least made possible an inward and spiritual restoration which might be reflected in the environment so far as the circumstances of the time permitted; and indeed the tales common to Christianity, Islam and Buddhism of the transformation of matter (or of concord between men and beasts) in the presence of the saints suggests that the environment has been restored to something of its primordial perfection at such moments. But the very fact that these moments have to be described as miraculous reminds us that time goes on.

It is as ferry-boats equipped to carry men across the stream of time (rather than as dams blocking the stream) that the world's religions have provided the means of salvation. What men are to be saved from is fragmentation, dismemberment and dispersal in multiplicity, and what they stand to lose in such a process of fragmentation is their real identity as human beings. The unity which a particular religion imposes upon its people is necessarily somewhat rigid, at least in its outward forms, but this is the nature of ferries, and it is only as rigid structures that they can serve their purpose. The fact that one religion forbids what another permits, or that sexual and alimentary regulations are not the same for all, in no way undermines the validity of these rules in their own context, as parts of a single, seaworthy structure which has been built in the light of a particular religious perspective. The perspective determines the blueprint and the method of construction, while the given environment provides the materials.

Those in our time who assert their right to approach God 'in their own way' and condemn all organised religion seem unaware that, even if they themselves are capable of making this approach (as, in the nature of things, some few might be), they are also asserting the right of other men to drown and perhaps condemning them to drowning. The question one must ask is not whether the possibility exists of a man breaking through to Reality on his own, without the assistance of traditional supports and a religious framework, but whether this in fact happens save in the most exceptional cases. The answer to the first question would necessarily be in the affirmative, since it deals only with possibilities and 'with God all things are possible'. But the second can only receive a negative answer. This is what matters. Churches and temples are necessary, not because God is what he is, but because we are what we are. Though present everywhere, he is most easily found wherever a particular religious crystallisation has, like a burning glass, focused the rays of his Grace.

Such words as 'structure' and 'crystallisation' suggest something rather more concrete than an ideal or an aspiration. As we have seen, the life of archaic peoples is so thoroughly determined by their myths, symbols and rituals that what happens outside this sacred framework can hardly be said to exist. For them there can be no opposition between sacred and profane, since they are unacquainted with the profane. Given the conditions of a later time and the increasing remoteness of our world from its divine source, the world's religions have had to face this opposition, although the extent to which they have acknowledged its existence varies greatly. The orthodox Hindu has much in common with archaic man and is scarcely aware of a profane sphere set over against his ritual practice. The Muslim who still lives in a tight-knit Islamic community knows the same cohesion of life-in-the-world with religious life. The case of Christianity is quite different.

The Hindus never questioned the subordination of the temporal power to the spiritual, and Islam brought its own corner of the world under the divine Law revealed in the Qurān. But Christianity came into being in a hostile environment which was therefore by definition profane. Unlike Hindus or Muslims, Christians were immediately in contact with things that were not sacred and had to compromise with the profane sphere (or suffer martyrdom).

Since the Christian religion did not contain within itself rules of conduct and of political organisation such as are set out in the Hindu scriptures and in the Qurān, it had to assimilate much of its worldly structure from the Hebraic environment into which it was born and from the Roman environment in which it grew to maturity. Even at the height of its power, when Christendom was mighty and unified, a distinction was admitted between the spiritual and the temporal (therefore profane) spheres which would have seemed intolerable to Muslims at the time when the Islamic civilisation was at its zenith.

It was always more natural to Christians than to others to suppose that there were aspects of human life which lay outside the immediate orbit of religion. These things could be kept in order— or neutralised—so long as men acted as good Christians in relation to them, but they did not in themselves belong to the sphere of the sacred. Through this loophole, unimportant so long as the majority of Westerners thought primarily in terms of being good Christians, has crept the entirely profane world of our age which goes its own way while permitting the survival of religion as a personal matter— so long as it does not interfere in more important domains.

Personal faith is one thing, religion another. The two are intimately bound up with one another, but the distinction must be made. A man may pursue a spiritual path in isolation from his social and economic environment, but the very idea of religion implies the incorporation of the public realm in a spiritually determined pattern so that not just a man but all men are assisted towards their goal by everything they do and everything they touch in the normal course of their daily lives. The ferry-boat is a world in itself, an ark supplied with all the necessities of life.

Things break away. First one aspect of living claims autonomy, then another, building themselves their own little ships; but these are ships constructed for sailing downstream, in accordance with the direction of time, not for crossing over. Politics, science, industry, art and literature go their way, each proudly independent of everything except the current itself and their own increasing momentum. Until finally one more little ship is added to the flotilla calling itself, perhaps, 'Religion Adapted to the Needs of

Our Time', equipped with certain regulations governing the personal life and a cargo of ideals. Somehow it never quite manages to keep up with the rest. Possibly some memory tugs at it, against the pull of the stream, or the strangeness of its cargo sets it apart.

To question the usefulness of any attempt to adapt religion to what are supposed to be the needs of our time is not to decry the intrinsic value of personal piety or, indeed, to underestimate the nobility of those who live a 'Christian life' in the contemporary context; what is questionable is the propriety of diluting truth for the sake of meeting error halfway and of applying evolutionary theory to the marks of eternity embedded in the matrix of the temporal world. To put the point bluntly, if God wished to speak to the modern world it may be supposed that he would find a way of doing so. There is a limit to how far men can go in interpreting the divine Word in terms of a language from which all the appropriate words have been excluded. If people have gone away from the central place that is their real home, then charity requires that they should be shown the way back. To imagine one can take the centre out to them—while they stay where they are—is folly.

The effort to make religion—and in this case it is Christianity with which we are specifically concerned—acceptable to as many people as possible has a way of defeating its own object. This has happened to a striking degree in the Protestant countries, where Christianity has too often been reduced to a matter of morality and idealism. But there are two quite separate factors which come together to undermine faith.

In the first place, there has been the refusal to admit that the very structure of contemporary life excludes religion, being profane in root and branch, and that there is no way in which Christianity could be integrated into this structure as it stands. Almost everything that is said and done in the modern world implicitly assumes the non-existence of any other dimension than the profane one. People imagine that this merely represents an attitude of neutrality towards religion. They are wrong. To exclude religion is to deny it, for all religion stands or falls on the claim that divine reality cannot be excluded from any corner of existence. The *more real* takes precedence over the *less real;* it dominates the latter. In order for that which is less real to escape this subordination it must refuse to recognise that there is any other reality but its own. A dreamer cannot hold onto his dream by telling himself that it is just as real as waking life; he can do so only by keeping his eyes closed and refusing to wake up.

Secondly, Protestants have to a large extent cast aside the metaphysical and intellectual heritage of Christianity for the sake of appealing to 'ordinary' people, and the Catholic Church now seems ready to follow their example. These 'ordinary' people may not be greatly concerned with intellectual considerations, but those from whom they take their cue—those who, in the long run, tell them what to think—are very much concerned with these considerations. There is a bitter irony here; Christianity has been simplified and de-intellectualised to make it more attractive to the majority, but instead of gratefully accepting this watered-down religion, the majority have looked to the more sophisticated and more intellectually demanding minority for guidance. The latter, after one glance at the pap that is offered, have rejected it.

This is, in itself, an over-simplification. There are members of the intellectual elite who have gone to the trouble of rediscovering the metaphysical roots of the Christian religion and have become convinced of its truth, while others have been content to go down on their knees in simple faith before the *mysterium tremendum* and have been surprised by joy. But it cannot be denied, particularly in this age of mass media, that a Church which does not or will not appeal to the leaders of opinion must sooner or later lose the masses. In our time the ignorance of Christian doctrine and of Christian symbolism displayed by otherwise highly educated people is so abysmal that one must assume they were never told anything more of Christianity than a simple-minded missionary might see fit to tell supposedly simple 'savages'. They cannot be said to have rejected religion. They have never heard of it.

Christianity or, for that matter, any other religion is completely at the mercy of the scientific point of view (understood in the crudest sense) as soon as its metaphysical and mystical dimensions are forgotten. But what is attacked and so easily destroyed is the religion of tiny tots, Sunday School Christianity. And the attack is met with Sunday School arguments which never dare to hint that terror encompasses a world which goes astray and that man is never a forgotten creature who might slip away into the comfortable darkness unobserved.

Although God has said to the Islamic world, 'My Mercy takes precedence over my Wrath', Muslims have never imagined that Wrath is abolished by its ultimate subordination to an all-embracing Mercy. Christianity however has drifted—partly in reaction to the hell-raising fulminations of preachers in the eighteenth and early nineteenth centuries—into a situation in which God is defined entirely in terms of the nicest human qualities, and anthropomorphic symbolism, true and necessary in its proper context, is taken so literally that it become indefensible. From this has come the bitterness of those who are unable to forgive God for not being a Christian as they were taught to understand the term, the anger of men betrayed by those whom they most trusted, the pathetic blasphemies of people who—seeing a sick world around them—ascribe its creation to a sick deity while, in the same breath, denying that any deity exists. Meanwhile, the gentle teachers of the good child's religion go gently on their way.

Since the perfect man was created in the image of God, it follows that his very existence proved the human Face of God and justifies the use of anthropomorphic images. But we go beyond this and tend to ascribe the qualities and limitations of fallen humanity to the deity, reducing the Absolute to humanoid proportions.

From the Catholic point of view, Thibon has written eloquently concerning 'the simple tale of the creation of God by man'. Dazzled by transcendence and otherness, it is natural that we should try to confine the divine nature within the most accessible of its multitudinous aspects and envisage God as Man writ large. The tiger no doubt knows a tigerish deity, and among men it is only those who have sloughed off the impediments of humanity and achieved within themselves a kind of total nudity who may know God otherwise than through their own image; but what is seen through this tinted glass is nonetheless there (for there is nothing positive that is not *there*), and the humanised image serves as a bridge to a region beyond all created images, provided it is recognised as a bridge.

The danger is that it may be mistaken for a stopping-place rather than a point of departure, and this is a danger to which Christianity in modern times seems to have been particularly exposed. Europeans have always been rather simple minded (as were the ancient Romans) and peculiarly inclined to take the symbol for the thing symbolised, attempting to reduce all that *is* to manageable proportions. They have finally reduced the Absolute to the dimensions of an Old Man in the Sky and are horrified to discover what a useless (and amoral) Old Man this is.

It is time to remember our heritage and to become alert to the ancient wisdom, to look upwards and to look within. The answers are always there, undisturbed by time, in the primordial gift of reminiscence, in all that is above us and, here and now, within our own deepest selfhood. We have only to look in the right direction.

# 8

## WHAT WE ARE AND
## WHERE WE ARE

Contemporary thought dismisses as naive or childish a great many of the beliefs which our ancestors regarded as essential elements of Christianity; but there is one particular notion which has been cast aside in anger and indignation. This is the doctrine that human acts have repercussions far beyond the frontiers of the human world and may provoke, in the very nature of things, reactions which our language defines in terms of punishment and suffering. In earlier times the process whereby these consequences come home to roost was seen as a divine Judgment and this suffering was described in the picturesque imagery—necessarily borrowed from the conditions of our own familiar world—of the pains of hell.

How could the God of the Sunday Schools allow his decent, well-meaning children to suffer in perpetuity for faults and weaknesses which are 'only human' and which, in any case, very often derive from environmental factors rather than from the ill will of the sinner? Obviously he could not. But then one is logically compelled to ask how he can permit many other things which do, undeniably, exist: war and oppression, the early death of loved ones, cancer and the wide spectrum of mental and physical 'handicaps'. If, as no one can deny, people suffer pain and grief in this world, then it is clearly illogical to maintain—as do some modern Christians—that God could not permit suffering to exist elsewhere.

Muslims, although by no means immune to modernism, have on the whole had less difficulty in reconciling the vicissitudes of earthly existence both with the divine Power and with the divine Mercy. They have been less disposed to fall into the trap which awaits those who push anthropomorphic symbolism to its extreme limit. 'Glorified be God with a Glory remote from all representations of him': this is one of the basic themes of Islam. Remote from the representation of a good man writ large and infinitely remote from the Dear Old Man in the Sky. Being human we have need of images as rungs on a ladder leading to That which is ultimately without image, incomparable; but when we try to rest too heavily upon these supports their provisional character becomes apparent.

The fear of hell has made countless men and women turn round, face their true goal and move towards it when, but for this fear, they might have wandered away into the shadows. If fear sets a man on the path to safety and towards the recognition of his real identity, then fear has a useful function; and, since human responsibility exists and acts do have owners to whom their consequences relate, there are indeed things to be feared (who, among the living, could doubt this?) and there is no deception in the imagery of fire and brimstone. It is, however, an imagery that suggests punishment coming exclusively from outside ourselves, quite alien to all that we are. In an age in which men are already profoundly alienated from their roots and from their world, this imagery threatens a further alienation, not because it is inherently false but because it is readily misunderstood by those who have lost all sense of unity and inter-connection.

Since the idea of responsibility carries little weight if it is confined entirely to the social realm and since any extension of responsibility beyond this realm implies that supernatural consequences attach to human acts, we need to be reminded that, in religious terms, we are judged, not by some alien despot who rules—or misrules—the universe, but by the Norm inherent within us.

'Fire will invade, envelop all,' says Thibon, writing from the Catholic point of view: 'All will be judged from within and, so to say, by its own self'.* 'Whosoever sins, sins only against himself,'† says the Qurān; and again, 'Read thy book. Thy soul suffices as a reckoner against thee this day.'‡ In every religious context we find the doctrine that divine Judgment (under whatever name it goes) is neither more nor less than the stripping away of every kind of falsehood and self-deception, with a consequent exposure of what we really *are*. Our identity had been mercifully veiled from us— this was our freedom and our opportunity to exercise responsibility

* *L'Echelle de Jacob:* Gustave Thibon, p. 94.
† Qurān, 4:3.
‡ Qurān, 17:14.

within our own field—but at the last the veils are drawn away, the comedy is over, and we face ourselves.

Our actions are the outward sign of what we are. This is their chief significance and this is why a change in a man's basic nature— 'repentance'—is said to free him from the burden of his past sins, however black they may have been. Those who regard as absurd the notion that a man could deserve supernatural punishment for some apparently trivial sin are right, so long as the situation is defined in this way. But it is not the sin that is punished. It is the profound inner warping which betrayed itself through this sin that stands revealed—and is to be measured against the Norm—when time and obscurity are brought to an end.

And yet our acts can never be disowned, any more than we can disown our limbs. 'This Day', says the Qurān, 'We seal up mouths; and hands speak out and feet bear witness to their acts.'* As was suggested earlier, the distinction commonly made between a hard core of individuality and the web of action within which it operates is a convenient but superficial distinction. The person as a whole, as the manifestation of a particular pattern in time and space, is not subject to chance or accident; whatever happens to him and—most important of all, in view of contemporary efforts to exempt from responsibility those who act 'under orders' —everything in which he takes part is an aspect of his total nature. The paradox in which human reason can find no reconciliation lies in the fact that this total nature, though already complete beyond our existential context, is—from our point of view and in our experience—in the process of formation, still malleable, still alterable. And our experience represents something inherent in the nature of reality. We do not merely have an illusion of freedom. We are free, but only relatively so. Absolute freedom is a quality that belongs to God alone.

There is no need to labour this riddle, for no amount of twisting and turning in the corridors of reason will solve it; but the emphasis upon experience—our consciousness of happenings, together with the ideas and feelings which they provoke—is essential to an understanding of what the traditional doctrines have meant by 'hell'. 'The damned souls are in Paradise', said Simone Weil, 'but for them Paradise is Hell'. It is in rather the same paradoxical spirit that the Zen Buddhists tell us that this present world of

* Qurān, 36:64.

space and time (and suffering) is none other than the timeless Nirvana. Hell is not a locality but a state of being and therefore, in our terms, a state of experience. The experience, perhaps, of the intractably imperfect in the presence of the Norm from which it has departed and to which it refuses to return. The damned soul, says Thibon, is 'an essentially refractory being, for ever consumed by flame and for ever powerless to become flame.'

Hell is an alienation so extreme that the only way in which the damned can experience their own totality is in terms of pain. Like the madman convinced that the person who loves him most is his deadliest enemy or like the victim of hydrophobia who dies in an agony of thirst though water is at hand, the damned are meshed in an evil dream which disguises the most benign objects in shapes of terror and malignancy. This infernal state is the result (from our point of view, here and now) of a misuse of our relative freedom, a refusal not only to be what we are—in terms of our Norm—but also to accept the burden imposed upon us as responsible beings and to face the fact that our actions and their consequences have a significance far beyond the narrow field in which they are initiated.

'Since we are "not other" than the Self,' says Schuon, 'we are condemned to eternity. Eternity lies in wait for us, and that is why we must find again the centre, that place where eternity is blessedness. Hell is the reply to the rim which makes itself centre or to the multitude which usurps the glory of Unity; it is the reply of Reality to the ego which wants to be absolute . . .' We are condemned to totality because no amount of wishful thinking and no amount of theorising, no sheltering under the earth's weight and no act of self-destruction, can make us less than we are. We can only pretend to be other than viceregal creatures with a viceregal responsibility, and this is the pretence that is to be stripped away on the Day of Judgment.

According to Martin Buber, 'The greatest evil is to forget that thou art the son of a King'. This forgetfulness is closely bound up with the desire of the human 'ego' to set itself up as a false absolute (on however petty a scale), which is why it has even been suggested that hell contains only those who prefer to be where they are and reject the offer of release. So it is sometimes said in Islam that the souls in hell enjoy, each of them, some particular pleasure or apparent advantage which roots them in their condition of misery, unwilling to break out of this dark dream and face the light.

In denying or forgetting his viceregal identity—his divine ancestry—man loses a dimension of his being, but through this amputation he gains an illusion of self-sufficiency and of freedom from responsibility, a robber baron who no longer recognises that his castle is held in fief and that he has an account to render. This deceptive freedom has made possible the development of contemporary science and technology and has led to the unprecedented exploitation of the natural world (both animate and inanimate). It has enabled modern man to commit monstrous crimes against his fellows and against his environment (therefore ultimately against himself) without any awareness of guilt so long as he has been acting as massman, as a member of an organised multitude 'doing his duty'. Yet this has in no way freed him from an obsessive sense of guilt in his personal life, as an individual acting alone, indeed there has never been a greater fear of taking risks than there is among the bourgeoisie of our time.

The exercise of human responsibility may well involve the readiness to take tremendous risks and to assume an unavoidable burden of guilt; but this burden is intolerable only so long as we refuse to see it as a condition of our existence. The soldier who kills because he is commanded to do so and the civil servant administering regulations which cause harm and suffering imagine themselves exempt from responsibility—'I didn't make the rules!' —without being able to say to whom their acts belong, if not to themselves, and imagining that so long as they are in uniform or dressed for the office they are less than men.

Do they suppose that responsibility rests solely with those who give them their orders? They are servants of God, not of their fellow men; and if they obey their fellow men this is their choice, and the responsibility is theirs. 'I had no power over you,' says Satan in the Qurān, 'except that I called to you and you obeyed me; so blame me not, but blame yourselves.'*

The Christian tradition has given an intensely emotional flavour to ideas of sin and guilt, partly by taking the view that the sinner is hurting a loving Saviour through such acts of disobedience and partly by the emphasis it has placed upon the fatherhood of God, so that emotions derived from childhood situations attach to the sins of the adult. This emotional attitude, perfectly in place within

* Qurān, 14:22.

the body of the Church, has persisted among those who are no longer Christians and for whom, therefore, there can be no confession, no expiation and no forgiveness. In the Christian guilt may be an aspect of health; in the ex-Christian it is often a sickness.

Awareness of guilt in the sense of a personal, intellectual recognition of what we are and where we are is the beginning of realism and of the knowledge that we are responsible beings. But guilt as an emotional condition tends to be at once paralysing (so far as the individual is concerned) and destructive (in terms of human relationships); it is in essence a feeling of alienation. Whereas the intellectual awareness of guilt is essentially a recognition that we are not what we should be; that we misuse our powers and misrule our kingdom. In Christianity it is bound up with the knowledge of an original sin constantly sustained, in Islam with the knowledge that the compact made by all souls 'when they lay within Adam's loins' has been broken, and in Hinduism with the doctrine of 'karma' and of the chain of actions and reactions which has brought us to this twilight place. To say that we should be better than we are reduces the question to the level of moralism and sentimentality. What we should be is other than we are, more truly ourselves in terms of our own Norm.

But since we can only start from where we are and only initiate action in the place in which we find ourselves, it is as sick men that we begin our work and the world with which we have to deal is a ruined paradise. Perfection is far off and, under the circumstances in which good is inextricably mixed with ill and every light projects a shadow, none but the saints can act responsibly without incurring some further burden of guilt.

What is required of us is not that we should try to achieve an impossible purity of action but that we should learn to discriminate between the relative goods presented to us as our field of operation, situating each thing in its place and at its proper level in the total order, reconnecting where connection has been broken and reuniting where unity has been shattered. This we can do only if we are prepared to understand our real situation and, at the same time, to turn our faces towards our own true centre and, by focusing our attention upon it, begin to draw the scattered elements of our present circumstances towards it.

Man is committed at birth to two journeys (or to journeying on two different levels). The first he cannot escape, for this is the journey of action and experience as he travels down the stream of his own lifetime and creates, as a man of his period (localised in time and space), a story which expresses, in this particular mode, his ultimate identity or the human possibility which is the reason for his existence.

The second journey, which can—at least in a certain sense— be avoided, is upstream, using time and locality only as starting points, leading beyond their zone. This is the journey described in countless myths and legends, the arduous, perilous way towards the centre of being, the passage from the ephemeral and illusory towards the eternally real. In terms of universal myths, it was to provide a landscape for this journey that the monster 'Chaos' was slain and an ordered world raised from the waters, and it was to provide a negotiable way through this landscape that the prophets laboured, Christ died and Muhammad led the people of the City into battle in the Arabian wastes.

In a normal society the circumstances of the first journey provide supports for the second, and it was man's aim in the past to build and maintain a physical and social environment in which every element had a dual character, existing as a 'thing' in terms of the first journey, standing as a symbol and signpost in terms of the second.

For a very long time now the routes of these two journeys have been diverging, and it is not by chance that the last of the great, world-transforming Revelations laid such particular emphasis upon the duty of pilgrimage. The pious Muslim on his way to Mecca is like a dancer who, by the steps he takes towards the physical symbol of all centrality, acts out the drama of his own inner, timeless journey, just as, in his obligatory prayers, he creates a tiny area of consecrated territory—confined to the dimensions of his prayer-mat—in an environment that has become almost totally profane. From this point of view it might be said that the sacred rules of Islam were specially designed to protect the traveller in a world which no longer offers him any foothold.

But the fact that the two paths have now diverged so far that they can scarcely any longer be related to each other is not, in the last analysis, a senseless accident. The human world, being what it is, could only decay in the course of time, but, since decay is itself a necessary aspect of a larger pattern and since there are possibilities which can only find existential expression in such a context as ours, this is where we belong. We live out our lives here and now (rather than in some paradisal environment) because it is our nature to be where we are. And we are told that there are compensations available to such as us which were not available to the less degenerate men of earlier times. 'You are in an age in which, if you neglect one-tenth of what is ordered, you will be condemned,' the Prophet of Islam told his Companions, 'but after this a time will come when he who observes one-tenth of what is now ordered will be saved.'

Modern man is weak, not to say feeble, and he is at the same time subject to pressures and to temptations unknown to the people of earlier times. Moreover he lives in an environment so hostile to religion and to the sacred in its terrestrial forms that divine Justice must allow for this and we cannot be judged by the standards which might fairly be applied to our ancestors, living, as they did, in an environment in which it was 'natural' to be religious. But if the wind is tempered to the shorn lamb and if we have a quite special claim to Mercy, there is still one vice, sin or crime which excludes the possibility of forgiveness, and this is refusal of the Mercy offered us. One might say that we are like drowning men to whom a hand is held out. If we refuse to recognise this hand for what it is and will not grasp it, then there is no hope for us.

The great revealed religions and the truths inherent in the ancient traditions of humanity are, by definition, 'a mercy to mankind'. So, to a lesser degree, are the saints and men of true piety. So also is the sacred in all its ramifications, whether in the form of temples and sanctuaries built by hand or in the splendour and beauty of virgin nature. To scorn sanctity when we find it among men or to defile the sacred is therefore the gravest form of what Christians call the sin against the Holy Ghost. It is to trample Mercy underfoot.

Here, in human terms, we meet with a paradox. The relative can make no impact upon the Absolute. Man, however much he may blaspheme or rebel, can do no injury to God. But the manifestations of Mercy in this world are, of necessity, more fragile than their author. The sacred is vulnerable. We have to tread very carefully upon this earth, for it is scattered with the signs of divine Mercy. We have to be aware of the wonders that surround us and take care not to damage them, both for our own sakes and for the sake of others who might find their salvation here or there, among the little things which are so easily destroyed.

On the one hand there are these 'little things' in which Mercy lies half-concealed; on the other, the daily trivialities which seem so important to the men of our time and which they cherish with blind devotion. What is required of us is an act of discrimination between gold and straw, between sacred and profane; required of us precisely because it is our nature to be capable of this act. And, in a world encumbered with distractions, such discrimination becomes increasingly necessary. The further the world moves from its source and is stripped—or appears to be stripped—of supernatural meaning, the greater the necessity to concentrate our attention upon essentials. For creatures who are here so short a time, whose powers decay just as they are learning to use them and who die long before they are ready to go, there cannot be many essentials. In our situation very little matters, but that little matters enormously.

The complexity of modern life is a surface complexity in that most of the strands which compose it are woven from artificial needs, unreal obligations, trivial ambitions and, above all, glossy but unsatisfying substitutes for the few things really necessary to the accomplishment of the human journey (in either of its aspects).

The hostility of all religions to 'riches', their praise of 'poverty', is to be understood primarily in a spiritual sense and is closely related to archaic man's indifference to actions and events which do not bear the stamp of That Time, the stamp of eternity. In both cases it is the unreal—or the less real—that is to be feared in so far as it threatens to dissipate man's energies (and his capacity for giving attention) in the wilderness of quantity. And it is precisely by giving the whole weight of our attention—an attention so powerful that it is said to be capable of penetrating the veils which hide the light of heaven from us—upon the realm of quantity and relativity that we have been able to build the scientific and technological wonders of our age.

Anyone, any race, could have done it, given the willingness to make the Faustian sacrifice upon which the whole edifice depends. It happened to be the Europeans who first turned their backs upon the light in order to conjure marvels out of the darkness, but other races have lost no time in following suit; the notion that it is possible to have the best of both worlds is ludicrous, since human attention cannot be focused in two opposite directions.

In the long run, we can get no effective purchase on quantity. We are real and need to be matched with reality, whereas the realm of quantity (as opposed to the world of unique and significant objects) becomes increasingly shadowy as we pursue it down the corridors of time. The danger lies in the fact that the more shadowy and unrewarding this realm becomes, the more feverish is our pursuit of a satisfaction which constantly eludes us and the more involved we become in haste and hullabaloo. The search for pleni- tude in the region of number, the pursuit of reality among husks and fragments which have become no more than units in a num- bered sequence, is dissipation, and its final outcome can only be a fierce and despairing destructiveness. Everything disappoints and so everything must be punished for not giving us the satisfaction we crave. The thirst for the Absolute which is inherent in human nature is focused with a terrible and distorting power upon the partial and the fragmentary, and under the blaze of this attention even the most harmless objects are twisted into monstrous shapes, as though the sun were concentrated upon them through a burning glass.

Simone Weil speaks of the 'monotony of evil', and monotony is one of the chief characteristics of the realms of quantity: 'Nothing new—all here is equivalent.' Evil as we know it in action is closely bound up with certain typical reactions to monotony; on the one hand an almost manic overvaluation of particular relative goods for their own sake and, on the other, boredom and despair in the face of a state of existence without grandeur and without ultimate significance. The man who clothes trivial things in splendour and projects upon them his huge appetite for the real and the truly important is, in fact, father to the disillusioned cynic who perceives the hollowness of all such inflated goods but does not know how to go beyond this perception and refill the empty gourds. Thus we gravitate between an idealism which refuses to face facts and a cynicism incapable of penetrating beneath the surface of the factual.

Given the peculiar conditions of our time, there is a need for disillusionment. Illusions are sticky things and hold a man in their web, content when he should be discontented, happy to be where he is and unaware that any further journeying is required of him. In other periods, in protected environments, a certain optimism, a certain tendency to see the best in everything and to ignore the worm in the apple, did no harm at all; but in our case, hemmed in by so many illusions and led astray by phantoms, a recognition that the profane world as such is 'a tale told by an idiot, full of sound and fury signifying nothing' may be the beginning of wisdom and recall certain men to their responsibility for re-consecrating a desecrated environment.

But disillusionment when it is entirely passive, and when it represents little more than the angry disappointment of the greedy 'ego', issues only in despair. And despair, in the sense of a dead-end to journeying and a profound alienation from destiny, is more common than might be supposed. 'Mon cas n'est pas unique : j'ai peur de mourir et je suis navrée dê'tre au monde.'* The term 'navré' suggest something more subtle than grief. It suggests the boredom and disappointment of the soul which finds only monotony where it looked for splendour and dry wells where water should have flowed. But despair is not necessarily a state of constant unhappiness. There are a great number of men and women in our time who are quite without hope, in the Christian sense of the word, seeing only grey days ahead and a meaningless extinction when the grey days are done, but who are reasonably happy most of the time, find a certain satisfaction in their families and friendships and an even greater satisfaction in their work.

Yet they lead lives of quiet despair and are happy only on condition that they discipline their minds to reject disturbing or 'morbid' thoughts. Less enterprising—perhaps less courageous—than those who seek satisfaction in danger, narcotics or sexual adventures, they are determined to make the best of a bad job. But this is not good enough, and under such sober and sensible attitudes there runs a current of bitterness which comes to the surface when certain notes are struck or when quite trivial ambitions are thwarted. It is in this context that ambition is so dangerous ; not so much the great ambition which is focused upon power and glory, but the little ambitions which are adjusted to the rungs of a promotional ladder or to 'keeping up with the Joneses'. In the first place, these offer a palliative to despair at times when despair should be squarely faced and transcended. Secondly, they force a

* Opening words of the novel *La Bâtarde* by Violette Leduc.

man to take seriously occupations so trifling as to be unworthy of his full attention. Thirdly, they lead ever further into the realm of quantity, their goal a will-o'-the-wisp that constantly recedes. And finally they provide a handle by which men are all too readily manipulated.

In a highly competitive society trivial ambitions force us to devote all that we have it in us to give—and more than we have any right to give—to entirely local and profane tasks. A man cannot serve two masters. Our energies are limited (and our time is short), which is why they have to be contained and directed and why the human communities of earlier times were concerned that the tasks of the practical life should reflect and even embody the spiritual or ritual work through which we make our way towards the central place.

When the activities which keep the community in being, keep the wheels turning and provide for men's basic needs, take on the character of distractions, when they are irrelevant to any purpose beyond the immediate, practical one, then it becomes important that people should be frequently distracted from distraction (as, for example, the Muslim is by the prayers which interrupt his day's work) if they are not to be completely absorbed into natural process. We do not have the right to use ourselves up in profane tasks unless under the spur of hunger or some equally urgent natural necessity.

It may be said that there is nothing to prevent a man combining intense spiritual concentration with an extremely active life in the world; many of the saints, both Christian and Muslim, have done so. But this is quite beyond the capacities of the majority of people, and a view which ignores the incapacities of the majority is a totally impractical view. The social factors which compel the majority to give their best to their jobs compel them also to ignore everything outside and beyond these jobs. This being so, the price we pay for the comforts and advantages of contemporary civilisation is too high. We cannot afford them.

Perpetuating into adult life the young child's competitiveness among his siblings, a society in which a man's position depends entirely upon his own efforts and talents (and in which these efforts and talents must be fully applied throughout his working life) is precisely the kind of society required if all our energies are to be exploited in the production of social wealth. But this can only be a society in which all values are subordinated to the productive process. No one can rest without falling behind in the race ; but it is only in rest from activities of this kind that a man can pursue the 'second journey' or, in Christian terms, take care of his own salvation. And only by turning his back upon the realm of quantity and of quantitative rewards so that he faces the centre, the human Norm, can he exercise the responsibility which—as king of his small castle—he is born to exercise.

Compromise is possible in many fields, and the paradoxical nature of the world itself (so far distant from heaven, and yet not-other-than heaven in its ultimate essence) makes compromise a condition of human living. But there is one matter in which no compromise is possible. We are not two-headed creatures, we cannot face two ways at once, and sooner or later we have to choose in which direction our basic attention is to be focused. In the end it is not in terms of relative good or relative evil that a man is judged, but in terms of the direction in which he faces.

The fact that we are creatures made for choosing is no longer apparent to the majority of people. As has already been suggested, the modern world is dominated by a sense of fatality, the kind of fatality inherent in natural processes, and those who find fault with it do so chiefly on the grounds that it is not all it might be in terms of its own aims and ideals. Bettelheim's view that we have a simple choice between renouncing freedom and giving up the comforts of modern technology is not widely shared, difficult though it is to ignore the evidence that the free society and the technological society are mutually incompatible.

Living so much closer to the operations of cause and effect than we do and believing in supernatural rewards and punishments as the ultimate repercussions of the choice they made in the course of their lives, our ancestors could not doubt the significance of their own decisions. We have no such certainty. Believing that the consequences of what we do are confined to our own locality, and overwhelmed by the complexity of this place in which we find ourselves, we interpret significance in quantitative terms and value action only as a contribution to some form of corporate achievement.

This is bound to be the case so long as we regard ourselves as no more than clever animals dwarfed by the immensity of a hostile universe and as self-contained units dwarfed by the multitude. It seems that the decisions which shape the only world in which we believe are made by a very few people and that our contribution is at most an infinitesimal fraction of the decisive act.

It is not that we deliberately reject the normal, traditional view that one man's action may shake the very fabric of the heavens and the earth, that the descendant of Adam (before whom, according to the Qurān, the angels were commanded to bow down) cannot be merely a contributor, and that our responsibility is to God alone. There is no occasion to reject it, since people have forgotten that it was ever normal to our kind. This is the measure of our diminution from man to manikin, from priest-king to monkey.

The world overwhelms us by sheer size and multiplicity. Our environment crushes us. We are faceless in a mob which numbers billions. Yet all this matches with perfect correspondence the beliefs and mental climate of our time. The whole fabric of our world is, in a very real sense, a projection of our ideology and of what we are within ourselves. It exists because it is, basically, what we want; or, to state this more accurately, it is the objective crystallisation of our wants and of their inevitable consequences. It is the desert which faces those who turn their backs upon the Mountain. A single centrifugal force is at work both within the most intimate recesses of our nature and throughout the theatre in which our life's experience unfolds.

This process is, in one sense, inevitable. In another sense it can proceed only by our permission. The traditional doctrines saw creation itself as a centrifugal process moving ever further from its centre, outwards into the wilderness, downwards into the abyss, until it reaches its limit ('a fraction of a degree above absolute zero') and is, in cataclysmic fashion, caught up, redeemed, brought back. The process is necessary because there are elements in the totality of Perfection which can only manifest themselves in distant places, like small lights which could never be seen in the neighbourhood of the sun, and there are values which are made complete only when tested among the fragments of a dissolving world. But, according to these same doctrines, man is made not only for choosing but also for returning and for bringing back. He alone of all that is created can maintain a direct connection with the centre and, by penetrating the thickening layers of cloud, remain aware of sunlight. So long as he holds to this, his viceregal function, the fragments are kept whirling in meaningful patterns. Only when he lets go can chaos come again.

What the Muslims call the Holy War is in fact the opposition of the unified and God-centred man to the forces of dissipation and chaos both within and outside himself. Such warfare is likely, in our times, to provide a history of defeats and failures—at least so far as our environment taken as a whole is concerned—but this is precisely why we are told that less is expected of us than was expected of the men of earlier periods. Defeat does not matter, because it is by fighting this war that we become what we are, and the achievement of integrity is not dependent upon the quantitative and temporal outcome of the struggle. Our concern is only with doing what we are capable of doing. The rest is out of our hands.

Defeat is one thing, abdication another. And despair grows out of abdication rather than out of defeat. 'What is the good of . . .', 'What is the use of . . .', are the catchwords of an age which measures everything in terms of immediate and seemingly objective success. We have the presumption to believe that we can foresee the ultimate effects of our actions, and this belief makes us impotent. Deprived in this way of our true function as men, there is nothing to prevent our being carried away downstream with the other debris of a broken world.

Ours is not a time for impotence. The events of the past fifty years suggest that the process to which Western man committed himself some centuries ago is speeding up at an all but uncontrollable rate and that the moment—the point of no return on the curve of progression—beyond which no real choice will be possible (short of the madman's compulsive decision to break free) is fast approaching. The world we have made is closing in upon us, the pressures are mounting, and techniques whereby men can be reduced to a condition only fractionally different to that of automata are improved year by year. The 'developed' world, as it is so curiously called, with the 'developing' world close on its heels, now seems to be possessed by an impersonal force quite outside the reach of our will, a force which means to prevail, regardless of the transformation this requires in man's nature and in his status. Development, understood in this sense, obeys its own laws. They are not ours—or God's.

Yet it is only the little man meshed in this process, frightened of shadows, aware of his own weakness and dependence, who can stand up against the great wind. The big men will not help, for present circumstances must inevitably bring to power chiefly those who co-operate wholeheartedly with the course events are taking and lend themselves as ready instruments to the prevailing force. It is not in their nature to cry 'Stop!'.

According to certain traditions, the burden of personality, which is also the burden of viceregal responsibility, was offered around creation in That Time, the time of the beginnings, and was refused on every side—the very mountains are said to have trembled and fallen back in fear—until, at last, man accepted it. We are not free to lay the burden aside. Whether we know it or not, we are accountable for what happens to our province.

And this means that neither a lack of worldly power nor subordination to many masters in a giant organisation suffice to exempt us from the necessity for choosing or to save us from the consequences of our choice. The little man in a big world may think himself weak as a kitten, seeking only to 'get by' and glad that the necessity for making great decisions devolves, not upon him, but upon those others, whose orders he so readily obeys. He is deceived. Those others cannot bear his burden for him. He was born to it, having been born a man, and it is as much a part of him as his own flesh. Those who think they have some kind of right to a quiet life have come to the wrong place.

The most menacing among the tendencies now at work in the world—menacing, that is, to what remains of man's freedom of movement—depend upon a general conviction that our responsibility is limited on the one hand to the realm of personal relationships and, on the other, to doing our duty, understood in the sense of conscientiousness towards our employers and towards the organisation in which we work. Behind this there is also a sense of obligation to keep the wheels turning, and we are subjected daily to a flood of propaganda aimed at strengthening this sense of obligation and persuading us to play our part in the 'march of progress' and to adjust to the 'needs of the modern world'. The notion that each individual man is accountable, not merely for what he does 'of his own free will', but also for every action in which he participates or assists is destructive of these limitations and calls into question the nature of this obligation. It is totally incompatible with the mechanism of the modern age and, above all, with the process whereby an age of complete human abdication—already prefigured in the Socialist societies—may be brought into being.

Accountability does not really diminish in proportion to the size of the organisation in which a man is enmeshed; but the personal sense of accountability withers away. If three or four men band together in some enterprise, each will have at least a certain power of decision and a certain sense of responsibility for what is done. The larger the organisation, the less scope there is for decision and the easier it becomes to forget that the consequences of our acts relate to us personally and directly. All that seems to be required of us is conformity.

And yet the conformist has made a choice, even if it was little more than the choice of abdication, and he is accountable for what is done with his co-operation. When a number of men unite to commit a crime which results in killing, all stand equally accused of murder. They are treated by the Courts, not as though a single act had been fragmented and the responsibility for it parcelled out among them, but as though each, individually, was the one murderer. There can be no corporate ownership of human acts and no diminished responsibility when a man is acting in concert with others. We stand alone, each of us, burdened with all that we have done and all that has been made possible through our presence in a particular place at a particular time. This is an aspect of the grandeur of the human state, and this is what we are fit for; and from this there is no escape.

No escape, that is, at the worldly level and within the purely existential frame of reference; no escape so long as we think ourselves alone, abandoned and without refuge. If the matter rested there we would indeed be solitary stars in a firmament of darkness. But there are other dimensions than these.

'I take refuge', says the Muslims; 'I take refuge with Thee from the evil of my hearing and the evil of my seeing; from the evil of my tongue and from the evil of my heart and from the evil of my sexual life. I take refuge with Thee, O God, from unprofitable knowledge and from a heart without reverence, and from an ever-demanding self, and from unheard petition. I take refuge with Thee from hunger, the worst of bedfellows, and from treachery that ruins friendships, and I take refuge with Thee from the evil

suggestions of the breast and from the frustration of affairs . . .',
until the final cry which completes the circle: 'Behold, I take
refuge with Thy good pleasure from Thy wrath and with Thy
pardon from Thy punishment; and I take refuge with Thee from
Thyself.'*

This belongs to the border country, where the human creature
sets foot on the bridge provided. Beyond lies a less fearful region,
and the 13th century Muslim saint, the Lady Rābiya, prayed, 'My
Lord, eyes are at rest, the stars are setting, hushed are the movements of birds in their nests, of monsters in the deep. And Thou
art the Just who knows no change, the Equity that swerves not,
the Everlasting that passes not away. The doors of kings are
locked, watched by their bodyguards. But Thy door is open to
him who calls on Thee. My Lord, each lover is now alone with his
beloved. And I am alone with Thee.'†

The taking of refuge is from an imperfect world in which even
heavenly fruit is worm-eaten and from a selfhood pitted and
riddled with the same imperfection; and in this world the man who
depends upon his own strength, the self-reliant man, is inevitably
a pathetic figure. There are a thousand ways in which his strength
may be destroyed. It is a question only of the degree of pain, fear
or deprivation required to reduce him to abject weakness. 'There is
no force and no strength save in Allāh!' is among the most common of Muslim sayings, and to forget it is to put all one's weight
upon a matchwood crutch.

The place of refuge—and the source of all strength—is at the
centre, where the grim dichotomies are resolved and man is supplied with all the strength he needs; and the 'evil' from which
refuge is taken is not an evil inherent in human faculties or in
their objects. It is the quality of obscurity which clings like a cob-
web to these faculties and these objects in so far as they are fragmentary and incomplete in themselves unless their connection
with totality is constantly renewed. Only through prayer, understood in its widest sense and ranging from the highest contempla-
tion to the most desperate cry for help, is that connection made
and maintained. Only in prayer is man fully himself.

Since the centre is the place of unity and the source of all such

* Quoted by Constance Padwick in *Muslim Devotions* (published by
SPCK).
† ibid.

peace and strength as we can know in our experience here, on the periphery, it is also the source of love; love's only source. Already, in our human experience, the lover's eye participates in the unifying clarity which belongs to all central (as against peripheral) vision.

The fact that some may think that what they saw when their sight was clarified was an illusion, a mere gloss on the ugly data of practical experience, alters nothing. For a person or a thing is, in truth, what God sees; not what we see with a cold eye, an avaricious heart and a jaundiced temper. Recounting the tale of Layla and Majnun, the heroic lovers of Islamic tradition, Rumi tells how Layla was brought before the Ruler and how he said to her: 'Art thou she by whom Majnun was distracted and led astray? Thou art no better than other fair ones'. 'Be silent', she said, 'for thou art not Majnun!'

All that has been said of viceregal power and of that shabby King of the Castle who tends the crumbling walls while the waves eat them away and all that has been said about responsibility as a dimension of our lives which cannot be measured against the standards which this world provides pre-supposes a doctrine of man's nature in terms of which his everyday personality is no more than the tip of an iceberg. It assumes his rootedness in a central place untouched by the winds and the tides we know and implies that the castle over which he rules is important only for the patterns which it briefly embodies in sand.

Meanwhile the supposed masters of this world, the leaders who have fought their way to the top of the human pile (and must fight without respite to stay on top), are too enmeshed in the processes now at work to look up for a moment from their eighteen-hour-day labours and see where they are going. Responding as best they can to crisis following upon crisis, and faced with logistic and administrative problems which are becoming increasingly unmanageable, they cannot afford to cultivate the lover's eye or the vision of the God-centred man.

They are no less competent than the average man-in-the-street, whom they officially represent, but the demands made upon their time and energy would incapacitate better men than these and effectively prevent them from giving serious thought to any issue. Yet it is not necessity which makes these demands. They are galvanised into ceaseless activity by a fever for change which is self-generating and serves no purpose. More and more laws are made for the sake of law-making; more and more interference in every aspect of human life prevents anything from functioning in accordance with its own nature; solid buildings are pulled down so that shoddy ones may be put up, and everything is out-of-date by the time it is ready for use.

In the grip of this fever and seized by the momentum of the world's descending course, they pull their carts as blinkered horses, seeing nothing but the small stretch of road immediately ahead. To stop now, even to pause for breath, would bring the turning wheels to a halt. To attempt to reverse the process or to check its gathering momentum would be to destroy the modern world as we know it. So the process continues and its momentum increases.

Anyone who could fling himself out of the vehicle and, in some last sanctuary, stand at the still centre of the world might expect to hear a huge din of overheated metal fading into the distance, in the direction of nothingness; a juggernaut with its great load of human souls.

And still, in the midst of unprecedented change, flurry and pandemonium, the human situation remains what it always was. Man is still either Viceroy or usurper, still noble when he achieves beauty of form both within himself and in his environment, and still able to look upon Layla with the eyes of Majnun. And Truth is what it has always been: accessible, in varying degrees, to those who focus their attention, their love and their deepest hunger in the right direction.

To say that it is possible for man to have access to the truth and so to pass beyond the region of mere opinion is to take great risks. The tolerance so highly valued in a number of Western countries rests upon a kind of agreement that no one can really be sure of anything and that all sincere opinions should therefore be respected. This, at least, is the theory. In practice there are many opinions which are firmly censored, and anyone in Britain or the United States today who expresses views totally at variance with the contemporary climate of opinion soon comes up against the limits of 'tolerance'. The fact remains, however, that the ideology of our time cannot admit that some people may be right in an absolute sense and others may be totally wrong.

There are good reasons for this. It is no longer commonly believed that the world, with all its business, rests in the hands of God. People think that everything depends upon themselves, or at least upon chosen leaders no better than themselves; they see some of the dangers which surround us—not least that of physical annihilation in nuclear war—and hope that if we all keep very quiet, do nothing to 'rock the boat', and tolerate evil and error for the sake of peace (or *détente*) we may survive. Unfortunately this is not an attitude shared by enemies of the free society, who tend to regard peace as a strategem of war and recognise weakness when they see it.

At the root of the contemporary gospel of tolerance lies a conviction that our earthly life is all that matters and that the peaceful ordering of human society takes precedence over every other consideration. The priests who fixed their gaze beyond the temporal realm are gone. So are the knights, the warriors, who valued glory and honour above life itself. Only the bourgeoisie and the proletariat remain, and for them piggery and trough are the sole reality. In this context a man's worth can be assessed only in terms of his usefulness to the society in which he happens to find himself, regardless of whether that society has any intrinsic worth in terms of our ultimate end, our *raison d'être*.

Truth, by its very nature, disturbs the peace when it breaks in upon the realm of error and relativity, taking possession of human minds which are by definition partial, limited and easily swayed by passion. In West Africa the tale is told of a trickster divinity, Edshu, one of those trouble-makers found in a number of mythologies who set snares for the foolish and, at the same time, enlighten the wise. This same Edshu walked one day down the path between two fields wearing a hat that was red on one side, white on the other, green in front and black behind (these being, for the Yoruba people, the colours of the four directions or four compass points). The farmers watched him pass and, meeting that evening in the village, discussed the odd-looking stranger they had seen. 'A little fellow in a red hat,' said one. 'Red? Nonsense! It was a white hat.' Another:'Green!' And another: 'Black!' The farmers came to blows, each knowing himself to be right, and they were brought before the headman for judgment. Now Edshu revealed himself, complete with multi-coloured hat; deceptive dancer, trickster, prankster.

Until 'Edshu' reveals himself, can we blame men for fighting on behalf of their partial truths? Passionate attachment to a particular formulation (and for many temperaments there can be no faith without passion) often involves intolerance towards other, complementary formulations; but to replace this narrow fervour with a tolerance based on agnosticism and indifference to everything that really matters is to substitute a greater evil for a lesser one.

Good will does not require us to overestimate the intelligence of ordinary people, whether in the West or elsewhere. Stupidity exists. Stupid people exist, and it is pointless to pretend (from a misplaced principle of charity) that they do not or should not exist. Now it is undeniable that the stupid believer, unless he has a quite uncommonly gentle disposition, is intolerant by nature. At least this is preferable to his being a stupid unbeliever. He has got hold of the right end of the stick, even if he is incapable of understanding what kind of stick this is. So long as he holds to it he will be drawn to the right destination.

The man who has grasped one aspect of the truth, seeing—for example—that 'Edshu's' hat is red (or green, as the case may be) has made effective contact with reality. He may have a long way to go, but at least he is not marooned in the desert. If we tell him that he is indeed right, but only up to a point (certainly the hat is red, but it is also green) we may leave him so confused that he no longer knows true from false. A certain narrowness of view can have a protective function and therefore has a right to exist, but we pay a price for this in terms of human conflict.

The risk, the potentiality for disorder in the social realm, which is inseparable from faith in an absolute truth attaches also to the doctrine of viceregal responsibility. If jobholders and petty officials are to take it upon themselves to question (whether inwardly or actively, according to circumstances) the orders they receive and the policies they are required to implement, we are indeed on dangerous ground. How is the machine to function unless its servants put aside all personal judgment and all sense of individual responsibility?

One can only reply that the question is irrelevant. We were not created to make such a machine work or to behave as automata in a collectivity. It is essential that first things should be put first. A civilisation which does not obey this simple and obvious rule—

within the limits of the possible—carries within itself the seeds of its own necessary destruction. There is little point in trying to preserve the furniture from damage if the result of our efforts is to bring the house down.

In any case, however much we may hanker after comfort and security, we have to face the fact that under the peculiar conditions of this age and, above all, under the conditions likely to be imposed in our children's time there are many worse things than disorder; and we do well to recall the nature of the obedience that made possible the existence and smooth-functioning of the Nazi concentration camps and the Soviet labour camps. What is most feared under present conditions is anything that interferes with the process which is carrying us so swiftly downstream. Organisational man wants a quiet life, freedom from real responsibility, an artificial world in which nothing is left to chance and, quite particularly, the absence of 'difficult' people who create 'complications'. We are under no obligation to give him what he wants.

What is being attempted in contemporary societies is the achievement of the kind of order and predictability that is characteristic of the machine, and this involves closing all the doors and windows through which a wayward breeze might bring disorder and unpredictability. Just as the laws with which our societies are encumbered are, in so many cases, designed to prevent a very few people from gaining an 'unfair' advantage over their fellows, so the structure of these societies is increasingly determined by the desire to eliminate risk from human life. It is no coincidence that a world which goes to such lengths to play safe now faces dangers greater and more threatening than any known in the past.

We do better to face the natural and, in a sense, providential hazards inherent in our condition as human beings, rather than huddle together in a hygienic prison of our own making. There is no freedom that is not open to abuse, and abuses cannot be abolished without abolishing the freedom we need to become what we are. The history of human sanctity, both in the Islamic world and in Christendom, suggests that civil disorder, social injustice, the breakdown of amenities or the disintegration of central authority have not, in the past, been an obstacle to the achievement of man's true end. The real threat comes from a society which attempts to be all-embracing—in effect, 'totalitarian', however democratic its forms—since such a society

threatens, by its pseudo-absolute claims, to suffocate those elements in man which are by their nature fitted to take him on his
'second journey', the only journey that truly matters.

We are, indeed, outwardly and partially social animals and,
through one aspect of our multiform nature, members of a herd ;
but this is not the whole story nor anything like the whole story.
Each of us stands alone before God, as though the earth were a
desert in which no other man or woman was to be found ; and each
of us is alone in death as though there had never been companions,
husbands, wives, children. Alone, too, in pain and in our inmost
and incommunicable thoughts.

'Now have you come unto us, solitary as We created you at the
first, and you have left what We conferred upon you behind your
backs, and We see not with you those—your intercessors—of
whom you claimed that they possessed a share in you. Now is
the bond between you broken, and that which you counted upon
has failed you.'*

When all is said and done, each goes his own way. The parents
who were once all people to him fade into the shadows, young
love becomes a sentimental memory, children grow up and take
their leave, and old friends die. This man plods on, and only one
thing does not change : the choice he has, the choice he makes while
it is still his to make.

The Hindus speak of 'the human state hard to obtain', and their
doctrine illuminates much that might seem obscure in the Muslim
and Christian teaching that human life presents a stark alternative : win or lose all. For the Hindus, a being may pass through
numberless states of existence—or, allegorically speaking, numberless 'births'—before reaching the moment of truth, the human
state, and standing upright before the door which offers an exit
from imprisonment in the chain of 'transmigration'. To arrive at
this door after such long travail and refuse to pass through it is
therefore a kind of suicide. It is as though a man, surfacing briefly
as he is carried along in a rushing stream, were offered the means
of coming to dry land yet missed this opportunity only to be submerged again in the raging waters.

Such doctrine may seem foreign to our thought, but here is a

* Qurān, 6:94.

solid English voice speaking: 'A life devoted to the interests and enjoyments of this world . . . may be truly called a dream as having all the shortness, vanity and delusion of a dream; only with this great difference; that when the dream is over nothing is lost but fictions and fantasies; but when the dream of life is ended by death, all that eternity is lost for which we were brought into being.'*

In so many different languages and in terms of different symbolisms it is said that a door onto all that lies beyond our 'bubble' opens when we are born. At death the door closes, the way is barred. There are therefore no words to describe the loss suffered by those who slide through their human life, getting by as best they can and content to do no better than this.

We are fashioned for passing through this door and an awareness of the reality behind the dream is implanted in our deepest nature, though for the most part only in embryonic form. A human environment, a culture or a political system, can only be judged in terms of whether it develops and nourishes this awareness or kills it. Children and adolescents, unless warped by an evil heredity or by quite monstrous circumstances, have a sense of glory which is, in essence, an inkling of what lies beyond the door, outside our 'bubble'. It is the nature of the modern world first to stultify and then to destroy this sense of the sublime (a word which is, significantly, among the most devalued in our language), doing so in the name of 'realism' and 'common sense'. Those whose eyes are thick-horned with cataract assure the sighted—immature and suggestible as they are—that their vision has nothing to do with the real world; and this monstrous process makes use both of the adult's gravity (for he takes life seriously) and his humour (for he takes it 'with a grain of salt').

Such humour is often no more than a malign instrument for pulling down all that is high and noble through belittlement and trivialisation, a mockery rooted in fear and expressed as a nervous snigger in the face of immensity. There is no fun in it and no joy. But the young are terribly vulnerable to its corroding effects. They do not know how to cope with a mockery directed against dreams and feelings and intimations associated with an innocence which seems to find no echo and no response in the adult world. They

* William Law.

want, after all, to qualify for entry into that world as soon as possible and, for lack of any better model, they must believe that this poor wisdom—narrow, obtuse and short-sighted—is the badge of maturity.

There is, on the other hand, a different kind of humour which serves a useful, sanitizing function in puncturing worldly pretensions and, perhaps, in cutting the adult world down to size. An irreligious age is also an age of sentimental idealism, of self-important people and pretentious trivialities; and, having lost so much, the humanist finds it necessary to pretend that men and women are wiser than they really are, 'nicer' and less selfish than the facts suggest.

The boy or girl whose inarticulate sense of glory is dismissed as no more than a symptom of immaturity, is nonetheless encouraged to believe palpable untruths about the adult world. The young are not so easily deceived and, before they consent to join the charade (persuaded that there is no alternative), they suffer a disillusionment which, only too often, spreads like a stain until it encompasses the noble as such, the sublime as such. It is a sad thing that so many modern Christians—forgetting that Christ himself said: 'Why callest thou me good? none is good save one, that is God'—make a virtue of sentimental falsehoods and therefore discredit religion as such in the eyes of the young. A proven liar is not readily believed when he tells the truth.

The sense of glory is therefore threatened both by a cynicism which claims to be realistic and by an idealism which refuses to accept the facts of human nature. Not that it could remain intact through the passage of the years. At the start it may be no more than a child's joy in a new present, the excitement of a holiday in a place full of wonders, or the miracle of first love. All this must wither away unless transformed into a sense of the sacred, nourished, stabilised and perpetuated through contact with an authentic religious tradition. But if the sense of glory is strangled at birth there can be no transformation. A fragile sapling, it requires the company of great trees if it is to come to maturity. Its truth needs to be confirmed and reinforced, as it is when the babble of present-day voices is silenced by the great voices out of our human past and when certitude, established in authority, stands firm against all passing opinions. 'The most ignorant of all people,' said a thirteenth century sufi Master, 'is the one who abandons the certitude he has for the opinion people have.'* Just so do the young grow into ignorance.

But the sense of the sacred implies a sense of awe, and one would have to be either more than human or less than human for fear not to have some part in this. The child knows fear as he knows glory. The mature man unites a noble fear—for how could something so small not fear the Tremendous?—with his sense of the sacred. 'The fear of the Lord is the beginning of wisdom, and knowledge of the holy is understanding', said the Psalmist, underlining the connection between fear and intellectual clarity. 'The fear of God,' says Schuon, 'is no more a matter of sentiment than is the love of God; like love, which is the tendency of our whole being towards transcendent Reality, fear is an attitude of the intelligence and of the will: it consists in taking account, at each moment, of a Reality which infinitely surpasses us, against which we can do nothing, opposing which we could not live, and from whose teeth we cannot escape.'†

Only the very simple, who trust as a child trusts ('I am too little to damn myself', said St. Thérèse of Lisieux) may think of God entirely without fear. Ultimately, no doubt, love casts out—or absorbs—fear, but this in no way alters the fact that fear is the realistic and rectifying point of departure. Nor is there understanding at any level without knowledge of the holy, at once lovable and awe-inspiring, since understanding cannot exist in the context of ignorance of that which is the supreme object of knowledge. It might be added that the fear of God casts out lesser fears, whereas love of God enriches and perpetuates lesser loves provided they are subordinated to it.

If it is stupid not to fear what is to be feared and not to love what is to be loved, the very root of stupidity is located in the lack of self-knowledge. Above all, to be quite unaware of our own weakness and of our dependence upon other-than-self is to be incapable of sound and realistic judgment in any sphere.

Modern man refuses to acknowledge his need for Mercy, his need for forgiveness and his total dependence upon other-than-himself. The Edwardian poet who wrote, 'I am the Master of my Fate, the Captain of my Soul' was a lonely and neurotic cripple

---

* *Hikam* of Ibn 'Atā' illāh (E. J. Brill, Leiden).

† *Spiritual Perspectives and Human Facts:* Frithjof Schuon (Faber & Faber), p. 207.

who deserves recognition as a great ironist; precisely because the absurdity of this claim stands out so clearly in Henley's case we can detect the corresponding absurdity in other, less immediately obvious cases. For all their addiction to psychology, our contemporaries dare not see either themselves or others in a clear light, hence the lethal combination of cynicism and idealism which tears them apart. They cannot believe in anything and yet they must believe in something; and this is a plain invitation to fantasy and illusion, which come flooding in to fill the space left behind by departing religious faith.

Even so, there is a corrective always close at hand. Pain, misfortune and bitter loss break in to awaken the man of our time from the slumberous passage of the days and to bring him face to face with an aspect of reality. This is always a moment of truth and therefore a moment of choice. He may, of course, burrow even deeper into the dream-haunted darkness, like a child diving under the sheets and making himself very small; but it is also possible that he will, in such a moment of truth, emerge from the coverings which define the *kafir's* situation and, in the unfamiliar land of real choice, seek for a direction, a way out, an answer.

Unless he combines folly and arrogance in so potent a combination that he imagines he can invent his own religion (in which case he is back under the covers again), he has no alternative but to turn to traditional religion and re-examine his forgotten heritage. His education and the conditioning of the period are likely to make this an act of condescension, in which case he will expect the full welcome accorded to the prodigal son. He may be disappointed. Moreover he will find no justification, in the religious doctrines which have come down to us, for picking and choosing in terms of personal taste and personal prejudices or for sifting through a religious doctrine in the hope of stealing certain 'nuggets of wisdom' which might come in useful. To possess what he wants to possess he will have to accept a great deal that he never thought he wanted.

If he is sincere it must be assumed that he has some desire to escape from the prison in which he finds himself rather than to prettify his familiar cell with a few embroidered mottos. To come out from this cell and from the vicious circle in which he finds himself trapped he will have to leave behind a whole complex of thoughts and prejudices (reflecting the current climate of opinion), together with many personal desires and ambitions. One does not slip out of prison with a cluster of suitcases; and if this escape were not, to some extent, a leap in the dark it would not be an escape.

There can be no new growth unless the ground is cleared. Our minds and hearts are so clogged with false opinions and false desires that there is a great deal of clearing to be done. This seemingly negative task is the essential chore upon which all positive spiritual progress depends. It cannot be undertaken without divine grace, but no man can say with certainty where personal effort ends and the activity of grace begins, and it is not our business to be over-concerned with this demarcation. We do what we can because it is what we can do. The rest is out of our hands.

There remains, however, what is probably the greatest of all obstacles facing the man whose mind and personality are moulded by this age : a profound distaste for the paraphernalia of organised religion and for its readiness to temporise with the forces of this world.

So far as the institutional side of religion is concerned, this is the necessary basis for its existence through the ages. An abstract and disembodied spirituality disappears like a whiff of smoke when the wind blows hard upon it, and institutions have a protective function which is, in practical terms, indispensable (whether we like it or not). One of the first things a man must know about himself is the fragility of his existence, which can be ended by a pin-prick, an air bubble in the blood or a moment's inadvertence ; and the institutions which embody traditional values are scarcely less vulnerable. People think it easy to survive in this world— easy for the human soul, easy for the Word of God—and seem not to realise how much depends upon the survival of certain repositories of truth and of divine grace (crystallised, as it were, in religious forms) in an environment entirely hostile to the other-worldly.

To withstand the destructive tide of time it is necessary to exercise certain practical skills, not least in the political realm, and compromise is both necessary and legitimate, always provided it does not extend to falsifying doctrine or tolerating systems and ideologies which kill the spirit. We do not live in a bland or sunny place, but in the midst of turbulent seas and clashing rocks. There have been periods of history when this fact might be overlooked. It can scarcely be ignored today.

Before, for example, condemning the historical manoeuvres of the Catholic Church or the 'political' Popes we do well to remember that, had there been no such strategems, there might by now be nothing left and little or no hope for men and women born into the Western world at this late stage. At the same time, there is always the danger that the Church, finding itself a prisoner of the unbeliever's world, may behave like those inmates of the concentration camps who came to accept their guards' scale of values and to cooperate willingly with the system. Here everything is a matter of judgment and tactics, governed by an implacable integrity.

The fact remains that there are many people born in our time who have no clear and immediate access to an authentic religious tradition. It may still be natural for the man born into the sector of the world shaped by almost two thousand years of Christianity to seek a traditional framework and spiritual home in Catholicism or in the Eastern Orthodox Church; but under present conditions, when competent spiritual directors are hard to find outside the monasteries and when the acid of modernism has bitten so deeply into the structure of the Churches, he may be frustrated in his search. Providence, however, has provided compensations for the decline of spirituality in our time; the destruction of the barriers which formerly separated one traditional 'world' from another has made it possible for us to look further afield if we must.

Those who do so run very real risks, like tourists wandering innocently in an unfamiliar land. They may expect to meet 'gurus' who claim to offer easy access to the peaks of Hinduism quite outside the enduring body of the Hindu tradition, neo-Buddhists who have little acquaintance with the orthodox schools of Buddhism, 'sufis' who have turned their backs on Islamic orthodoxy, and even certain 'geniuses' who have borrowed bits and pieces from every religion under the sun (adding a little magic for good measure) and offer some brand new religion to the brand new people of this age. One way or another, these false prophets make their appeal to pride and ignorance, inflating the ego with a poisonous wind. One need only place such 'masters' and their adepts beside an old peasant telling his beads to make a very fair guess as to which is the more likely to be pleasing to God.

Even so there are certain people who find themselves compelled, under the quite abnormal circumstances of our time, to turn away from the Christian heritage and to seek their home in

Islam, Buddhism or elsewhere. Only in appearance is this a choice made by the individual; in truth the choice is made for him, the way indicated by unmistakeable signs and the matter concluded without too much fuss. But no one should assume, from the doctrine of the transcendent unity of the religions, that there are no real differences between them. If this were so, they would have no *raison d'être*. Each represents a unique Revelation and a unique perspective, and each creates around it a unique psychological and emotional climate, moulding the most intimate contours of the human personality.

Unity between the religions lies at the centre or, in effect, at the journey's end. Here and now diversity predominates and, as we have already seen, one perspective necessarily excludes all others on the purely human level; a man cannot be in two places at once. It is no more possible to mix the religions together and produce some kind of Highest Common Denominator than it is to express oneself eloquently in a mixture of Arabic, Sanskrit and Latin. No one denies that the same truths may be expressed in any one of these different languages, but no one imagines that the vocabularies are the same.

From the firm standpoint of his own religion, however, anyone can look around and find both confirmation of his faith and illumination of his doctrine in other shapes of wisdom as he does in the divine messages imprinted upon the phenomena of nature and of destiny. 'All wisdom', say the Muslims, 'is the believer's lost camel'. Whatever our path—provided it is authentic and founded upon Revelation—we have an owner's rights over every riding beast and every milk-giver that comes our way. Adhere to one synthesis of the human heritage, and you have access to the whole of that heritage and may seek knowledge in every corner of the globe.

Just as surely as they seek the treasures of this world, men seek the truth, though often enough they fall asleep on the way or are diverted by counterfeits and forget where they were going. It is as much our nature to look upwards as it is the cow's nature to look down at the grass she is cropping. But to follow our nature in this respect means to conform ourselves to the human Norm and, in an entirely abnormal age, this is hard, uphill work. Spiritual life is not theory, although it is the more firmly established when backed by theory; it is not sentimentality, although it requires the support of sentiment, nor idealism, although it makes use of our capacity for idealism. Spiritual life is primarily an effort to drag our attention away from the pandemonium and uproar which rivet it and to turn towards the 'open', towards the splendour of the Real. It is also a work of transformation—alchemist's work—since our leaden nature is to be turned into gold, a metal fit for heaven.

Every day is a good day to begin this work, but every day provides its crop of reasons for delay and hesitation—we are busy, we have problems—and time passes. We behave, many of us, like senile old people who, when the house is on fire, mumble over small possessions, fuss and natter, while their end roars all about their ears.

It is said in Islam that when a man takes one step towards God, then God himself comes down from the Throne of Power and Dominion and takes ten steps towards this man. The taking of that first step however requires both a child's spontaneity and a grown man's decisiveness; one must indeed 'become as a little child', undoing all the false maturity which was so ill done and learning to walk again. The man who is truly seized by the sense of the sacred and by the 'divine attraction', as iron shavings are drawn to a magnet, is concerned with the object of his love, the infinitely desirable Beauty which he recognises again and again in all contingent and delegated loveliness. We have been given eyes, and we must look; ears, and we must listen. There is much to be seen and heard if we are attentive and not entirely absorbed in the buzzing of our own thoughts and the itch of our own needs. But, above all, we have been given the power of movement—'Had We willed it so, We would indeed have fixed them in their place, unable to go forward . . .,' says the Qurān—and the power of decision. Having taken a first step, it is by placing one foot in front of the other that we advance; and it is by travelling that we arrive.

Seen from here it may look like a hard journey and a lonely one; yet none can number the multitude who have gone before us on this way and reached the other shore, and we are told in so many traditions—in religious doctrine, in universal myths and under the subtle disguise of 'fairy tales'—that the traveller, far from being alone, is surrounded by helpers and that the very forces which once seemed most hostile now come to his aid. So it is often said that he does not, in truth, leave the world behind him, but draws it after him into the pattern of unity and reconciliation for which it craved. The self-enclosed man is friendless in a necessarily hostile environment, whereas the traveller, like those ancient heroes who were aided in their moments of greatest peril by birds and beasts and plants, is nowhere rejected and everywhere at home.

'Just as it is the nature of fire to burn,' says a contemporary Buddhist writer, 'it is the nature of man—would he but remember it—to become Awake.' We sleep, troubled by a multiplicity of dreams, but the traveller walks towards an awakening in which are known, at last, and fully enjoyed the realities foreshadowed in his dreaming; until his night is done and an unimaginable daylight encompasses him.

It is from a man's choice between sleeping and waking or between drifting with the tide and making his way upstream that the pattern of his destiny is built up. Here we stand, as creatures made for choosing; and we do not know, until the veils are lifted, how much depended upon our choice.

# SUGGESTIONS
## FOR FURTHER READING

A significant feature of the current climate of opinion is the manner in which books that go against the trend of the times are buried under the weight of ephemeral material issuing from the world's printing presses. They seldom receive the publicity which might bring them to the attention of their potential audience.

Some years ago, when René Guénon's major works were first translated and published in the English-speaking world, many of us who had read him in the original French waited anxiously for the Press reaction to this momentous event, aware that he might arouse fury in some quarters but hoping for a positive response in a few journals and newspapers. What we could not have foreseen was that he would be completely ignored. Guénon's considerable influence in spite of this conspiracy of silence gives a hint of the impact he might have had if his work had been brought to the attention of a wider public.

Frithjof Schuon's books, although more widely read, have been generally ignored by the media. Since there is no more challenging nor more significant voice to be heard in the present age, this suggests that thousands of potential readers are deprived of access to a body of work which might satisfy their most urgent spiritual and intellectual needs.

I propose therefore to draw attention to a few authors whose books may be of interest to any reader who finds that the principles and point of view put forward in *King of the Castle* strike a chord of reminiscence, sympathy or assent.

At present (1977) only two of Guénon's books are readily available, but these are among the most important of his works: *Crisis of the Modern World* (Luzac), written fifty years ago but still timely, and *The Reign of Quantity* (Penguin Books, USA).

Ananda Coomaraswamy's collected papers and essays are to be reissued in a collected edition by Pantheon (USA), but any book of his that can be found in libraries or elsewhere is a treasure worth the seeking.

Frithjof Schuon's work is easier of access. *The Transcendent Unity of Religions* (Harper & Row, USA), *Stations of Wisdom* (Perennial Books), *Light on the Ancient Worlds* (Perennial Books) and *Logic and Transcendence* (Harper Torchbooks, USA) are at present in print, as are at least two of his major works on Islam. *Spiritual Perspectives and Human Facts* is to be reissued by Perennial Books.

Titus Burckhardt has written a number of outstanding works on sacred art including, in particular, *Sacred Art in East and West* (Perennial Books). Martin Lings, best known for his book on the Shaikh al-'Alawī, *A Moslem Saint of the Twentieth Century* (Allen & Unwin), is the author of *Ancient Beliefs and Modern Superstitions* (to be reprinted in 1978 by Allen & Unwin). Also deserving of special mention is *The Encounter of Man and Nature* (Allen & Unwin) by Seyyed Hossein Nasr, whose numerous books on Islam are justly recognised throughout the Muslim world and elsewhere as among the most profound and illuminating studies to have appeared in recent years. *The Way and the Mountain* (Peter Owen Ltd.) by Marco Pallis, Lord Northbourne's *Looking Back on Progress* (Perennial Books), and the recently published *Forgotten Truth* (Harper & Row, USA) by Professor Huston Smith of Syracuse University complete the list.

For those however who question the unanimity of traditional wisdom there can be no better corrective than Whitall N. Perry's monumental *Treasury of Traditional Wisdom* (Allen & Unwin), the most comprehensive anthology of its kind ever compiled.

Most of these authors contribute from time to time to a quarterly magazine, *Studies in Comparative Religion* (published by Perennial Books Ltd., Pates Manor, Bedfont, Middlesex). A selection of articles from this quarterly has been published by Penguin Books (USA) under the title *The Sword of Gnosis* (edited by Jacob Needleman); this includes a series of articles by Titus Burckhardt on 'Cosmology and Modern Science' which is of outstanding importance. Their work also appears in the bi-annual journal, *Sophia Perennis* (Editor, Peter L. Wilson) published in Tehran by the Imperial Iranian Academy of Philosophy (Director, Seyyed Hossein Nasr) and distributed outside Iran by Kraus-Thomson Ltd. (FL-9491, Nendeln, Liechtenstein); the French originals of Frithjof Schuon's articles are published in this journal.

These books and articles present variety in unity, very different voices speaking from a single standpoint. Few readers respond to them in a neutral or tepid fashion. For some they open up new horizons, often with a sense of shock, discovery and delight, while others, who cannot bear to have their ingrained habits of thought and all the cherished assumptions of the age so ruthlessly challenged, are angered and outraged. They provoke, in other words, a polarisation of perspectives which serves to clarify thought and to define the demarcation line between the basic tendencies of our time, the traditional and the modernist; and justice requires that people today should be offered a clearer view of the alternatives before them than is commonly available before they choose their way and fix, once and for all, the orientation of their lives.